THE JINGSHAN REPORT: OPENING CHINA'S FINANCIAL SECTOR

CHINA FINANCE 40 FORUM
RESEARCH GROUP

THE JINGSHAN REPORT: OPENING CHINA'S FINANCIAL SECTOR

CHINA FINANCE 40 FORUM
RESEARCH GROUP

TRANSLATORS: HU BING, GAO ZHENG, TAO MENGYING,
WANG MENGHAN, XIE YUELAN, YE FENG, ZANG ZIMING,
SHAO SUYA, ZHAO CHUNMEI, LI SHUANGSHAN

Australian
National
University

PRESS

ANU PRESS

Published by ANU Press
The Australian National University
Acton ACT 2601, Australia
Email: anupress@anu.edu.au

Available to download for free at press.anu.edu.au

ISBN (print): 9781760463342
ISBN (online): 9781760463359

WorldCat (print): 1135070092
WorldCat (online): 1135070276

DOI: 10.22459/JR.2019

Cover design and layout by ANU Press

Contents

Abbreviations vii

Introduction: Proactively and Steadily Advancing China's
Financial Opening. 1
Huang Yiping

1. China's International Strategic Environment 25
    Zhang Yuyan, Feng Weijiang and Liu Wei

2. China's Financial Development: A Global Perspective. 51
    Zhu Min, Chen Weidong, Zhou Jingtong, Gai Xinzhe
    and Xiong Qiyue

3. Further Expanding the Opening Up of China's Financial
    Industry 109
    Zhu Jun, Guo Kai, Ai Ming, Zhao Yue and Bai Xuefei

4. RMB Exchange Rate: Moving Towards a Floating Regime 145
    Zhang Bin

5. China's Cross-Border Capital Flow Management 175
    Guan Tao, Zhang Antian, Xie Yaxuan, Gao Zheng and Ma Yun

6. Promoting China's Financial Market Reform and Innovation
    with Opening Policies. 229
    Xu Zhong, Zhang Xuechun, Cao Yuanyuan, Tang Yingwei
    and Wan Tailei

7. Building China's Overseas Investment and Financing
    Cooperation 261
    Zhu Jun, Guo Kai, Ai Ming, Bai Xuefei and Zhao Yue

Abbreviations

ABC	Agricultural Bank of China
AGBI	Asian Government Bond Index
AMC	asset management company
BBVA	Banco Bilbao Vizcaya Argentaria
BOC	Bank of China
BOCOM	Bank of Communications
BRIC	Brazil, Russia, India, China
BRICS	Brazil, Russia, India, China and South Africa
CBRC	China Banking Regulatory Commission
CCB	China Construction Bank
CDB	China Development Bank
CFETS	China Foreign Exchange Trade System
CIRC	China Insurance Regulatory Commission
CIRR	commercial interest reference rate
COFER	currency composition of official foreign exchange reserves
CPC	Communist Party of China
CRCC	China Railway Construction Corporation
CSRC	China Securities Regulatory Commission
EBRD	European Bank for Reconstruction and Development
EIBC	Export-Import Bank of China
EM	Emerging Market
EMGBI	Emerging Markets Government Bond Index
EU	European Union

FDI	foreign direct investment
GDP	gross domestic product
GEM	Growth Enterprises Market
GFC	global financial crisis
G-SIB	global systemically important bank
ICBC	Industrial and Commercial Bank of China
IFFO	Infrastructure Financing Facilitation Office
IMF	International Monetary Fund
IPO	initial public offering
M&As	mergers and acquisitions
MOFCOM	Ministry of Commerce
MPA	macroprudential assessment
MRF	Mutual Recognition of Funds
NBS	National Bureau of Statistics
NEEQ	national equities exchange and quotations
NPL	non-performing loans
ODI	outward foreign direct investment
OECD	Organisation for Economic Co-operation and Development
OTC	over-the-counter
PBC	People's Bank of China
QDII	Qualified Domestic Institutional Investor
QFII	Qualified Foreign Institutional Investor
ROA	return on assets
ROE	return on equity
RQDII	RMB Qualified Domestic Institutional Investor
RQFII	RMB Qualified Foreign Institutional Investor
SAFE	State Administration of Foreign Exchange
SDR	special drawing right
SFC	Securities and Futures Commission
SME	small and medium enterprises
SOE	state-owned enterprise

SPDB	Shanghai Pudong Development Bank
SSE	Shanghai Stock Exchange
SSVB	SPD Silicon Valley Bank
STRI	Services Trade Restrictiveness Index
SZSE	Shenzhen Stock Exchange
UK	United Kingdom
URR	unremunerated reserve requirement
US	United States
USD	United States dollars
WTO	World Trade Organization

Introduction: Proactively and Steadily Advancing China's Financial Opening[1]

Huang Yiping[2]

China has consistently pursued the opening of its financial sector over the past four decades. In the 1980s, the Chinese Government tried to improve economic relations with foreign countries by reforming the exchange rate regime, establishing special economic zones to pilot the market economy system and implementing an opening policy. In the 1990s, the government actively employed a 'market-for-technology' strategy to attract foreign direct investment. It also adopted a managed floating exchange rate regime after aligning official and market exchange rates in 1994. When entering the World Trade Organization (WTO) in 2001, the Chinese Government promised to open the domestic financial sector and provide foreign-owned financial institutions with pre-establishment national treatment. After the global financial crisis, the government took the initiative to accelerate RMB internationalisation, established the Asian Infrastructure Investment Bank and launched the Belt and Road Initiative.

---

1   This article is the overview of the 2017 China Finance 40 Forum Jingshan Report. Authors of the report include Huang Yiping, Zhang Yuyan, Zhu Min, Zhang Bin, Xu Zhong, Guan Tao and Zhu Jun. All the experts participated in their personal capacity. Huang Yiping authored the overview, which combines the main analysis and conclusions from seven sub-reports. Not all of the views expressed in the overview are identical to those held by the authors of the sub-reports. Guan Tao, Zhang Bin, Xu Zhong and Zhu Jun provided valuable comments on the overview. Huang Yiping takes full responsibility for any errors or oversights found in this overview.
2   Chairman of China Finance 40 Forum Academic Committee and Deputy Dean of the National School of Development, Peking University.

China's financial opening over the last 40 years has several notable characteristics. First, progress has been slow, with several reversals; second, the government has shown great determination, but implementation has been difficult; third, policy coordination has been insufficient. These characteristics are related to China's gradual approach to reform. Our overall assessment of China's financial opening up policy is that much has been achieved, but many problems remain. The exchange rate regime reform has moved consistently in the direction of allowing two-way fluctuations of the currency value and letting market forces decide the exchange rate. However, to this day, the exchange rate still lacks flexibility. Liberalisation of the capital account and internationalisation of the RMB have also made substantial progress, but some reversals have occurred over the past two years. Granting market access to foreign-owned financial institutions remains 'long on talk but short on action'—little progress has been achieved, and to some degree retrogression is apparent. Opening of the financial market is severely restricted by the differences between domestic and international market rules and systems, as well as China's 'channelised' mode of opening. China has just started to engage in foreign investment and financing cooperation. China's financial institutions are far behind the enterprises in going global, and their capabilities for providing cross-border financial services are rather limited.

Despite all these problems, financial opening has not affected China's economic growth and financial stability as yet, although many emerging economies have experienced financial crises after instituting opening policies. Should China further open up the financial sector? Currently, China's financial openness lags behind that of other emerging economies; it is also below the degree of openness in the real economy. In addition, there are at least three reasons for China to further open up its financial sector. First, financial opening is essential to sustainable economic growth. Economic growth requires economic innovation, and economic innovation is dependent on financial innovation, which can be boosted by financial opening. Second, financial opening is an important way to prevent and control systemic risks. Expanding financial openness can not only instigate advanced managerial concepts, skills and rules, but also strengthen market discipline and reduce financial risks. Third, financial opening is an important way for China to participate in international economic governance. China must align itself with the international financial system to uphold economic globalisation and promote internationalisation of the RMB and the Belt and Road Initiative.

The Chinese and global economies have undergone many changes in the past 40 years. It is necessary for the Chinese Government to consider ideas and strategies that align with today's economic realities when formulating financial opening policies. First, as a major economy, China should consider fully the spill-over effect of opening policies on other economies and the international market. Second, while actively liberalising the capital account, authorities should consider establishing a moderate and temporary cross-border capital flow management mechanism to ensure financial stability and monetary policy independence. Third, the exchange rate can influence the real economy through both trade and financial channels, with the latter becoming increasingly important. Fourth, reform and opening complement and reinforce each other. China should promote progress on both fronts.

To proactively and prudently open up China's financial sector, we propose the following policy recommendations.

First, the Financial Stability and Development Committee under the State Council should coordinate financial reform and opening policies. 'Promoting reform through opening' is vital, but 'facilitating opening with reform' is also indispensable. Coordination of financial and non-financial reforms is essential. For example, reform of state-owned enterprises (SOEs) is an important condition for interest rate marketisation and capital account liberalisation. Additionally, coordinating domestic and foreign financial policies is required. For example, the opening of financial institutions to the outside world depends on whether foreign-owned financial institutions can truly enjoy pre-establishment national treatment in China. Finally, the coordination of various financial opening policies, especially the 'troika' of financial sector opening, exchange rate regime reform and financial deregulation must occur.

Second, the exchange rate should be more flexible and market forces should play a bigger role in determining the exchange rate. Since the end of 2016, RMB depreciation expectations have subdued, and the real economy has remained relatively stable, providing an important opportunity for the long-expected reform of increasing exchange rate flexibility. If China allows the exchange rate to be determined by market forces in due time, it will provide an important foundation for China to expand financial opening and improve financial regulation. It will also send a very positive signal to the international community, giving China more status in international financial affairs.

Third, China should establish a management framework for cross-border capital flows at both the macro and micro levels, while steadily accelerating RMB internationalisation. At the micro level, it is important to promote capital account convertibility and facilitate trade and investment. The focus of regulation should shift from ex-post regulation to ex-ante and concurrent regulation. At the macro level, a two-dimensional management framework—one on capital control and one on macroprudential management—should be established. Regulatory tools such as the macroprudential monitoring mechanism and stress test should be improved, and capital control measures such as the Tobin tax should be maintained as counter-cyclical instruments. However, capital controls should only be temporary measures to buy time for further reform.

Fourth, China should fully implement the pre-establishment national treatment towards foreign financial institutions and relax the cap on shares owned by foreign investors. When foreign-owned financial institutions enter China, they become resident business entities and are subject to the supervision of Chinese regulators. Their influence on financial stability is completely different from that of short-term capital flows. The Chinese authorities should treat local and foreign institutions equally in terms of ownership percentage, forms of incorporation, shareholder qualifications, business scope and the number of licences allowed, to provide a level playing ground for foreign investors.

Fifth, China should respect international rules and practices to achieve a higher level of financial opening. Opening the domestic market is essential to enhancing China's international competitiveness and achieving RMB internationalisation. A substantial gap exists between the openness stipulated by policies and those that are achieved. This is mainly due to misalignments between domestic and international rules and regulations. China should open up the credit rating market and foreign issuers should be given more flexibility in choosing auditing and accounting standards. Taxation issues faced by foreign investors in the Chinese bond market should be clarified as soon as possible. In addition, the financial infrastructure should be based on Chinese conditions, but should adapt to international practices.

Sixth, the opportunities presented by the Belt and Road Initiative and domestic industry upgrading and restructuring should be seized. This could help construct a framework for outbound investment and financing. In addition to development finance and policy, China should also create a comprehensive commercial financial services system. Regulators could guide Chinese financial institutions to plan their overseas presence rationally and encourage financial institutions to expand the scope and depth of their cross-border financial business. Overseas investment and financing services can be improved by using the correspondent banks, syndicated loans, assistance provided by host countries and multilateral development banks, capital markets in developed economies and international financial centres.

Finally, a macroprudential regulatory framework that matches an open financial system should be established. This will prevent and mitigate risks that could occur in the opening process. An open financial system can enhance efficiency, but may also increase risk. The regulatory framework should be expanded based on rules regarding cross-border financing risks in the People's Bank of China's (PBC) macroprudential assessment (MPA) system. Consideration should be given to the roadmap, timetable and coordination of financial opening policies. The authorities should adjust policies to adapt to different stages of development, reduce the volatility of capital flows, maintain external debt at a reasonable level and optimise its structure.

Overview

Four decades of financial opening

When the Third Plenary Session of the 11th Communist Party of China Central Committee decided to shift the government's focus to economic development in late 1978, China had only one formal financial institution—the PBC. The PBC performed the functions of both the central bank and commercial banks. The distribution of funds was based on central government planning, while the role of commercial financial institutions was almost negligible. However, the government established three specialised commercial banks in 1978: the Bank of China, China Construction Bank and Agricultural Bank of China.

For nearly four decades since 1978, the reform and opening up policy has brought tremendous changes to China's financial sector. China's financial reforms have not followed a simple linear process; they have been successful in increasing the quantity of financial services provided, but the quality has not improved much (Huang, Wang, Wang & Lin, 2013). The types and quantity of financial institutions have increased significantly, and the scale of financial assets has also expanded dramatically. All types of financial institutions can now be found in China. China now ranks first in the world in terms of commercial bank assets, second in terms of stock market capitalisation and third in terms of private sector bond market capitalisation, although most derivatives markets are still at an early stage of development, except for commodities futures. Judged only by these quantitative indicators, China's financial system is already a leader in the world (Zhu, Zhang et al., 2017).

In contrast, market mechanisms for the pricing and allocation of funds are faced with many constraints (Huang & Wang, 2017). The government intervenes in many areas. Some examples that challenge market discipline include the rules for benchmark deposit and lending rates, intervention in the foreign exchange market, guidance on fund allocation in the credit and capital markets, control over cross-border capital flows, government holdings in large financial institutions, soft budget constraints of SOEs and guaranteed payment on financial products. Economists at the International Monetary Fund (IMF) used 2005 data to create a financial repression index measuring the degree of government intervention in the financial system; China ranked fourth out of 91 countries (Abiad, Detragiache & Tressel, 2010).

Since the beginning of China's economic reform, financial opening has become increasingly important in policy considerations. China's financial opening can be divided into four stages.

The period from 1978–1991 was an exploratory stage for financial opening, and the most important move during this period was the launch of 'special economic zones' and adjustment to the exchange rate system. The focus of economic reform at this stage was first on rural regions. It gradually shifted to urban areas after 1984. In 1979, Japan Export-Import Bank became the first foreign bank to set up an office in Beijing. In 1982, CITIC Bank issued the first foreign bond since 1978 in Japan's financial market, with help from Nomura Securities. In 1979, Deng Xiaoping called forth establishment of 'special economic zones'. The first one was set up in Shenzhen in 1980. These special economic zones rolled out favourable policies like tariff exemption, aiming to create a beneficial environment to attract foreign investment. Meanwhile, the authorities tried to increase the proportion of market allocation of foreign exchanges by adopting a dual exchange rate system, where both an official exchange rate and a market rate existed. To support export growth, the government gradually devalued the RMB exchange rate against the USD from 1.498 in 1980 to 5.323 in 1991.

The period 1992–2000 was the foundation stage for financial opening, and the most important move during this period was the implementation of a managed floating exchange rate system and the effort to attract foreign direct investment. Deng Xiaoping's visit to South China in early 1992 opened a new era for economic reform. In October 1992, the 14th National Congress of the Communist Party of China made it clear that the objective of China's economic reform was to establish a socialist market economy. In 1993, the government introduced the 'market-for-technology' policy to attract foreign investment. In the following 22 years, China attracted more foreign investment than any other developing country. In early 1994, the central bank cancelled the dual exchange rate system and unified the official exchange rate with the market rate to establish a single managed floating exchange rate system based on market demand and supply. Current account convertibility was achieved in December 1996. When the Asian financial crisis broke out in 1997, the government tried to maintain the stability of the RMB and adopted a temporary exchange rate policy that pegged the RMB to the USD. In the meantime, the government accelerated reform of state-owned commercial banks.

The period 2001–2008 was an expansion stage for financial opening. The most important move at this stage was to open the domestic market to foreign-owned financial institutions. China's official accession to the WTO at the end of 2001 prompted the government to increase its efforts at economic reform. The government promised to open RMB business to foreign banks completely within five years, and similar commitments were made to foreign securities and insurance companies. To open up channels for investment in domestic and foreign capital markets, Chinese regulators set up the Qualified Foreign Institutional Investor (QFII) scheme in 2003 and the Qualified Domestic Institutional Investor (QDII) scheme in 2006. In 2004, the government began to encourage Chinese enterprises to 'go global'. Soon, China became one of the world's largest home countries of direct investment. In July 2005, the central bank dropped the RMB's peg to the USD. At the end of 2003, the central bank issued a notice on providing clearing arrangements for personal RMB business in Hong Kong, and then expanded such arrangements to Macau in 2004. By then, the cross-border circulation and use of the RMB entered a new stage. In October 2005, the International Finance Corporation and the Asian Development Bank issued the first RMB-denominated bonds (commonly known as 'Panda bonds') in China; in June 2007, the first RMB bond was issued in Hong Kong (commonly known as 'Dim Sum Bonds'). At this point, although the internationalisation of the RMB was not yet a national strategy, China had been quietly testing the waters.

The period 2009–2017 saw steady advancement of financial opening, and the most important move was accelerating RMB internationalisation and introducing the Belt and Road Initiative. Since early 2009, the central bank has actively expanded the offshore RMB market and supported RMB settlement for cross-border trade and investment. In July 2015, the central bank opened the interbank bond market to foreign central banks, international financial institutions and sovereign wealth funds; schemes such as the Shanghai–Hong Kong Stock Connect, Shenzhen–Hong Kong Stock Connect and Bond Connect were established to bridge the domestic and foreign capital markets. On 1 October 2016, the RMB was officially included in the IMF's special drawing right (SDR) basket. However, reform of the RMB central parity formation mechanism on 11 August 2015 led to prevalent depreciation expectations. President Xi Jinping proposed the Belt and Road Initiative in 2013, and the first multilateral development institution initiated by China—the Asian Infrastructure Investment Bank—was established in Beijing in December 2015.

Great achievements but many problems

From the perspectives of economic growth and financial stability, China's financial reform and opening up in the past four decades have undoubtedly been successful. Notably, China's gross domestic product grew at an average annual rate of nearly 10 per cent in the first three decades. Additionally, China is the only country of the major emerging market economies that has not experienced a serious financial crisis. However, if a thorough analysis is conducted on China's financial opening policies, many problems can be identified, despite the evident progress. Understanding regarding the appropriate degree of openness in areas like financial institutions is also lacking. Regarding exchange rate policies, although a certain consensus has been reached on the objective of a more flexible exchange rate, it has been difficult to put such policies into practice.

In some areas, such as foreign investment and financing cooperation, the opening process is still at a very preliminary stage. The following presents a brief assessment of the financial opening policies in a few major areas.

First, the problem with the exchange rate policy is that the authorities have tried to let market forces play a bigger role in determining the exchange rate level, but the flexibility of the exchange rate is still inadequate (B. Zhang, 2017). The RMB exchange rate policies (including the exchange rate regime) have undergone many changes, from consistent devaluation in the early days to gradual appreciation, from pegging the RMB to the USD to pegging it to a basket of currencies, and from the once fixed regime to a managed floating system. A lasting theme can be found in the process over the past four decades, which is the desire to increase the flexibility of the exchange rate and gradually move towards a market-determined exchange rate system. In fact, China's exchange rate policies have achieved much. The exchange rate is moving towards equilibrium level without wild fluctuations. The exchange rate has also effectively supported export growth, helping China maintain a healthy balance of payments and accumulate massive foreign exchange reserves.

However, China's exchange rate policy seems to have fallen into a dilemma of 'hate to fix but fear to float' since 2005. A managed floating exchange rate regime that lacks flexibility is rarely adopted by large economies. While the Chinese authorities have long claimed that market factors should play a bigger role in determining the value of the currency, they took measures to stabilise the exchange rate quickly whenever fluctuations were apparent. Over the past decade, the central bank either tried to reverse the expectations of unilateral RMB appreciation or eradicate unilateral depreciation expectations, except for some rare periods. The lack of flexibility not only affects monetary policy independence and macroeconomic stability, but also impedes economic restructuring, RMB internationalisation and the 'going global' efforts of Chinese enterprises.

Second, despite considerable progress in capital account liberalisation and RMB internationalisation, the past two years have seen some reversals (Guan, Zhang, Xie, Gao & Ma, 2017). The Third Plenary Session of the 16th Communist Party of China Central Committee proposed a policy objective of 'gradually achieving capital account convertibility'. Since then, capital account liberalisation started to accelerate and expanded from direct investment to external debt and credit, securities investments and other cross-border capital and financial transactions. The regulation of the capital account also shifted from 'lax on inflows and strict on outflows' to 'balanced management on bidirectional flows'. The number of items more than partially convertible on the capital account increased from 34 in 2012 to 37 by the end of 2016, and the share in total transactions by these items increased from 85 per cent to 92.5 per cent, while only three items were left unconvertible. A traditional puzzle with capital account liberalisation is how to balance the benefits and risks, including how to open up the account and to what degree.

Policies on RMB internationalisation were introduced in 2003. In late 2003, the central bank began to provide clearing arrangements for Hong Kong banks with individual RMB business. In 2009, cross-border RMB use for current account transactions was expanded to the whole country, while cross-border RMB use for capital account transactions was also greatly liberalised. Meanwhile, RMB offshore centres, represented by Hong Kong, developed rapidly. On 1 October 2016, the IMF officially announced the inclusion of RMB in the SDR basket. According to the IMF's data on the currency composition of official foreign exchange reserves, the RMB accounted for 1.1 per cent of the total reserves by the end of 2016. However, since mid-2015, part of the RMB internationalisation effort was reversed to encourage stability in the foreign exchange market. SWIFT data shows that the RMB's ranking in international payment fell from fifth in 2015 to sixth by the end of 2016, and its share declined from 2.31 per cent to 1.67 per cent.

Third, the opening of the financial services sector—especially to foreign-owned financial institutions—is basically 'long on talk and short on action' (Zhu, Guo, Ai, Bai & Zhao, 2017). After China joined the WTO in 2001, the country gradually relaxed restrictions on the form of incorporation, location and business scope, allowing for foreign-owned financial institutions. By the end of 2016, the assets of foreign banks accounted for 1.3 per cent of the total assets of banking institutions in China; joint-venture securities companies accounted for 10 per cent of securities companies, and their assets accounted for 4.5 per cent of the total; foreign-owned property insurance companies and joint-venture life insurance companies accounted for 30.4 per cent of the total. Meanwhile, Chinese financial institutions were 'going global' proactively, with networks covering the Asia-Pacific, North America and Europe. They also collaborated with an increasing number of banks globally in providing financial services, using various approaches.

However, China's openness with regard to foreign-owned financial institutions lags significantly behind the international average. Regarding the banking sector, the share of foreign bank assets in China is much lower than the average level of OECD countries (above 10 per cent), and is lower than the level of 2 per cent when China joined the WTO. The share of foreign assets in the insurance sector also fell to 5.6 per cent in 2016 after reaching a peak of 8.9 per cent in 2005. The decline of foreign shares is an indication of China's poor business environment and multiple policy barriers faced by foreign institutions. China is one of the few countries that impose restrictions on foreign ownership in the banking, securities and insurance sectors. Restrictions on business scope and licensing rules also constrain the development of foreign-owned financial institutions in China. For example, foreign securities firms can only enter China as joint ventures, and can only conduct very limited types of business, such as underwriting and the brokerage of foreign shares and bonds. Foreign-owned financial institutions are not really given pre-establishment national treatment.

Fourth, the opening of China's financial market is restrained by regulatory and institutional differences at home and abroad, and by China's 'channelised' mode of opening (Xu, Zhang, Cao, Tang & Wan, 2017). The bond market opened up by allowing foreign institutions to issue RMB bonds or invest in the interbank market; the stock market opened up by introducing a series of schemes such as QFII, QDII, the Shanghai–Hong Kong Stock Connect and the Shenzhen–Hong Kong Stock Connect to encourage two-way investment; the interbank foreign exchange market opened up by introducing 66 foreign institutions. However, the openness of these markets is generally limited. For example, total foreign shareholdings through schemes like QFII, RMB Qualified Foreign Institutional Investor, the Shanghai–Hong Kong Stock Connect and the Shenzhen–Hong Kong Stock Connect account for no more than 5 per cent of the stock market, much lower than 30 per cent in South Korea. Foreign holdings in China's bond market account for less than 2 per cent, while 10 per cent of Japan's treasury bonds are held by foreign entities. In China, transactions by foreign investors account for less than 1 per cent of the total trading volume in the interbank foreign exchange market.

The relatively low degree of openness in China's financial market can be largely attributed to regulatory and institutional differences between the domestic and international markets. This difference has caused much inconvenience to foreign issuers and investors and has dampened their enthusiasm to participate in the Chinese market. China's stock market opened up in a 'channelised' approach and the foreign exchange market is a managed market based on demand. Such practices have suppressed the degree of openness. The bond market is even more problematic, as foreign institutions struggle with different accounting and auditing requirements. China's bond market differs from the international market in that it requires filing for market access and adopts approaches such as single-tiered custody and centralised trading. Moreover, China's rating agencies generally lack credibility, and the variety of bond-related foreign exchange and derivative products is quite limited.

Finally, China has just started to establish a framework for overseas investment and financing cooperation. China's financial institutions clearly lag behind the enterprises in their 'going global' efforts, and their capabilities to provide cross-border financial services remain quite limited (Zhu, 2017). While China remains a large recipient of capital inflows, it has gradually become an equally powerful exporter of direct investment. The focus of overseas investment and financing cooperation has gradually expanded from Asian economies to advanced economies in Europe and North America, and the sectoral distribution has also shifted from the mining industry to business services, financial services and manufacturing. Investments made by non-SOEs rose from 19 per cent of total investment in 2006 to 49.6 per cent in 2015. However, Chinese enterprises investing overseas face substantial financing difficulties, as their investment projects are often long term, large scale and involve high risks. Moreover, many host countries are short of funds themselves. Chinese enterprises lack sufficient credit in foreign countries, and the overseas presence of Chinese financial institutions is mainly concentrated in developed economies, rather than in the developing and emerging economies where Chinese companies are investing heavily.

Many problems have surfaced as Chinese financial institutions have 'gone global' to conduct investment and financing cooperation. Some financial institutions have 'rushed forward' to seize new projects, resulting in distorted market competition. Some companies are ignorant of the host country's environmental and social norms, but invest in the country despite possible significant risks. It is also quite common that responsibilities, rights and interests are not properly aligned among stakeholders, especially in relation to public and concessional funding, as an ongoing tracking and accountability mechanism is missing.

The overseas distribution of domestic financial institutions does not match that of Chinese enterprises, and the overseas branches of Chinese financial institutions lack the strength and capability to provide sufficient service to companies investing overseas. Although the size of cross-border merger and acquisitions activities initiated by Chinese investors has increased rapidly, Chinese companies have a relatively high ratio of debt financing. The median ratio of debt to EBITDA for Chinese cross-border merger and acquisition deals is 5.4, while the global median is 3.

Government policies aiming to open up the financial sector over the past four decades have several prominent features. First, they are slow with reversals. China has been trying to open up its capital account for more than 20 years since the RMB became convertible under the current account in 1996. For more than a decade, the authorities repeatedly proposed a more flexible exchange rate, but the tolerance for exchange rate fluctuations remained low. The Chinese Government made a strong commitment to financial opening when China entered the WTO, but has been slow in fulfilling its promises.

Second, the government has shown great determination, but implementation has been difficult. When China joined the WTO, people in the domestic financial sector were largely pessimistic about the impact of foreign competition. However, it seems that foreign shares in the domestic banking and insurance sectors have declined rather than increased. In more recent years, the PBC has opened up the interbank bond market vigorously to international organisations, sovereign funds and commercial financial institutions. However, the actual degree of openness is still surprisingly low, due to gaps between domestic and international rules, systems and infrastructures.

Third, policy coordination is insufficient. China's financial reforms are ahead of its economic reforms, and RMB internationalisation is ahead of the financial reform. This lack of coordination has often reduced the effectiveness of opening policies for the financial sector. Financial policies and institutions are intrinsically related. They should be coordinated in the process of reform, or they will hinder each other and possibly trigger new risks. In the last two years, the authorities have suppressed the implementation of some existing policies for capital account liberalisation and RMB internationalisation in order to stabilise the foreign exchange market.

The aforementioned characteristics of financial opening policies can be attributed to many factors, including sectoral interests and policy ideas. The slow progress or even retrogression of financial opening may be explained by concerns over the perceived harm to the vested interests of domestic financial institutions. It is also obvious that policies discriminate against foreign-owned financial institutions in terms of shareholdings and business scope. Many people worry that financial opening may be detrimental to China's financial security and stability. Some of these worries are unnecessary, but some make sense. For example, massive short-term capital flows can easily trigger financial risks or even financial crises. If China is to further open up, it needs to put in place an efficient mechanism to prevent and respond to these potential risks.

Policy ideas and strategies should evolve with the times

Should China continue opening up the financial sector and, if so, how should the country achieve this? Once no doubts existed, but now this is a pressing question. Although China's financial openness is still relatively low, its economic and financial performance is highly regarded globally. If China's policies are working, why should they be changed? Conversely, China has taken developed countries in Europe and North America as a model for its financial reforms, but these economies have experienced serious financial crises in the past, and the progress of economic globalisation has slowed down or even reversed. Moreover, some developing countries, such as Indonesia and Mexico, have experienced financial crises after opening up their financial sectors. All these indicate that China needs to balance efficiency and stability when formulating financial opening policies.

However, China should continue to open its financial sector for at least three reasons.

First, further opening of the financial sector is an important condition for achieving sustainable economic growth. Currently, the openness of China's financial industry is not only far below the openness of the real economy, but is also significantly below the openness of the majority of emerging economies. While repressive financial policies, including capital account control, contributed to economic growth in the 1980s and

1990s, the impact of such policies has been negative since the turn of the century (Huang & Wang, 2011). China's future economic growth needs innovation to obtain new momentum, and economic innovation needs support from financial innovation. As China's WTO entry experience shows, the more developed, competitive and internationalised sectors are usually those that are opened up more thoroughly to the outside world and are more actively involved in global resource allocation. Financial progress also relies on further opening, even though problems in the financial sector are more complicated than in other sectors. At present, Chinese financial institutions are far behind Chinese enterprises in their 'going global' efforts.

Second, financial opening is also an important means to prevent and control systemic financial risks. The recent increase of systemic financial risks can be attributed to many factors. The continued economic slowdown has caused the deterioration of corporate balance sheets, and government bailouts for financial products and enterprises have worsened the moral hazard problem. Government bailouts seem to stabilise the financial market in the short term but may instigate further financial crises. Further opening the financial sector can not only introduce advanced management concepts, technologies and rules; raise economic efficiency; and strengthen competition and market discipline (thus lowering financial risks), but can also facilitate the diversification of risks. Clearly, financial opening measures should not be implemented all at once, but need a carefully designed roadmap and a prudential regulatory framework.

Finally, financial opening is also crucial for China to participate actively in international economic governance. Since 2008, some 'black swan' events have occurred in the international political and economic arena. However, peace and development remain the major theme of our time, and China is expected to see an extended period of strategic opportunities for reform and development (Y. Zhang, 2017). Over the past four decades, China has been a major beneficiary of economic globalisation, and it is in the country's interest to maintain an open global economic order. China today can hardly assume the role of a rule maker for international economic affairs, but it can be active as a key participant. The new initiatives recently launched by the Chinese Government—including the Belt and Road Initiative, Asian Infrastructure Investment Bank and RMB internationalisation—should be progressed on the premise of closer integration with the international economic and financial system.

The Chinese and global economies have undergone many changes compared with the early days of reform and opening up almost 40 years ago. It is necessary for the Chinese Government to consider ideas and strategies that are adapted to today's new economic realities when formulating financial opening policies.

First, as a major economy, China should take full account of the spill-over effect of its financial opening policies on other economies and the international market. A few years ago, it was quite common for experts to regard RMB exchange rate policies as China's internal affairs that did not involve other countries. This argument was incorrect then and is even more so in today's context. The exchange rate is the relative price between currencies, and an undervalued or overvalued yuan will affect other countries. More importantly, China has evolved from a small economy to the world's second largest. The international economic environment has changed from an exogenous variable to an endogenous variable of the Chinese economy, and its economic policy has become an important part of the international system. Studies have found that China's monetary policy can have a significant impact on the Asian economy through the real economy and financial channels (Cho, Huang & Kim, 2017). This was not so 40 or even 20 years ago.

Second, on the premise of further liberalising cross-border capital flows, moderate and temporary management of cross-border capital flows can maintain financial stability and enhance monetary policy independence. After the establishment of the Bretton Woods system in 1944, the IMF supported capital account control. When the US removed the gold standard in 1971, the IMF supported the free flow of cross-border capital. After 2009, the IMF's stance on the free flow of capital shifted again towards allowing governments to take appropriate management policies for financial stability (IMF, 2011). Recent studies have found that many developing countries only have the dilemma between free flow of capital and independent monetary policy. Therefore, appropriate management of cross-border capital flows could also enhance monetary policy independence (Rey, 2013). However, the IMF believes that China's capital flow management is stricter than that of most developed economies. The future direction would be for China to gradually lift capital controls, shifting from quantitative control and a quota system to price control, from residence-based administrative control to currency-based regulatory measures, and from ex-ante approval to ex-post reporting and supervision.

Third, exchange rates used to affect the real economy through trade channels, but now the financial channel is becoming increasingly important. Undervalued currencies usually increase exports and reduce imports, thereby improving trade balance and supporting economic growth. Recent studies have determined that exchange rates can affect the economy through financial channels in addition to trade channels (Hofmann, Shim & Shin, 2016). Since mid-2015, the depreciation of the RMB forced many Chinese enterprises to accelerate repayments of their foreign debt; this is equivalent to capital outflows and is detrimental to economic growth. In the past, China's economic activities with foreign countries mainly involved trade. Now, with a more open financial sector, an undervalued currency may not stimulate economic growth. Neither can an overvalued currency be assumed to support economic growth. Instead, China should aim for exchange rates that align with its economic fundamentals, while maintaining adequate flexibility.

Fourth, China should combine 'promoting reform through opening' and 'facilitating opening with reform' to promote both financial reform and opening up. One of the most important lessons from China's experience in joining the WTO is to 'promote reform through opening'. For over a decade, China's policymakers have often applied this concept of governance to the financial sector and made much progress. As the links between various elements of the financial sector are very important, policymaking should pay particular attention to the sequencing issue 9 (McKinnon, 1993). For example, the Chinese central bank removed restrictions on the floating range of deposit and lending interest rates at the end of 2015, but the problems with risk pricing and interest rate transmission mechanism have not yet been resolved so interest rate marketisation has barely been accomplished. Another example is the internationalisation of the RMB. After the global financial crisis, the international community became more sceptical about the USD-dominated international monetary system, and expectations for the RMB rose. The Chinese central bank seized the momentum and propelled RMB internationalisation to a new level. However, supporting reforms, such as exchange rate regime reform, lag far behind, which has seriously restricted the progress of RMB internationalisation. The troika of financial sector opening, reform of the exchange rate formation mechanism and reduction of capital controls must be promoted in a coordinated manner.

Promoting reform through opening; facilitating opening with reform

Throughout the process of economic reform and opening, the Chinese Government has actively advanced financial opening, but the degree of openness still lags behind that of China's real economy and the financial sectors in most countries. Historically, this would not have had much of a negative effect on China's economic growth or financial stability. However, now it is constraining further growth. From the perspective of maintaining economic growth, controlling financial risks and participating in international financial governance, China should further open up its financial sector. New policy ideas should be considered in formulating and implementing policies. Here, we propose seven policy recommendations.

First, the Financial Stability and Development Committee under the State Council should coordinate financial opening policy, design the roadmap, and implement the policy proactively and steadily. 'Promoting reform through opening' is very important, but 'facilitating opening up with reform' is also indispensable—a one-sided financial opening policy should be avoided. Of course, this does not mean reform policies cannot be advanced concurrently. However, the success of reform policies in certain areas depends on the completion of reforms in other areas. China has accumulated some experience and has also learned lessons from bringing in foreign banks, opening up the bond market and advancing RMB internationalisation. Now that a high-level committee has been established, it should aim for strengthened coordination. Financial and non-financial reforms should be coordinated. For example, solving the issue of soft budget constraints of SOEs is an important condition for interest rate marketisation and capital account liberalisation. Domestic and foreign financial policies should also be coordinated. For example, the opening of financial institutions to the outside world depends on whether foreign-owned financial institutions can enjoy pre-establishment national treatment and fair competition. Additionally, the promotion of financial opening policies should be coordinated. For example, opening financial institutions and financial markets, reforming the exchange rate formation mechanism and reducing capital controls are highly interconnected. The top priority now is to have a more flexible exchange rate.

Second, exchange rates should be more flexible and market factors should play a bigger role in determining the exchange rate levels. The RMB is still not flexible enough. Once the market shows signs of trouble, the authorities will act to fix it. Government intervention has become a key source of financial instability. However, since the end of 2016, RMB depreciation expectations have almost disappeared, and the real economy has remained relatively stable, providing an important opportunity for the long-expected reform of increasing exchange rate flexibility. Both domestic and international practices show that if China is to let the market decide the exchange rate and achieve a 'clean' float of the yuan, China should do so in favourable conditions when risks are low. China should seize the current opportunity to push forward reform decisively. Missing a good opportunity once again is inadvisable. In the meantime, China should have response plans ready for all sorts of possibilities: prepare for the worst and strive for the best. If China can achieve the leap of exchange rate reform in good time, it will provide an important mechanism for China to expand financial opening and improve financial regulation. It will also send a very positive signal to the international community, giving China a stronger voice in international financial affairs (Y. Zhang, 2017).

Third, China should establish a management framework for cross-border capital flows at both the macro and micro level and steadily accelerate the process of RMB internationalisation. China's 13th Five-Year Plan has promised to 'expand two-way opening of the financial sector, achieve RMB capital account convertibility in an orderly manner, and increase the convertibility and free use of the RMB'. The macro-control function of capital flow management will continue to decline in importance. The micro-supervision function will decouple from the macro-control function. The future reform of capital flow management will be characterised by decentralisation and diversification. The establishment of a dual-pillar framework for cross-border capital flow management is proposed. At the micro level, it is important to promote capital account convertibility and trade and investment facilitation; the focus should shift from ex-ante supervision to concurrent and ex-post supervision, while emphasising authenticity and compliance checks. At the macro level, a two-dimensional management framework—one on capital control and the other on macroprudential supervision—should be established. Upgrading the policy toolkit and improving the macroprudential assessment mechanism and stress tests is urgently required. Capital control measures such as the Tobin tax should be retained as instruments for counter-cyclical control and ex-post regulation. However, cross-border capital controls should only be temporary measures, as they will cause market distortions and increase transaction costs. China should use cross-border capital flow management to buy time for other reforms such as improving monetary policy independence and boosting economic growth. China should take immediate action to manage financial risks and support the orderly adjustment of the balance sheets of the private sector so that they can become better adapted to a more flexible exchange rate. At the same time, measures regarding RMB internationalisation should be steadily promoted. Such measures include providing more RMB liquidity in offshore markets, promoting RMB settlement in international trade and investment, expanding the proportion of RMB in international payments and reserves, and promoting the use of RMB in pricing products in the international market (Guan et al., 2017).

Fourth, China should fully put into practice pre-establishment national treatment of foreign financial institutions and liberalise the restrictions on foreign holdings of financial institutions. When a foreign financial institution enters China, it becomes a domestic business entity and is subject to the supervision of Chinese regulators. This is equivalent to foreign institutions conducting direct investments in China. Their impact on financial stability is completely different from that of short-term cross-border capital flows. In this sense, the Chinese authorities should treat local and foreign financial institutions equally in terms of ownership percentages, forms of incorporation, shareholder qualifications, business scope and the number of licences allowed. This would provide a fair competitive environment for foreign investors in the Chinese market. China could relax restrictions on foreign ownership in the banking, securities and insurance sectors and allow the establishment of wholly foreign-owned securities companies and insurance companies. China could cancel the requirement on total assets for foreign bank shareholders, the requirement for minimum years of operation for foreign banks to start RMB business, and the requirement that at least one Chinese shareholder of a joint-venture securities company should be a securities company. China should no longer restrict the development of joint-venture life insurance companies by limiting the number of licences granted and could consider giving new regional operation licences to wholly foreign-owned life insurance companies. At the same time, to encourage Chinese financial institutions to 'go global', China should remove restrictions on the overseas locations of commercial banks. It is suggested that newly established branches be subject to filing procedures only, rather than review and approval procedures. Moreover, applications to incorporate should be allowed to proceed simultaneously in the home country and host country to increase efficiency (Zhu, Guo et al., 2017).

Fifth, China should respect the rules and practices in the international market to achieve a higher level of financial opening. Opening of the financial market is a necessary requirement for China to enhance its international competitiveness and achieve the goal of RMB internationalisation. China should establish an orderly and open credit rating market as well as a uniform registration management system that covers international rating agencies. The specific market management requirements should be clarified and take into account the conditions of international rating agencies. Foreign rating agencies should be allowed to either establish a commercial presence in China or conduct business as foreign corporate entities. Moreover, international rating agencies can be permitted to gradually engage in the domestic bond rating business (beginning with Panda bonds) and foreign issuers should be given more flexibility in auditing and accounting. For private placement bonds issued to institutional investors, it is recommended that a regulatory cooperation agreement between China and the home country of the accounting firm not be a prerequisite. Otherwise, it should be sufficient for the accounting firm hired by the issuer to submit a regulatory confirmation letter to the Ministry of Finance. Accounting firms formed in European Union countries and Hong Kong may be exempt from filing with Chinese regulators. Uniform management measures, including relevant auditing and accounting policies and higher transparency and standardisation requirements, should be released as soon as possible for foreign governments, international developmental agencies and foreign commercial institutions issuing RMB bonds in the interbank market. Finally, tax issues concerning foreign investors in the Chinese bond market should be clarified as soon as possible. At the same time, financial infrastructure construction should take into account both China's conditions and international practices (Xu et al., 2017).

Sixth, China should take the opportunity presented by domestic industry upgrade and restructuring, as well as the Belt and Road Initiative, to construct a comprehensive foreign investment and financing framework. The basic principle is to reduce uncertainties and increase economic returns of overseas investment through reasonable financing arrangements, appropriate risk-sharing mechanisms and proper financial instruments.

China should promote development finance vigorously. Development finance emphasises the commercial viability and financial sustainability of projects rather than maximising profits. It emphasises support for infrastructure investment and other long-term investment projects. China is already a world leader in this field. China should continue improving the export credit mechanism for policy finance. China's export credits lean more towards 'South-South cooperation', rather than 'concessional loans' in the traditional sense. Therefore, China should promote the reform and improvement of international rules on export credit. Finally, China should establish a comprehensive commercial financial service system. Regulators could take the opportunity to guide Chinese financial institutions with planning their overseas presence rationally. They can also encourage financial institutions to expand the breadth and depth of their cross-border financial business, such as experimenting bank-enterprise cost-sharing mechanisms, improving exchange rate risk hedging tools for long-term investment, and relaxing sovereign guarantee requirements for host country project financing. They could also make use of correspondent banking operations, syndicated loans, assistance provided by host countries, multilateral development banks, the capital market in developed economies and international financial centres and employ a variety of investment and financing arrangements, such as equity investments, to improve overseas investment and financing services (Zhu, Guo et al., 2017).

Seventh, a macroprudential regulation framework that matches an open financial system should be improved to effectively prevent and mitigate risks that could occur in the opening process. Financial opening can enhance efficiency; it can also cause more instability to the financial market. Therefore, a key point for financial opening policy is to find a balance between efficiency and stability. Establishing a macroprudential regulation framework is an important way to achieve this balance. The Chinese central bank has proposed an MPA system that monitors seven categories of indicators. One category is cross-border financing risks, indicated by the weighted average of cross-border financing risk exposures. Macroprudential regulation on financial opening can follow this system, but it should include more assessments. For example, financial opening policies should be coordinated to avoid progress on a single front. The opening process should follow a well-designed roadmap and timetable to achieve a balance among opening, development and stability. Opening policies should be adjusted to adapt to different stages of development, and special attention should be paid to the potential risks brought about by opening up, especially the risks of cross-border capital flows. Finally, external debt should be kept at a reasonable size, and its structure should be optimised (Guan et al., 2017).

References

Abiad, A., Detragiache, E. & Tressel, T. (2010). A new database of financial reforms. *International Monetary Fund Staff Papers, 57*(2), 281–302.

Cho, C., Huang, Y. & Kim, S. (2017). *International transmission of Chinese monetary policy shocks to Asian Countries* (Draft Paper). National School of Development, Peking University.

Guan, T., Zhang, A., Xie, Y., Gao, Z. & Ma, Y. (2017). *Managing China's cross-border capital flows: 2017 Jingshan Report.* China Finance 40 Forum.

Hofmann, B., Shim, I. & Shin, H. S. (2016). *Sovereign yields and the risk-taking channel of currency appreciation* (Working Paper No. 538). Monetary and Economic Department, Bank for International Settlements.

Huang, Y. & Wang, X. (2011). Does financial repression inhibit or facilitate economic growth? A case study of Chinese reform experience. *Oxford Bulletin of Economics and Statistics, 73*(6), 833–855.

Huang, Y. & Wang, X. (2017). Building an efficient financial system in China: A need for stronger market discipline. *Asian Economic Policy Review, 12*(2), 188–205.

Huang, Y., Wang, X., Wang, B. & Lin, N. (2013). Financial reform in China: Progress and challenges. In Y. Park & H. Patrick (Eds), *How finance is shaping the economies of China, Japan and Korea* (pp. 44–142). New York, NY: Columbia University Press.

International Monetary Fund (IMF). (2011). *Agreement of the International Monetary Fund.*

McKinnon, R. I. (1993). *The order of economic liberalization: Financial control in the transition to a market economy.* JHU Press.

Rey, H. (2013). Dilemma not trilemma: The global financial cycle and monetary policy independence. *Federal Reserve Bank of Kansas City Economic Policy Symposium, 2013,* 285–333. Retrieved from www.kansascityfed.org/publicat/sympos/2013/2013Rey.pdf

Xu, Z., Zhang, X., Cao, Y., Tang, Y., Wan, T. (2017). *Promoting the reform and development of the financial market by opening up to the outside world: 2017 Jingshan Report*. China Finance 40 Forum.

Zhang, B. (2017). *Moving towards a floating RMB exchange rate formation mechanism: 2017 Jingshan Report*. China Finance 40 Forum.

Zhang, Y. (2017). *The international strategic environment China is facing today: 2017 Jingshan Sub-report*. China Finance 40 Forum.

Zhu, J. (2017). *Constructing a cooperative framework for overseas investment and financing: 2017 Jingshan Report*. China Finance 40 Forum.

Zhu, J., Guo, K., Ai, M., Bai, X. & Zhao, Y. (2017). *Further opening up China's financial sector to the outside world: 2017 Jingshan Report*. China Finance 40 Forum.

Zhu, M., Zhang, Y., Guan, T., Zhang, B., Zhong, X., Zhu, J. & Yiping, H. (2017). *China's financial development from a global perspective: Jingshan Report 2017*. China Finance 40 Forum.

1

China's International Strategic Environment

Zhang Yuyan,[1] Feng Weijiang[2] and Liu Wei[3]

Introduction

The international strategic environment refers to the external environment in which a country designs and implements its national strategies. The international strategic environment determines China's medium- and long-term development strategy and foreign policy and constitutes the background of financial reform and opening up. This chapter analyses the international strategic environment from three perspectives: peace, development and governance. These three perspectives cover a wide range of issues including new approaches, factors with a sustained influence, material, ideological and institutional factors, and the tactical characteristics of actors. Moreover, with China's increasing role in the global system, China's own development and behaviour is affecting the external environment more significantly. As a result, examining variations in the external restrictions China is facing and evaluating the external response to China's influence are equally important in judging and analysing the international strategic environment.

---

1   Director of the Institute of World Economics and Politics at the Chinese Academy of Social Sciences.
2   Staff researcher at the Institute of World Economics and Politics at the Chinese Academy of Social Sciences.
3   Staff researcher at the Institute of World Economics and Politics at the Chinese Academy of Social Sciences.

Part 1: Although overall global peace can be maintained, the international security environment is becoming increasingly complicated

Peace and war are both closely related to a country's survival. They also lie at the centre of a national strategy. A revolutionary change in international relations has significantly decreased the possibility of war between major powers. As a result, overall global peace can be maintained. However, local security risks and unconventional security threats are increasing and have become an important source of threats to national stability and prosperity. In particular, the continuous extension of people's activities and communication has a spill-over effect in various realms, including the economy, society, culture, healthcare and information. This is seen across different countries and appears to be increasing.

Normalisation of peace among major countries

Since the first half of the twentieth century, four revolutionary changes have weakened the motives for major powers to resort to war and have restrained many indirect or accidental causes of war. They provide a basis for long-term group values that make lasting peace among the major powers possible. These four changes are outlined below.

First, with the advent of nuclear deterrence and other new-type weapons (e.g. long-range, precision munitions), wars among major powers are no longer a reasonable option to gain war benefits such as annexation of land and securing of resources. Second, wars among major powers are no longer the only way to secure a country's war interests, as countries are more effectively using their economic and social means to enhance their influence. Third, the decision-making systems and processes of modern foreign policy have progressed rapidly, inhibiting the incentives for wars among major powers. Fourth, information technology, globalisation and consumerism enhance anti-war values in the populations of major powers.

For China, the 'new normal' of long-term peace among major powers has the following strategic implications.

First, the long-term judgement is that World War III will never happen and peace and development is the theme of the time. Specifically, the overall external environment for China's reform and development will remain stable. China must also consolidate its foundations, coordinate the domestic and international situations, promote the stable development of its economy and a society driven by reform and innovation, and advance modernisation in the national governance capacity. On this basis, China will steadily enhance its influence on the world stage, while avoiding aggressive strategies.

Second, competition between major powers under the 'peaceful new norm' will be enduring and complex. Specifically, in the next five to 10 years, hegemonic states will increase the structures around China and across the world to improve their influence and increase their involvement in regional issues. China's situation in relation to global and peripheral affairs may worsen, crises may break out more frequently and pressures on safety will increase. China may be placed in a disadvantaged position in relation to longstanding and multidirectional enemies. This requires more sophisticated forecasting and assessment capabilities in the short to medium term, and the comprehensive use of diplomatic, economic and other responses.

Neighbouring regions are 'disordered without battle, fighting without splitting up'

Despite overall peace among the major powers being maintained, China still faces increasing uncertainty from its neighbouring regions, along with a more diversified and dispersed security risk. Non-traditional security threats have become prominent. China's neighbouring countries and the Asia-Pacific region are regarded as a key battlefield for shaping future international patterns. Strategic mutual trust among major countries is reduced, and the security problem is highlighted. The region's security issues seem more complicated with the involvement of foreign powers. Heated issues frequently and increasingly escalate into crises. However, the situation is generally controllable.

Although the United States (US) has abandoned the Asia-Pacific rebalancing strategy as such, the overall trend of concentrating US resources in the Asia-Pacific region will continue. In recent years, with its diminished comparative advantage in national strength, the US has continued to draw India, Australia and Singapore to its side, forming an arc that encourages these three nations to take an active role in achieving 'shared responsibilities'. This makes the security threat faced by China even more complicated. Disputes over neighbouring territories and territorial waters will become more serious. Connections between the proliferating geopolitical issues of the South China Sea and South Asia will be significantly enhanced. In the future, the South China Sea and South Asia will represent a significant crisis for China. Fortunately, in the foreseeable future, South Asian countries will be greatly restricted by their internal affairs and resources, ensuring that their capacity for intervention is limited. They will be unable to affect the security environment of China's neighbouring regions in a fundamental way. In the long term, the US's deployment of the Terminal High Altitude Area Defense system will significantly damage the strategic balance and mutual trust between China and the US. In the meantime, North Korea has made many breakthroughs in its research and development of nuclear missiles and, in theory, has the ability to launch nuclear attacks on the contiguous US. Responding to and settling the North Korean nuclear issue requires all parties to focus on the long-term and comprehensive use of various policy instruments.

The comparative strengths of major powers are undergoing substantial change

Currently, global patterns are undergoing profound changes. With an increase in their strengths, developing countries and emerging economies are entering the global stage at a rapid pace. Conversely, the vested interest groups of developed countries have gradually lost absolute dominance in the global system due to a decrease in their relative national strengths. Despite this, the US will assume the position of a superpower in the long term. With its expanding economic scale, China's economic strength is approaching that of the US. The gap between other countries and the US or China will be further widened.

The most important actors globally are the US and China. China's gross domestic product (GDP) has grown rapidly from a volume equivalent to that of Japan to more than twice the GDP of that country, and as much as 60 per cent of the US's GDP. Even if calculated using the 'inclusive wealth' concept, which includes human, physical and natural capital, the speed at which China is catching up with the US is amazing, despite the significant gap. Developed countries, led by the US, have already reached the plateau of their overall national strength. The growth of the national strength of developed countries is generally slowing down. One explanation for this may be the financial difficulties that industrial countries generally face. Fiscal conditions not only influence people's welfare and extend or restrict space for policy decisions, but also have a direct effect on the implementation of a country's foreign policies, especially for major powers or groups of states. Fiscal pressure has, to some extent, influenced the strategic contraction of the US in the Middle East and other regions. The situation is similar in regard to challenges from Russia in relation to Syria, and influence from the Philippines and Malaysia in relation to China. US President Trump wants to renegotiate the North Atlantic Treaty Organization and North American Free Trade Agreement with the US's allies because the US cannot afford to 'play this game' financially.

Although the US is experiencing stagnation or even a decline in power, it will remain the most important global player over the next decade. Having witnessed a rapid economic development for one-third of a century, China has risen to become the only country able to challenge the current and future global hegemony of the US. With the narrowing gap between China and the US, and the widening gap between these two and other countries, the global order is likely to become polarised. The rapid rise of China has worried the US, forcing it to treat China as a genuine competitor. As the US has a relative advantage, it may be the only country that can impede China's modernisation process. Strategic competition between the countries is likely to fall into the 'Thucydides Trap'. Fortunately, the existence of nuclear weapons has significantly decreased the possibility of a Sino–US war, because nuclear weapons change the rules of the games played by major powers. The nuclear deterrence strategy ensures that large-scale wars are less likely to develop. This means that the major global players have few choices for resolving disputes other than nonviolent means. The competition between nuclear states has, as a result, become even more complex.

Against this background, China is shifting from relying on exogenous strategic opportunities to creating endogenous opportunities. As the second-largest economy with a significant potential for development, China's foreign policies reverberate internationally. When China proposed 'a period of strategic opportunities' a decade ago, it emphasised the exogeneity of strategic opportunities. The shift from exogeneity to endogeneity is, to some extent, a result and signal of the substantial changes in the relative strength of China and the US.

The 'double-edged sword phenomenon' of cyber technology is becoming evident

Generally, people regard technological innovation as an indicator of human progress, because it can increase the productivity of labour, promote welfare and improve living conditions. However, the uncertainty (or even destruction) created by technology can be significant, at least in certain historical periods. This is the 'double-edged sword phenomenon' of technological progress.

Technological innovation is changing people's way of production and lifestyle rapidly in the twenty-first century. The rapid development of information technology has expanded the way people acquire information, stimulated the spread of various values and ideologies and facilitated interaction and collective action among humans. Due to such characteristics as openness and anonymity, the internet has evolved into a major platform for groups to obtain information and express emotions. Some extreme or even distorted information has spread quickly through the internet. This situation could lead to accidental and violent mass incidents at any time.

The 'double-edged sword phenomenon' also applies to cyber technology. Due to the lack of relevant laws and the fact that users can remain anonymous, the general public has resorted to the internet more often to voice their concerns, which can gradually evolve into anti-establishment grassroots movements. These bottom-up movements question and challenge existing rules. Many extreme phenomena, such as trade protectionism among blue-collar workers in the US, the integration of ultra-nationalism and populism in Western society and the religious extremism represented by the Islamic State (also known as ISIS or ISIL) are not recent developments. However, the values related to these developments are now disseminated and exaggerated through the internet and have influenced the political orientations of larger groups. The world is now exposed to the danger of cyber war because of the global network.

The rise of terrorist attacks signals the clash of civilisations

Terrorism was one of the most important unconventional security issues in the realm of international relations during the twentieth century. Despite the large amount of personnel and capital invested in international counter-terrorism alliances, terrorist activities are still on the rise and have evolved into new forms. Under pressure from international counter-terrorism alliances, the Islamic State has begun to establish branches and alliances, leading to the spread of terrorist organisations to other countries such as Libya, Egypt, Nigeria, Afghanistan and Pakistan. The Islamic State has also used new technology and social media to incite radicals to initiate terrorist strikes in several cities around the world. They mainly target train stations, ports, hotels, sports stadiums and other public facilities, causing considerable loss of life and property, as well as social panic.

The rise of terrorism reveals not only the conflict created by economic inequality, but also the conflict of values created by different civilisations. The 'clash of civilisations', coined by Huntington, states that the root of future international conflict will be related to culture instead of ideological or economic issues. The confrontations and conflicts between civilisations will become the major battle lines. The competitive coexistence and confrontation among different civilisations will become the dominant theme of international politics.

Demographic structures and the racial composition of a society can undergo substantial changes. With intensified religious beliefs, integration in multi-ethnic countries becomes increasingly difficult. This affects not only international relations, but has also led to the rise of nationalism in developed countries. Currently, there are more than 50 million Muslims in Europe. Half of all newborn babies in the Netherlands and Germany are from Muslim families. At the current growth rate, in 2050, Muslims will account for more than half of the population in France and Germany, and 50 million of the total population in the US. Currently, there are about 10 million Muslims in the US, along with 30 million Hispanics. This figure is still increasing. Demographic changes in the twenty-first century have made conventional 'white' elites in Europe and the US anxious. They attribute social crises and domestic challenges to the clash of civilisations, an approach that eventually strengthens the strain between mainstream Western society and Muslim immigrants. Thus, the 'conflict of civilisations' becomes a self-perpetuating prophecy.

It is worth noting that religious nationalism is not exclusive to Islam. Racism in some forms of Christianity has long been a political undercurrent in Western society. This racism is restricted and concealed by political correctness. Trump's rise to political power has revealed the religious conflict hidden in US society. With the rise of nationalism in developed countries, the pressure related to nationalism and populism that has accumulated over a long time is released in election cycles or social movements. This may result in social unrest and terrorist activity, or even international conflict due to the transfer of domestic problems abroad.

Part 2: International strategic environment: A development perspective

Development is a basic demand of human society, as well as the key to solving all problems. Only with development can we eradicate the roots of conflict, ensure people's basic rights and meet citizens' demands for a better life. However, lack of development is still a challenge faced by many. A number of problems, such as income inequality, either between or within nations, the energy and resource bottlenecks that developing countries face, and a lack of global economic growth are constraining economic and social development.

The global economy shows signs of short-term recovery, but long-term sustainable and balanced growth faces challenges

The prospect of global economic growth is an important condition for China's economic development. China's foreign trade and investment are dependent on strong, sustainable growth in the global economy. Recently, global economic growth has improved markedly, the labour market has continued to improve, the price level has risen moderately globally, and the growth of international trade has increased. However, long-term factors supporting the rapid growth of international trade have not yet been formed. The adjustment of the US's fiscal and monetary policies will have a spill-over effect on the world economy; anti-globalisation, especially protectionist trade and investment policies, continues to strengthen; the debt problem has become more serious; and asset bubbles are rapidly accumulating and may burst at any time. Geopolitical risks and terrorism remain, indicating the lack of a solid foundation for sustained, stable and balanced growth (Zhang & Yao, 2018).

During the decade before the global financial crisis (GFC) (1998–2007), the annual global GDP growth was 4.2 per cent. In the nine years following the GFC (2008–2016), the annual global GDP growth rate fell to 3.2 per cent (International Monetary Fund [IMF], 2017). At present, global economic growth is dramatically variable. Since mid-2016, the global economy has entered an upward cycle, and this momentum has accelerated. According to the IMF (2017), forecasts for 2017 and 2018 global economic growth rates have been raised by 0.1 percentage points to 3.6 per cent and 3.7 per cent respectively. However, economic recovery remains uncertain: 'The short-term recovery is still fragile and robust growth may not be sustainable, and the medium and long-term prospects in many areas are not satisfactory' (IMF, 2017). From a longer-term perspective, the medium-term growth rate of most developed countries is still below pre-GFC levels. As a result, the current economic recovery remains fragile, and uncertainties may be intensified. Sustainable growth faces long-term challenges.

One of the biggest problems faced by global economic growth is the slow increase in labour productivity. According to data released by the Conference Board, the average annual labour productivity growth dropped from 3.2 per cent between 2003 and 2007 to 1.8 per cent between 2012 and 2016. In 2017, global labour productivity growth witnessed a slight increase to 2.2 per cent. The slow or even stagnant growth is caused by a number of reasons, such as the slowdown of technological advances and investment growth, slow technology diffusion because of inadequate market competitiveness and institutional inertia, slowdown of human capital accumulation and population aging in major economies, and misallocation of resources resulted from the quantitative easing policies in many countries (Zhang & Yao, 2018).

The slow recovery of global direct investment is also an important factor affecting economic recovery. Global direct investment is an important force in promoting the international division of labour, as well as economic integration and prosperity. According to the United Nations Conference on Trade and Development, global foreign direct investment (FDI) inflows increased by 5 per cent to 1.8 trillion dollars in 2017, thus reversing the negative growth in 2016. However, while a series of investment promotion policies have been introduced, some countries have strengthened restrictive policies for foreign investment, such as unilateral termination or reassessment of international investment agreements, so the increase of global transnational direct investment is likely to be small in 2018. The downturn in global direct investment activities has been associated with slow progress in promoting investment access and openness, as well as the policies of advanced economies that encourage manufacturing to go back to home countries.

Additionally, the continued rise of global debt levels has not only increased the vulnerability of financial markets, but also slowed recovery of consumption, hindering economic recovery. During the GFC, to eliminate liquidity panic in financial markets, central banks did not reduce their debts. Instead, they injected liquidity into the market and expanded the debt scale. After the GFC, central banks continued to use an expansionary monetary policy, including quantitative easing to stimulate economic recovery. Monetary expansion does not lead to a decline in debt levels. Rather, it created higher debt levels.

The uncertainty of global economic recovery and sustainable development will form the background of China's participation in the international division of labour in the future. Over the past three decades, China has relied on the international competitiveness of its labour-intensive and export-oriented manufacturing industries to meet the growing demand in the global market. Consequently, China has developed into the world's largest exporter. However, demand in the global market has been sluggish and the traditional comparative advantages of China are diminishing. Long-term structural problems with the Chinese economy have become prominent. Thus, China must adapt to the 'new normal' of slow global growth and vigorously promote technological innovation and structural reform. In the highly integrated global economy, national structural reform policies have significant spill-over effects. In addition to promoting supply-side reform, China should also actively promote coordinated reform among countries. At the G20 Hangzhou Summit in 2016, China proposed 48 guiding principles in nine priority areas, including boosting trade and investment liberalisation, promoting labour market reform, encouraging innovation and promoting fiscal reform. China provided the other G20 member states with guidance for these reforms.

Income distribution inequality leads to the rise of anti-globalisation forces

Economic globalisation is the most obvious trend since the Cold War. Globalisation is conducive to expanding the world market and improving the efficiency of global resource allocation. It is also conducive to developing the international division of labour and global production capacity. Global prosperity and development depend largely on the advance of globalisation. China has become a significant beneficiary of globalisation through its reform and opening up policy by participating in the global division of labour. However, since the GFC, discussions about globalisation have changed direction. 'Globalisation', as a frequently used word after the Cold War, has begun to be replaced with 'de-globalisation' or 'anti-globalisation'.

An important reason for the rise of anti-globalisation forces is the growing imbalance among countries and the widening gap between the rich and poor within countries. The imbalance between developed and developing countries is still an important issue that the international community must face. According to the IMF, the per capita GDP of developed countries based on purchasing power reached US$49,111 in 2017, equivalent to 4.2 times the average level of developing countries (IMF, 2017).

Meanwhile, economic globalisation has widened the income gap between individuals within countries. The failure of governments to implement effective redistribution and social security policies has aggravated income inequality. Although the US has always been the largest beneficiary of globalisation, its domestic wealth distribution gap is expanding significantly. The net gainers and net losers in US society are highly divided. The richest families, which account for only 0.1 per cent of the total population, have accumulated ever-increasing amounts of wealth. Today, they own 22 per cent of the total wealth in the US; that is, 0.1 per cent of the US population holds roughly the same amount of wealth as 90 per cent of the US population (Saez & Zucman, 2016). In *Capital in the Twenty-first Century* (2014), French economist Thomas Piketty showed (through statistical data) that income inequality is evident in all nations that have participated in globalisation. The continual widening of the gap between rich and poor has become a global phenomenon. In developed countries, scepticism has emerged around economic globalisation, with some commentators complaining that their

THE JINGSHAN REPORT

country's trading partners have taken local jobs. Calls have been made for governments to adopt protectionist trade policies. The inequality of wealth distribution caused by globalisation is eroding the domestic social basis of global economic integration.

It is natural that such dissatisfaction can result in attributing unemployment to economic opening. However, the idea of free trade will ultimately prevail, because the global division of labour brings massive trade benefits. No country can bear the cost of trade protectionism or achieve economic growth on its own; rather, countries must remain in an integrated global system. Although income inequality is not a sufficient reason to reverse economic globalisation, it has exposed problems with the current process. We need to make globalisation more inclusive.

Deepening economic interdependence continues to change the connotation of opening

Global economic integration can promote optimal allocation of production and increase in global, as well as national, welfare. Thus, along with intensified economic interdependence, the construction of an open and free international economic system has become a common interest of all states. As the core of economic globalisation, the free flow of goods, services and capital without discrimination demands institutional support. A free and open economic system should be based on international rules negotiated and agreed to by all states. At the domestic level, the market economy demands a system that protects property rights and ensures contracts are enforced. At the international level, a free and open international economy requires all states to negotiate, cooperate and forgo 'beggar-thy-neighbour' policies, such as trade protectionism, competitive devaluation and lack of coordination of financial regulatory policies. In the meantime, with globalisation, the spill-over effect of nations' policies is enhanced, which necessitates increased coordination of macroeconomic policies. As a result, with increasing interdependence, all states must make a collective effort to protect a multilateral trade system, construct an open global economic system and promote the free flow of production factors globally.

Currently, with the development of information technology and deepening of global value chains, mankind has entered a highly interdependent period. China's dependence on the rest of the world is also at the highest level in history, especially in relation to technology, market and resources. In the 1990s, global exports totalled US$5.7 trillion per year. This rose to US$14.6 trillion between 2000 and 2012. At the same time, the scale and speed of global capital flows have increased. In the 1990s, the global FDI outflow was about US$400 billion per year. This has increased to about US$1.5 trillion over the past 10 years. Against this background, economic integration has moved across borders, requiring countries to coordinate public policies and regulatory standards. In the current trade pattern, the global value chain has been normalised. Integrated transnational production needs all states to shift from conventional open measures, such as tariff concessions, to cross-border measures and regulatory coordination. The profound integration of the global economy has given opening up a new connotation. Some countries are trying to upgrade their systems, build up new competitive advantage, promote innovation and explore new approaches to opening. China should steadily press for reform through opening, build an open economy and push forward reform in 'deep-water' areas such as financial services and public services. China should enhance the level of opening of the financial industry; steadily promote RMB internationalisation; expand the scope, method and scale of cross-border RMB use; and accelerate RMB capital account convertibility with caution. Additionally, China's opening strategy should not only focus on itself, but also coordinate with other countries through actively preserving and developing multilateralism. This will create a stable and open environment for its reform and development.

Emerging economies emulating the development patterns of developed countries are restricted by resources and environmental factors

Resources and environmental factors place constraints on long-term economic growth. Human beings have consumed too much and have begun to 'pay' for the excesses.

There are two types of emerging economies: resource importing and resource exporting. The former is represented by China and India, and the latter by Russia, Brazil and South Africa. Resource-importing countries do not have enough resources to meet their development needs, so they are very constrained by resource availability. Resource-exporting countries are rich in resources, but their economic development is seriously affected by international energy and resource prices; as such, they are prone to resource dependence or the 'resource curse'.

Resource-importing countries face two types of risks. One is availability; that is, whether the country can obtain the necessary energy and raw materials from the international market. The other is price; that is, the impact of energy and resource price fluctuations on the international market. Take China as an example. With a great demand for energy and resources, China possesses increasing bargaining power in the international market. However, China must work hard and maintain strategic patience to alleviate the energy and resource bottleneck when considering such factors as the rise of economic nationalism in resource-rich countries, obstruction from multinational corporations, containment by strategic competitors and lack of capacity to protect waterway safety.

For resource-exporting countries, an economic model that relies heavily on resource exports renders their domestic economies vulnerable to fluctuations in international commodity prices. In a time of declining prices, the economic growth of these countries is generally slower. Russia and Brazil even experienced negative growth between 2015 and 2016. Conversely, when domestic capital and technology are concentrated on resources, other industries develop slowly. Due to an overdependence on gold, coal, iron ore and other resources, the economies of Russia, Brazil and South Africa were significantly damaged when global commodity prices plummeted in 2013. This led to a sharp decline in government revenue, and some departments, such as education and energy, have become seriously underfunded as a result.

With global warming, environmental pollution, rapid population growth and other issues becoming global problems, environmental issues have become a common constraint on both resource-importing and resource-exporting countries. China, Russia and South Africa are significant producers and users of coal, and China has the highest carbon dioxide emissions of any country. The key to reducing the proportion of coal consumption in emerging economies (and, thus, reducing carbon emissions and the irreversible damage caused by environmental pollution) is to promote the use of alternative renewable energy and clean energy; accelerate large-scale production of shale gas, nuclear and other new energy; and upgrade the energy industry's structure. Emerging economies and developing countries remain at a stage of high population growth. This rapid growth places much pressure on economic development and the natural environment. In China and India, population growth rates have dropped significantly, but due to the large population base, tens of millions of people are still added each year.

Resource and environmental constraints made it impossible for emerging economies to replicate the growth and consumption models of developed countries without regard to ecological factors. The development models of emerging economies have been adjusted, but the transformation will be difficult and take a long time. Development will still be a priority for China in the foreseeable future, but with the country's development moving into a new stage, the goals are being upgraded. China should no longer simply pursue GDP growth, but should instead seek 'green', inclusive and sustainable development.

Part 3: International strategic environment: A global governance perspective

In an era where global interdependence has reached an unprecedented level, humanity is facing a series of increasingly pressing global issues. These issues are characterised by their cross-border nature, great externality and spill-over effects, among other things. During the process of economic globalisation, problems such as trade protectionism, turbulent financial systems, environmental pollution, infectious diseases and terrorism have had a stronger spill-over effect, threatening the interests of various global actors. Resolving these issues is beyond the capacity of one or even several countries. These problems must be solved through broad global cooperation. Since the end of World War II, with the joint efforts of the international community, the global governance system has been continuously improved and perfected. However, due to continuously emerging global issues and changes of national strengths, the existing system has encountered severe problems in relation to its legitimacy, validity and representativeness, showing a lack of ability to adapt to the ever-changing situations. Therefore, the international community must reform this system urgently.

The dilemma of collective action has aggravated the global governance deficit

In his speech at the opening ceremony of the Belt and Road Forum for International Cooperation in May 2017, Chinese President Xi Jinping acknowledged that global governance deficit was one of the most serious challenges for humanity. The deficit is manifested mainly in the following two aspects. First, the contradiction between the growing demand for global governance and the inadequate supply of global governance or global public goods is becoming increasingly prominent. Second, flaws in the current governance mechanism have become increasingly serious, while reform of the system is uncertain.

Global public goods have a non-exclusive feature. Maintaining world peace, global trade and financial stability and promoting sustainable development is costly, while all the countries can have access to these products. In other words, even if a country does not contribute to the provision of these products, it can still enjoy the benefits. This gives countries an incentive to let other countries bear the costs of providing public goods while becoming 'free riders' themselves. As a result, the supply of global public goods is impeded. Therefore, a core issue to be addressed is how to coordinate the different players in the international community to increase the supply of public goods as much as possible.

In addition to the inadequate supply of public goods, there are cases of ample or excessive supply of some other types of public goods, such as biased international trade and investment rules. This can be explained by Mancur Olson's 'logic of collective action'. With a lack of incentive and the absence of a global government, a small number of players who are willing, capable and highly concerned with their own interests will form small action groups operating according to cost–benefit calculations. These groups will participate actively in the supply of public goods that can bring the maximum interests or minimal loss. Once a narrow interest group driven by selective incentives gains a dominant position, the resulting global governance will be biased and non-neutral. Through using non-neutral global public goods, group leaders will enhance their own interests, even at the expense of most other stakeholders. In some ways, global public goods in the form of international organisations or global order have been 'privatised' and become the tools of certain interest groups to achieve their goals.

The current global governance mechanism was mainly established by developed countries after World War II. To a certain extent, this mechanism has maintained a peaceful and stable world and a free and open international economic order. However, it should be noted that conflicts in some 'hot spots' still arise. Various forms of trade, investment and financial protectionism remain prevalent. There are increasing challenges in new areas such as climate change, cyber security, polar region and space issues. In particular, the GFC in 2008 exposed, in a profound manner, many weaknesses of the current global governance mechanism. Due to the lack of effective collective action, some traditional mechanisms have been unable to adapt to new situations.

Changing distribution of global power stimulates reform of global governance

As the comparative strengths of the world's major players have changed drastically, it is increasingly necessary to engage emerging economies in solving global issues. They have become important stakeholders in the current system and their awareness about maintaining and expanding their own interests through the global system is also growing. In this context, a need to adjust the existing order and make the global system more unbiased has emerged. However, at the same time, countries with vested interests in the current system wish to maintain their dominant positions.

Emerging economies should enhance collaboration through platforms such as the BRICS (Brazil, Russia, India, China and South Africa) cooperation mechanism and G20 to promote representation of the rights and voices of emerging market economies and developing countries in relation to global governance. However, the structures of some global governance mechanisms have not been improved for a long time and have been obstructed by countries (or groups of countries) with vested interests, especially the US and European countries. Even if a consensus on reform is achieved, it is often difficult to realise such consensus in a timely and effective manner due to the national interests of involved countries. For example, the US Congress did not approve the IMF's 2010 quota and governance reform program until December 2015, and further attached a condition of greater supervision over the IMF. Besides obstructing emerging economies from increasing their voices in international institutions, developed countries have begun to worry about the trend of developing countries catching up through multilateral rules and international division of labour. Some countries have used a unilateral strategy to stimulate reform of the multilateral system to preserve their advantages.

China will play an active role in the historical process of global governance reform. First, development is the key that China will provide to the international community to solve various global problems. China's greatest contribution to global governance has been its exploration of a development path of reform and an opening with Chinese characteristics. The country has been a role model and led the world in development. Second, China will adhere to the principle of achieving shared growth through discussion and collaboration and strive to build a more inclusive international order. In the face of global governance reform, China should always retain its mission of maintaining world peace and promoting common development. China does not seek to overturn the current system, but will actively promote its reform and improvement. China will firmly uphold the international order with the United Nations Charter as its core. It will also promote the reform of unjust and unreasonable arrangements in the global governance system, striving to make the system more balanced, beneficial and reflective of the will of most countries.

The waning of ideology in global governance ideas

Globalisation has brought about significant economic and cultural shocks to countries. Trump's populism highlights the division between income, social class, racial groups and cultures in US society. The social foundation for anti-globalisation is thus further strengthened. Trump's campaign promises and policies are largely against multilateralism. Some researchers even claim that Trump has subverted the post-war values of the US and is likely to put an end to the 'liberal international order' created by the US. However, Trump's hit on the multilateral system focuses on the idea of liberalism instead of the multilateral coordination system. Trump is trying to change the tradition of US liberalism and cultural pluralism in various realms such as immigration, climate, democracy and human rights; he is also challenging the basis of US foreign policy values.

The shock instigated by Trump's election reveals that the norm of international order, which has long been dominated by Western countries, is being challenged. This challenge originates from the complex problems of Western countries and is related to the social split caused by economic globalisation. It is also caused by the competition of different development modes and paths in emerging economies.

The GFC in 2008 gave people a chance to reflect on the effectiveness of the policy framework based on the 'Washington Consensus' and to appreciate the experiences of emerging economies. Under the leadership of the G20 Group and the Financial Stability Board, Basel III, which emphasises both macroprudential and microprudential measures, replaced the Anglo-Saxon model that was centred on relaxing financial regulation.[4] The IMF, an advocate of capital account liberalisation, has also begun to recognise the validity of capital flow management measures.[5] The principles advocated by emerging economies, such as sovereignty equality, inclusive development, diversity of development models and culture, and 'common but differentiated responsibility', are becoming core values of the international community and mainstream norms of global governance. The success of the Chinese model, which discards ideological differences and concentrates on development, provides sharp contrast to the US model, which has become inflexible and less effective. The influence and appeal of China's model has also significantly increased worldwide.

The world has expected and demanded China to participate in global governance

After 40 years of reform and opening up, China's economy and society have undergone unprecedented changes. China has developed into the world's largest trading nation, second-largest economy and second-largest investor. The biggest change has been the rapid growth of the Chinese economy and the substantial increase in China's overall strength. In other words, China's development has brought enormous shock and made the world order increasingly complex.

China's impact on the international order is manifested mainly in the following four aspects. First, is the impact at the physical level. This mainly refers to the significant increase of China's demand for energy and resources. Second, is the impact at the monetary level. The process of RMB internationalisation has already begun. In the next 30 years, the RMB is expected to become a currency for international trade and reserves, and a key currency in the international monetary system. If this goal is achieved, the international monetary and financial system will be significantly altered. Third, is the impact at the institutional level. Although a fundamental change in international rules is not possible in the short term, the rapid increase of China's national strength will enable

---

4   Basel III relies mainly on market discipline, self-regulatory hedge funds and financial derivative trade to join the international regulatory framework. See Helleiner and Pagliari (2010).

5   In February 2010, the IMF released a report on the regulation of international capital flow, recognising the appropriateness of capital account management and setting a guide for how to use it effectively. See Ostry et al. (2010).

and require China to seek fairer international rules. Fourth, is the impact at the conceptual level. At this level, China's impact on the contemporary world is reflected mainly in the country's development mode. Therefore, the certainty of China's future development is an important background for the interaction between China and the rest of the world.

The long-term rapid growth of China and other emerging economies has given the US and its Western allies a difficult choice. The latter wishes to place China and other emerging economies in an open trade and investment system with higher standards and stricter enforcement. As such, they will be able to use biased rules that are more favourable for them to constrain China. Additionally, they fear that China and other emerging economies will seek to establish a new set of international institutions in parallel to those dominated by the US and its allies. To prevent China from using its increasing influence to change the international order, Western countries—in particular, the US elite class—will more actively seek to have China accept the various international rules or institutions designed and dominated by developed countries. However, these rules are biased and favour developed countries.

When developed countries shift their focus to domestic issues, the international community raises its expectations for developing countries, especially China, in addressing global issues. Although quickly becoming a key player in the global arena, China is still a developing country. It should safeguard its own interests while taking on more international responsibilities. As the country's reform and opening up enters their later stages, its goals are also changing significantly. This has a profound impact on China's relations with the rest of the world. The Chinese economy is becoming increasingly dependent on the international system, while the US's leadership and support for a free and open international economic order is diminishing. International economic and trade rules are being restructured, and an open economic system urgently needs new momentum. This calls for China to shoulder more responsibility in developing a free and open multilateral system.

Part 4: China's strategic options for shaping the future global landscape

Engage in cooperation to disperse external pressure

The pressure China currently faces mainly relates to international rules. China should establish new platforms to address this. For example, it could strengthen cooperation among the BRICS countries and the Shanghai Cooperation Organisation, and promote negotiations on the China–Japan–South Korea Free Trade Agreement.

Shoulder appropriate responsibilities and participate in economic globalisation

Along with China's rapid economic development and rising global impact, there is a growing call for China to be a leader in the international order. An emerging economy like China should take on international responsibility according to its own conditions. The responsibilities must be in proportion to its national strength and development level. In doing so, China should follow three principles. First, responsibilities must correspond to rights. The principle of parity of responsibility and authority is commonly recognised in international law. In the current system, global governance rules and mechanisms were established under the auspices of developed economies, which are the major beneficiaries of the system, while the majority of emerging and developing economies do not enjoy fair treatment, nor can they wield influence commensurate to their power. Although China became the world's second-largest economy in 2010, its power of discourse is far weaker than that of the US and other developed economies. Second, China must take on responsibilities based on its own conditions, capabilities and needs. China will continue to be the world's largest developing country for a long time. According to the IMF, China's per capita GDP in 2017 was US$8,677, ranking 75th in the world. The number rose to more than US$9,580 in 2018, ranking 72nd. Third, China should properly balance short-term and long-term interests, as well as localised and national interests.

Strive for inclusive development

China should seek not only peaceful development, but also inclusive development, which means one country's development will benefit the entire world, and all countries will share the opportunities for welfare improvement. Inclusiveness is an important part of China's commitment to international responsibility. China's development has both positive and negative externalities. Compared to peaceful development, inclusive development emphasises strengthening positive externalities while minimising negative externalities.

Inclusive development also means China participates in global governance based on the principles of 'extensive consultation, joint contribution and shared benefits'. Consultation means that all participants form consensus on the basic principles, key areas, mechanisms and development planning of global governance based on discussion and consultation. Joint contribution means all members of the international community give full play to their advantages and potential to jointly promote reform and innovation of the global governance system. Shared benefits means that all countries have a fair share of the benefits of global governance. These principles embody openness and inclusiveness in global governance and conform to the global trend of democratic development. In practice, they actively involve all members of the international community, especially developing countries, heeding their concerns, better safeguarding their legitimate rights and ensuring they share in the benefits of global governance. The practice could enhance the trust between China and the rest of the world, and is a reliable path for burying doubts and achieving expectations.

Promote gradual reform of global governance

As an expanding country, China is a taker, rather than a maker, of existing international rules and institutions. Previously, interactions between China and international institutions were mostly conducting coordination under the current system and internalising the rules. As the legitimacy and effectiveness of the global governance system face more challenges, and as China plays an increasingly important role in the global economic system and security affairs, China has become a major force in promoting reform of global governance. In this regard, some may have unrealistic expectations that the increase in China's national strength will bring fundamental changes to international rules and the international order. In fact, the evolution of the international system is a long-term process. It is not realistic or necessary to make revolutionary changes to unreasonable international order or rules, especially those that favour vested interest country groups.

In its participation in global governance, China does not wish to establish an entirely new system or instigate a revolution of the existing system. Rather, it seeks modest reform of existing multilateral mechanisms. In doing so, China should take a cooperative path and emphasise the rise of emerging economies and developing countries and focus on complementing, not replacing, the current mechanisms (i.e. improvements, rather than revolution). To deal with mechanisms in various areas, China should employ differentiated approaches based on its own conditions, national interests and the characteristics of those mechanisms. China should promote the concept of inclusive development to improve the current system. The system is influenced by Western values and institutional patterns and does not adequately acknowledge the diversity of development paths and national conditions.

As China grows, it may seek reform of rules and institutions. In the next decade, China should seize opportunities and work with other emerging economies to make improvements to the current system and exert a larger influence.

Rationally respond to external challenges

China is on the road to 'great rejuvenation'. A peaceful global environment is critical to accomplishing this mission. While defending its territory and marine rights, China should exercise care and take appropriate actions. China should also be aware of the harmfulness of extreme nationalism and the danger of falling into an arms race trap. In addressing global issues, China must be patient and properly identify priorities.

In terms of foreign relations, China has two priorities. First, is the establishment of a new major power relationship based on mutual respect, mutual benefits and win–win cooperation. This is a new way of dealing with conflicts and contradictions between emerging countries and existing powers. The major obstacle to China's long-term development is the US, which intends to bring China into the existing system using the rules dominated by and favourable to itself. In engaging with the US,

China should consolidate risk management to avoid a lose–lose situation and promote win–win cooperation to establish a new major power relationship.

The second priority involves creating a stable peripheral environment. Peripheral instability is still a threat to China's security. Pressing issues in relation to islands, seawaters and resources in surrounding areas will continue or become worse. China should prioritise establishing a new regional security mechanism with Northeast Asia. While protecting its national sovereignty and core interests, China could enhance its influence in the region and explore new ways to solve disputes, break deadlocks and create new and favourable situations.

Specifically, China should reconsider the practicality and feasibility of some foreign policy objectives and respond to changes in the external environment in a flexible manner. China should improve weak links in foreign policymaking—for example, improving coordination among government departments, information sharing, intellectual support and personnel training mechanisms—to enhance the effectiveness of decision-making. Multiple policy instruments and contingency plans should be employed to respond to uncertainties in the external environment.

Actively seek support from the international community

As developed countries currently dominate international public opinion, China should enhance communication with other countries, actively express its voice and create an atmosphere beneficial to the dissemination of China's ideas of 'peaceful development' and 'inclusive development'. In particular, it is necessary for China to articulate how its rejuvenation contributes to the welfare improvement of all countries, so that the international community accepts China's development.

The Chinese Government should enhance the impact of its communication with the rest of the world, equip itself with modern communication technology and make full use of communication resources. This can be achieved by using new media tools and adopting multiple perspectives and narrative forms to shape China's international image more vividly. At the domestic level, China should promote cultural prosperity by establishing institutions and creating a favourable cultural environment. At the international level, the government and the public should actively use multilateral and bilateral communication channels to conduct cultural diplomacy. China should also leverage its position as the host country of global conferences to raise Chinese topics, concepts and plans and shape the agenda. Additionally, in the process of promoting international economic cooperation, China should disseminate knowledge of Chinese enterprises that have met social obligations and promoted people's livelihoods abroad, and tell success stories of the Belt and Road Initiative.

References

Helleiner, E. & Pagliari, S. (2010). The end of self-regulation? Hedge funds and derivatives in global financial governance. In E. Helleiner, S. Pagliari & H. Zimmermann (Eds), *Global finance in crisis: The politics of international regulatory change* (pp. 74–90). New York, NY: Routledge.

International Monetary Fund. (2019, October). *World Economic Outlook, October 2019: Global Manufacturing Downturn, Rising Trade Barriers*. Retrieved from www.imf.org/en/Publications/WEO/Issues/2019/10/01/world-economic-outlook-october-2019

Ostry, J. D., Ghosh, A. R., Habermeier, K., Chamon, M., Qureshi, M. S. & Reinhardt, D. B. S. (2010, February). *Capital inflows: The role of controls* (IMF Staff Position Note 10/04). Washington, DC: International Monetary Fund.

Piketty, T. (2014). *Capital in the twenty-first century* (Arthur Goldhammer trans.) Harvard University Press. (Original work published in 2013)

Saez, E. & Zucman, G. (2016). Wealth inequality in the United States since 1913: Evidence from capitalized income tax data. *Quarterly Journal of Economics, 131*(2), 519–578.

Zhang, Y. & Yao, Z. (2018). Global economic recovery accelerated while foundation needs to be enhanced. *Qiushi, 2.*

2

China's Financial Development: A Global Perspective

Zhu Min,[1] Chen Weidong,[2] Zhou Jingtong,[3]
Gai Xinzhe[4] and Xiong Qiyue[5]

Introduction

China's responses to the shocks of the 2008 global financial crisis (GFC) and its endeavours to rectify market order have led to significant reforms and developments in the financial industry. In or around 1996, the banking industry faced problems related to a high ratio of non-performing loans (NPL). Further, the stock, bond and insurance markets were underdeveloped and in a chaotic state. During this time, many authoritative international media commentators denigrated China's financial sector, claiming that China's commercial banks were technically insolvent and that this would stall economic growth. To promote stable and sustained economic development, China has striven vigorously to reform its financial system. In doing so, profound changes have been made to the financial sector.

---

1   Chair of the National Institute of Financial Research, Tsinghua University.
2   Researcher at the Institute of International Finance, Bank of China (BOC).
3   Researcher at the Institute of International Finance, BOC.
4   Researcher at the Institute of International Finance, BOC.
5   Researcher at the Institute of International Finance, BOC.

Today, China's financial sector plays an increasingly important role in the global financial system. It has evolved from playing a little-known 'supporting role' to a 'leading role' and is now the subject of significant international attention.

Part 1: China's banking industry: Development history, international status and future directions

Banking plays a crucial role in China's financial system. Since the launch of its reform and opening up policy, China's banking industry has undergone historic changes, including the separation of functions, resolution of bad loans and joint-stock reforms. Such endeavours have enhanced the banking industry's competitiveness and improved its international status significantly. In the global banking system, the role of Chinese banks has become increasingly important. However, unlike other large global banks, Chinese banks continue to rely on savings and loan business. Consequently, interest remains the major source of income for Chinese banks. In the future, the banking industry will continue to dominate China's financial system. Universal banking represents a future development direction. A major theme of regulatory reform will be to strengthen regulations related to bank capital, behaviours and functions.

Development history

The banking industry began to develop after it broke away from the 'unified administration system'. In 1979, China established or re-established three national specialised banks: the Agricultural Bank of China (ABC), the Bank of China (BOC) and China Construction Bank (CCB). In 1984, the Industrial and Commercial Bank of China (ICBC) was established to undertake industrial and commercial credit and savings business, a function previously performed by the People's Bank of China (PBC). Thus, a national professional banking system was formed with a clear division of responsibilities. Under this system, the four specialised banks (the ABC, BOC, CCB and ICBC) conducted four major types of businesses (rural finance, foreign exchange, construction projects, and industrial and commercial loans respectively).

In the early 1980s, the Chinese Government began to liberalise market access restrictions to satisfy the need of funds and financial services for rapid economic development. Several new credit cooperatives and commercial banks were restored or established in major regions and cities. For example, in July 1986, the Bank of Communications (BOCOM)—China's first joint-stock commercial bank—was established. Subsequently, a number of other national joint-stock commercial banks, including China Merchants Bank, the Shenzhen Development Bank and CITIC Bank (formerly CITIC Industrial Bank), were established. The establishment and development of joint-stock commercial banks broke the monopoly held by the national specialised banks under the planned economy system. Thus, a multitype and multilevel banking system that met the needs of China's socialist market economy gradually formed.

Since 1994, China has established three policy banks—the China Development Bank (CDB), Export-Import Bank of China (EIBC) and Agricultural Development Bank of China—to separate policy-oriented services from commercial banking services. These three banks are responsible for funding policies related to national key investments, foreign trade and rural reform respectively.

In 1995, China promulgated the Law of the People's Republic of China on Commercial Banks and legally defined the four specialised national banks as commercial banks. The four banks took this opportunity to accelerate the process of becoming true commercial banks. However, due to some policy-related services, ineffective management, economic overheating and other factors, China's banking industry suffered a sharp increase in NPLs. In or around 1997, the NPL ratio reached approximately 30 per cent.

In 1999, to increase public confidence in the financial industry, reform state-owned banks and address the NPL issue, China established four financial asset management companies (AMCs): China Great Wall Asset Management Co. Ltd; China Cinda Asset Management Co. Ltd; China Huarong Asset Management Co. Ltd; and China Orient Asset Management Co. Ltd. These AMCs received and disposed of non-performing assets (approximately CN¥1.4 trillion) divested from the four large banks. Following this, the NPL ratio of the four state-owned commercial banks decreased significantly.

On the basis of this restructuring, the Chinese Government proposed a four-step plan to further reform the commercial banks. This comprised implementing joint-stock reforms, increasing the disposal of non-performing assets, strengthening capital and creating the right conditions for listing. On 30 December 2003, the Chinese Government invested US$45 billion in the BOC and CCB through the Central Huijin Investment Company (Central Huijin). In June 2004, the Central Huijin injected another CN¥3 billion into the BOCOM. In 2005, the Central Huijin and China's Ministry of Finance jointly injected US$30 billion (50 per cent each) into the ICBC. Additionally, since 2004, the ICBC, CCB, BOC and BOCOM have divested CN¥1 trillion in non-performing assets. After restructuring, the financial burden of the four banks was reduced significantly. The substantial increase in asset quality and capital strength created favourable conditions that allowed the banks to transform into joint-stock companies and be listed. In 2015, the CDB and EIBC received US$48 billion and US$45 billion respectively to improve the corporate governance mechanism, of which the capital adequacy ratio was the core factor.

The BOCOM was listed on the Hong Kong Stock Exchange in June 2005 and on the Shanghai Stock Exchange (SSE) (A-share market) in 2007. The CCB was listed on the Hong Kong Stock Exchange in October 2005 and on the SSE (A-share market) in September 2007. The BOC was listed on the Hong Kong Stock Exchange in June 2006 and on the SSE in July 2006. The ICBC was listed on the SSE and the Hong Kong Stock Exchange simultaneously in October 2006 through the 'A + H' model, the world's largest initial public offering (IPO) at that time. The ABC was listed on the SSE (A-share market) and the Hong Kong Stock Exchange in July 2010, setting a new record for the world's largest IPO.

China's banking industry has moved from the edge of 'technical insolvency' to being on track for positive development. Further, the overall strength, profitability and competitiveness of China's banking industry have improved greatly.

First, the asset scale has continued to expand. At the end of 2016, China's total banking assets had reached CN¥226.26 trillion, 1,206 times that in 1978 (CN¥187.65 billion) and 7.2 times that in 2003 (CN¥27.7 trillion). In 2016, the assets of the domestic banking institutions reached CN¥208.92 trillion, 6.9 times that in 2003 (CN¥26.6 trillion) (see Figure 2-1).

(Trillion RMB)

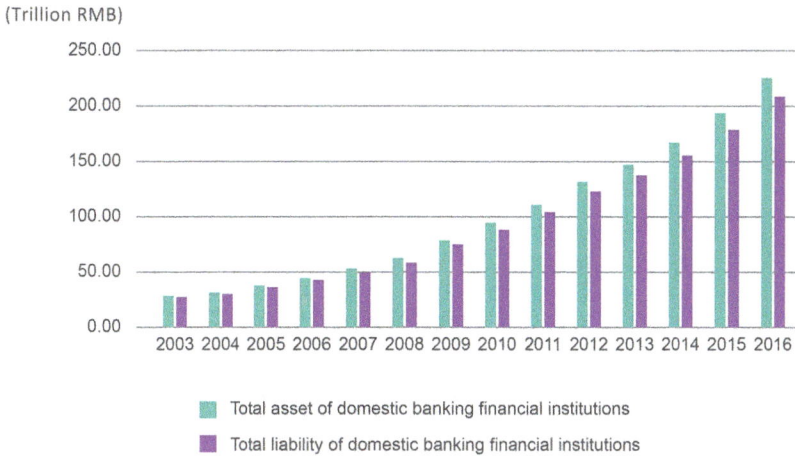

Figure 2-1: Total assets/liabilities of China's banking industry (2003–2016).
Source: Wind (2017).

Second, operational efficiency has improved significantly. In 1978, China's commercial banks achieved a loss of CN¥1.66 billion; in 2016, they achieved a net profit of CN¥1.65 trillion. Return on assets (ROA) was 1.1 per cent in 2016, compared to 0.1 per cent in 2003. Return on equity (ROE) was 14.8 per cent in 2016, compared to 3 per cent in 2003. The cost-to-income ratio dropped to 27.8 per cent, significantly lower than that of a decade ago. In addition to realising higher profits, the listed banks paid out ample dividends to their shareholders. Indeed, since being listed, the five major banks have achieved an average dividend ratio of more than 30 per cent.

Third, asset quality has fundamentally improved. Non-performing assets have shown a 'double decrease'; the NPL balance and NPL ratio dropped from nearly CN¥2 trillion and 20 per cent respectively at the end of 2003 to CN¥1.17 trillion and less than 1.5 per cent respectively at the end of 2013 (of this, the NPL ratio of commercial banks was only 1 per cent). In the past three years, due to the economic slowdown and some other factors, the NPL balance and NPL ratio have increased, but have remained stable overall, with the NPL ratio remaining low (see Table 2-1). By the end of 2016, the NPL balance of China's commercial banks was CN¥1.51 trillion and the NPL ratio was 1.74 per cent. This is low by international standards.

Fourth, risk resistance capacity has substantially increased. The capital adequacy ratio of Chinese commercial banks increased from a paltry level in 2003 to 13.28 per cent in 2016. With a provision balance of CN¥2.67 trillion, the provision coverage ratio of commercial banks rose from under 30 per cent 20 years ago to 295.5 per cent in 2012. Despite a subtle decline in 2016 (to 176.4 per cent), it has remained at a high level.

Table 2-1: NPL of commercial banks (2012–2016)

Indicator	2010	2011	2012	2013	2014	2015	2016
NPL balance (trillion yuan)	4336.0	4279.0	4929.0	5921.0	8426.0	12744.0	15122.0
Subprime (trillion yuan)	1562.6	1725.0	2176.0	2537.0	4031.0	5923.0	6091.0
Doubtful (trillion yuan)	2120.7	1883.0	2122.0	2574.0	3403.0	5283.0	6640.0
Loss (trillion yuan)	670.9	670.0	630.0	809.0	992.0	1539.0	2391.0
NPL ratio (%)	1.10	1.00	0.95	1.00	1.25	1.67	1.74
Subprime (%)	0.40	0.40	0.42	0.43	0.60	0.78	0.70
Doubtful (%)	0.50	0.40	0.41	0.43	0.50	0.69	0.77
Loss (%)	0.20	0.20	0.12	0.14	0.15	0.20	0.28

Note: NPL = non-performing loans.
Source: Wind (2017).

International status

In recent years, China's banking industry has consistently propelled reform and opening up and sustained the shocks of the GFC. As a result, its overall strength and international competitiveness have significantly increased. In just a few decades, China's major banks have developed into world-class financial institutions, and have adopted international accounting and regulatory standards. The rise in the international status of these banks can be observed in the following five areas.

Assets

In 1996, in a ranking of the world's top 10 banks by assets, only one Chinese bank (the ICBC) ranked (at number 10). It had assets of US$373.6 billion, 74 per cent of that of Deutsche Bank (the largest bank at that time). Conversely, 10 years later, in 2016, all four of China's major state-owned banks were included in the ranking of the world's top 10 banks by assets, all ranking in the top five. In 2016, the ICBC was the world's largest bank with assets of US$3.42 trillion (1.9 times that of Deutsche Bank) (see Table 2-2).

Table 2-2: Rankings of the world's top 10 banks by assets (1996 and 2016)

1996				2016			
Rank	Bank	Country	Assets (billion USD)	Rank	Bank	Country	Assets (billion USD)
1	Deutsche Bank	Germany	503.4	1	ICBC	China	342.22
2	UFJ Bank	Japan	501.0	2	CCB	China	282.73
3	Sumitomo Bank	Japan	499.9	3	ABC	China	274.14
4	Dai-Ichi Kangyo Bank	Japan	498.6	4	Mitsubishi UFJ Financial Group	Japan	264.85
5	Fuji Bank	Japan	487.3	5	Bank of China	China	259.10
6	Sakura Bank	Japan	478.1	6	HSBC Holdings	UK	240.97
7	Bank of Tokyo-Mitsubishi	Japan	475.0	7	JP Morgan Chase & Co.	US	235.17
8	Norinchukin Bank	Japan	429.5	8	BNP Paribas	France	216.76
9	Crédit Agricole Group	France	386.4	9	Bank of America	US	214.74
10	ICBC	China	373.6	10	Crédit Agricole	France	184.66

Note: ICBC = Industrial and Commercial Bank of China, CCB = China Construction Bank, ABC = Agricultural Bank of China.
Source: The Banker (2019).

Capital

In 2016, according to *The Banker's*[6] list of the world's top 1,000 banks, China had 119 banks ranked by tier 1 capital, of which 17 were ranked in the top 100. Of the world's 20 largest banks, China had five, and the ICBC, CCB, BOC and ABC ranked in the top five. Conversely, in 1996, no Chinese banks were ranked in the top 20. In 1996, the BOC was ranked 26th (the highest of all Chinese banks) and the ICBC was ranked 28th. In the 1985 list, no Chinese banks were listed (see Table 2-3).

Table 2-3: Presence of China's banks in *The Banker*'s top 1,000 world banks

	1985	1987	1990	1995	2000	2005	2010	2016
Number of banks in top 1,000	0	1	8	5	9	19	84	119
Number of banks in top 25	0	0	1	1	3	2	3	5
Number of banks in top 10	0	0	0	0	1	0	1	4
Highest ranking	0	51st	16th	23rd	10th	11th	7th	1st

Note: Only the world's top 500 banks were counted before 1987.
Source: *The Banker* (1996, 2016).

Profit

In 1996, only one Chinese bank (the BOC) was listed among the world's 20 most profitable banks, ranking 17th with a profit of US$1.86 billion. The BOC's profit was about one-third of the HSBC's profit (the most profitable bank at that time, with a profit of US$5.69 billion). Of the total profit of the 20 most profitable banks, the BOC's profits accounted for only 3.2 per cent. By 2016, of the world's 20 most profitable branks, China had nine. The ICBC became the world's most profitable bank in 2016, with a profit of US$35.68 billion (1.9 times that of HSBC). Of the total profit of the 20 most profitable banks, the profits of Chinese banks accounted for nearly 54 per cent (see Table 2-4).

6   *The Banker* releases its list of the top 1,000 banks around 1 July each year. It is one of the most authoritative and credible global banking rankings. The list removes national and regional restrictions and assesses the operating results of the majority of the world's banks. The rankings are largely based on banks' capital strength as defined by the Basel Accords. The rankings also evaluate banks' profit growth and risk resistance capacity by measuring their capital adequacy situations. The tier 1 capital of commercial banks is an important index for measuring banks' abilities for business development and risk tolerance and is also an important guarantee in realising sustainable development.

Table 2-4: Top 10 world banks by profit (1996 and 2016)

1996				2016			
Rank	Bank	Country	Assets (billion USD)	Rank	Bank	Country	Assets (billion USD)
1	HSBC Holdings	UK	56.9	1	ICBC	China	559.7
2	Citigroup	US	56.1	2	CCB	China	459.7
3	Banco do Brasil	Brazil	45.8	3	Bank of China	China	356.8
4	Bank of America Corp	US	45.7	4	ABC	China	355.7
5	Barclays Bank	UK	32.3	5	Wells Fargo & Co	US	336.4
6	NationsBank (see Bank of America)	US	29.9	6	JP Morgan Chase & Co	US	308.1
7	Chemical Banking Corp	US	29.8	7	Citigroup	US	248.0
8	National Westminster Bank	UK	27.2	8	Bank of America	US	221.5
9	Lloyds TSB Group	UK	25.6	9	HSBC Holdings	UK	188.7
10	Deutsche Bank	Germany	24.9	10	Mitsubishi UFJ Financial Group	Japan	133.1

Note: ICBC = Industrial and Commercial Bank of China, CCB = China Construction Bank, ABC = Agricultural Bank of China.

Source: *The Banker* (2019).

Chinese banks deemed global systemically important banks

In November 2011, the Financial Stability Board began publishing a list of global systemically important banks (G-SIBs). The list divides financial institutions across five levels based on their systemic importance, which correspond to 3.5 per cent, 2.5 per cent, 2 per cent, 1.5 per cent and 1 per cent of additional capital buffering requirements respectively. Only one Chinese bank (the BOC) was included in the first-level G-SIBs and it was required to take an additional 1 per cent capital buffer. In 2014, the number of Chinese banks listed as first-level G-SIBs rose to three. In 2016, four Chinese banks were listed as G-SIBs, with the ICBC listed as a second-level G-SIB to meet an additional 1.5 per cent capital buffer requirement (see Table 2-5).

Table 2-5: G-SIBs (2012, 2014 and 2016)

Bucket (Capital requirement)	2012	2014	2016
5 (3.5%)	–	–	–
4 (2.5%)	Citigroup, Deutsche Bank, HSBC, JP Morgan Chase	HSBC, JP Morgan Chase	Citigroup, JP Morgan Chase
3 (2%)	Barclays, BNP Paribas	Barclays, BNP Paribas, Citigroup, Deutsche Bank	Bank of America, BNP Paribas, Deutsche Bank, HSBC
2 (1.5%)	Bank of America, Bank of New York Mellon, Credit Suisse, Goldman Sachs, Mitsubishi UFJ Financial Group, Morgan Stanley, Royal Bank of Scotland, UBS	Bank of America, Credit Suisse, Goldman Sachs, Mitsubishi UFJ Financial Group, Morgan Stanley, Royal Bank of Scotland	Barclays, Credit Suisse, Goldman Sachs, ICBC, Mitsubishi UFJ Financial Group, Wells Fargo
1 (1.0%)		Bank of China, BBVA, Groupe BPCE, Groupe Credit Agricole, ING Bank, Mizuho FG, Nordea, Santander, Société Générale, Standard Chartered, State Street, Sumitomo Mitsui FG, Unicredit Group, Wells Fargo Agricultural Bank of China, Bank of China, Bank of New York Mellon, BBVA, Groupe BPCE, Groupe Credit Agricole, ING Bank, Mizuho FG, Nordea, Santander, Société Générale, Standard Chartered, State Street, Sumitomo Mitsui FG, UBS, Unicredit Group, Wells Fargo	Agricultural Bank of China, Bank of China, Bank of New York Mellon, China Construction Bank, Groupe BPCE, Groupe Credit Agricole, ING Bank, Mizuho FG, Morgan Stanley, Nordea, Royal Bank of Scotland, Santander, Société Générale, Standard Chartered, State Street, Sumitomo Mitsui FG, UBS, Unicredit Group

Note: ICBC = Industrial and Commercial Bank of China, BBVA = Banco Bilbao Vizcaya Argentaria, ABC = Agricultural Bank of China, CCB = China Construction Bank.

Source: Financial Stability Board (2016), Institute of International Finance Research, BOC (2016).

Significant improvement of degree of internationalisation of Chinese banks

Following the intensification of China's opening up, the pace of internationalisation of Chinese financial institutions accelerated significantly. By the end of 2016, the overseas assets of the five major banks reached CN¥10.59 trillion, 3.02 times that in 2009 (i.e. an increase of CN¥7.96 trillion). In 2016, the five major banks achieved an overseas pre-tax profit of CN¥120.3 billion, 2.37 times that in 2009 (i.e. an increase of CN¥84.6 billion). At present, the share of overseas assets and pre-tax profits in the five banks' total assets and total pre-tax profits account for 11.6 per cent and 10.1 per cent respectively; these figures represent an average increase of six to seven percentage points from 2010 (see Table 2-6).

Table 2-6: Overseas assets and pre-tax profits of China's five major banks (100 million yuan)

Bank	Item	2009	2010	2011	2012	2013	2014	2015	2016[1]
ICBC	Asset	3,857	5,888	9267	12,344	15,994	19,195	19,412	21,262
	Pre-tax profit	69	88	102	120	166	246	220	225
ABC	Asset	544	973	1,549	2,825	4,116	5,904	7,823	8,704
	Pre-tax profit	6	12	11	28	30	42	54	36
BOC	Asset	17,568	23,283	27,737	31,356	38,462	4,5591	48,308	50,690
	Pre-tax profit	250	283	360	349	412	532	548	814
CCB	Asset	2,327	2,711	4,411	5,166	7,299	9,356	11,495	16,664
	Pre-tax profit	13	32	3	32	39	63	53	68
BOCOM	Asset	2,025	2,429	3,348	3,860	5,256	6,451	6,671	8,559
	Pre-tax profit	19	20	25	32	38	62	61	60

[1] The overseas revenue and assets of the ICBC were calculated by the RMB central parity against the USD on 31 December 2016 (i.e. 6.937 RMB = 1 USD).

Note: ICBC = Industrial and Commercial Bank of China, ABC = Agricultural Bank of China, BOC = Bank of China, CCB = China Construction Bank, BOCOM = Bank of Communications.

Source: Annual reports of the five major banks.

Chinese financial institutions are 'going global' and achieving fruitful results; however, the development of foreign banks in China has been relatively slow. At the end of 2016, the assets of foreign-owned banks in China totalled CN¥2.9286 trillion, 4.03 times that in 2004 (i.e. an increase of CN¥2.34631 trillion). During the same period, the assets of Chinese banks increased 6.35-fold, from CN¥31.599 trillion to CN¥232.2532 trillion. Foreign bank assets as a percentage of total bank assets fell from 1.84 per cent in 2004 to 1.26 per cent in 2016. From a profitability perspective, foreign banks in China achieved a net profit of CN¥12.8 billion in 2016, 4.38 times that in 2004 (i.e. an increase of CN¥10.42 billion). During the same period, China's banking sector saw a net profit increase of 1,903 per cent. Foreign banks' net profits as a percentage of the banking sector's total net profit fell from 2.30 per cent in 2004 to 0.62 per cent in 2016 (see Table 2-7).

Table 2-7: Assets and profits of foreign-owned banks in China

Item	2004	2006	2008	2010	2012	2014	2016
Foreign bank asset (100 million yuan)	5,822.9	9,278.7	13,448	17,423	23,804	27,921	29,286
Banking asset (100 million yuan)	315,990	439,500	631,515	953,053	1336224	1,723,355	2,322,532
Proportion of foreign capital (%)	1.84	2.11	2.13	1.83	1.78	1.62	1.26
Foreign bank net profit (100 million yuan)	23.8	57.7	119.2	77.8	163.4	197.2	128
Banking net profit (100 million yuan)	1,035	3,379.2	5,833.6	8,990.9	15,115.5	19,227.4	20,732.4
Proportion of foreign capital (%)	2.30	1.71	2.04	0.87	1.08	1.03	0.62

Source: China Banking Regulatory Commission (2007, 2009, 2011, 2013, 2015, 2017).

Comparison of the operation characteristics of Chinese and international banks

After years of development, China's banking sector continues to consolidate its strengths. Its international status has improved significantly. Chinese banks have formed distinctive operation characteristics and development strategies. Compared to the global banking industry, the operations of Chinese banks have a number of notable characteristics.

Percentage of deposits and loans in the assets–liabilities structure is comparably high

At the end of 2016, the assets and liabilities of Chinese G-SIBs totalled US$11.92 trillion and US$11 trillion respectively. These figures accounted for 24.73 per cent and 24.62 per cent of G-SIBs' total assets and liabilities respectively. The structure of assets and liabilities of large Chinese banks indicates dominance of the traditional deposit and loan business. At the end of 2016, the proportion of deposits in Chinese G-SIBs' liabilities was 80.75 per cent, 23.65 percentage points higher than the average G-SIB level (57.1 per cent). The proportion of loans in Chinese G-SIBs' assets was 53.7 per cent, 14.5 percentage points higher than the average G-SIB level (39.2 per cent) (see Table 2-8).

Table 2-8: Assets–liabilities structure of large Chinese and foreign banks (2016)

Bank	Assets (US$100 million)	Liabilities (US$100 million)	Deposits/ Liabilities (%)	Loans/ Assets (%)
ICBC	34,732.4	31,881.6	81.4	54.1
CCB	30,165.8	27,878.3	80.5	56.1
ABC	28,160.4	26,258.7	83.4	49.7
BOC	26,115.4	23,975.5	77.7	55.0
HSBC Holdings	23,749.9	21,924.1	58.0	36.6
Barclays	14,976.0	14,095.0	37.1	31.9
Royal Bank of Scotland	9,859.4	9,249.5	47.2	41.0
Standard Chartered	6,466.9	5,980.3	62.2	40.1
UniCredit	9,065.5	8,610.0	48.5	52.5
Banco Santander	14,123.8	13,040.6	52.4	60.9
UBS	9,192.1	8,658.2	48.1	32.8
Credit Suisse Group	8,060.0	7,644.0	45.8	33.8
Nordea Bank AB	6,493.4	6,151.5	29.2	48.9
Mitsubishi UFJ Financial Group	27,248.0	25,751.4	63.5	36.6
Mizuho Financial Group	18,013.5	17,180.4	68.3	40.0
Sumitomo Mitsui Financial Group	17,769.4	16,760.2	69.5	41.4
JP Morgan	24,909.7	22,367.8	61.5	35.9
Bank of America	21,877.0	19,208.6	65.6	41.9
Wells Fargo	19,301.2	17,296.2	75.5	51.5
Citigroup	17,920.8	15,659.3	59.4	36.5

Bank	Assets (US$100 million)	Liabilities (US$100 million)	Deposits/ Liabilities (%)	Loans/ Assets (%)
Goldman Sachs	8,601.7	7,727.7	39.9	13.5
Morgan Stanley	8,149.5	7,377.7	46.9	17.3
Bank of New York Mellon	3,334.7	2,938.9	75.4	19.3
State Street Corp	2,427.0	2,214.8	84.5	8.1
ING Bank	8,913.1	8,381.5	65.8	67.3
BNP Paribas	21,905.7	20,795.9	38.7	37.3
Crédit Agricole	16,076.1	15,401.7	35.4	23.2
Société Générale	14,578.5	13,885.5	30.2	31.8
Banque Populaire	13,028.1	12,298.9	45.6	55.0
Deutsche Bank	16,775.5	16,091.8	36.1	26.0
Average	16,066.3	14,889.5	57.1	39.2

Note: ICBC = Industrial and Commercial Bank of China, CCB = China Construction Bank, ABC = Agricultural Bank of China, BOC = Bank of China.

Source: Wind (2017) and Institute of International Finance Research, BOC (2016).

Interest is the main revenue source and the net interest margin is at a medium level

On average, interest income comprised 71.8 per cent of the income of Chinese G-SIBs in 2016, 24 percentage points higher than the average G-SIB level (47.8 per cent). From 2011–2014, the net interest margin of Chinese G-SIBs (all of which ranked in the top 10 G-SIBs) remained at a comparably high level across all G-SIBs. However, since 2015, numerous factors (e.g. the rapid progress of domestic interest rate marketisation) have led to the net interest margin of Chinese G-SIBs declining significantly. In 2016, the net interest margin of Chinese G-SIBs was 2.1 per cent, equal to the G-SIB average level in the same period (see Table 2-9).

The non-interest income of Chinese G-SIBs is relatively low, only accounting for 28.2 per cent of the total G-SIB income in 2016, 24 percentage points lower than the G-SIB average (52.2 per cent). One important reason for this is the lack of income channels. Additionally, average service fee and commission income account for more than 80 per cent of the non-interest income of Chinese G-SIBs, while for the average G-SIB these account for less than 60 per cent of non-interest income. A significant gap remains in net investment income between Chinese and other G-SIBs.

Table 2-9: Net interest spread and proportion of interest income of G-SIBs (2016)

Bank	Net interest margin (%)	Proportion of interest income (%)	Proportion of non-interest income (%)
ICBC	2.2	71.8	28.2
CCB	2.2	74.0	26.0
ABC	2.3	76.2	23.8
BOC	1.8	65.3	34.7
Barclays	1.5	46.5	53.5
HSBC Holdings	1.7	57.3	42.7
Standard Chartered	1.7	55.5	44.5
Royal Bank of Scotland	1.7	65.6	34.4
UniCredit	1.4	56.6	43.4
Banco Santander	2.8	64.9	35.1
Swiss Bank Corp	0.9	21.5	78.5
Credit Suisse Group	1.0	39.4	60.6
Nordea Bank AB	1.0	44.6	55.4
Mitsubishi UFJ Financial Group	0.9	43.9	56.1
Sumitomo Mitsui Financial Group	1.1	41.5	58.5
Mizuho Financial Group	0.6	33.8	66.2
JP Morgan	2.3	48.5	51.5
Wells Fargo	2.9	55.8	44.2
Bank of America	2.2	48.1	51.9
Citigroup	2.8	63.1	36.9
Goldman Sachs	0.3	6.9	93.1
Morgan Stanley	0.7	10.7	89.3
Bank of New York Mellon	1.1	20.6	79.4
State Street Corp	1.1	20.4	79.6
ING	1.7	72.5	27.5
Crédit Agricole	1.6	45.6	54.4
Société Générale	0.9	34.6	65.4
Banque Populaire	0.9	55.2	44.8
Deutsche Bank	1.4	44.8	55.2
Average	2.1	47.8	52.2

Note: ICBC = Industrial and Commercial Bank of China, CCB = China Construction Bank, ABC = Agricultural Bank of China, BOC = Bank of China.

Profit level is relatively high and leverage ratio remains at the global average

In 2016, the average ROE of Chinese G-SIBs was 14.17 per cent, the average equity multiplier was 12.63 and the average ROA was 1.12 per cent. During this period, G-SIBs had an average ROE of 5.5 per cent, an average equity multiplier of 11 and an average ROA of 0.5 per cent. The ROE of Chinese G-SIBs was 8.67 percentage points higher than the G-SIB average, their ROA was 0.62 percentage points higher and their equity multiplier was 1.63 times higher. From this perspective, the high profitability of Chinese banks can be explained by strong asset profitability and an average overall leverage ratio (see Table 2-10).

Overall asset quality is good, but capital adequacy needs to be improved

At the end of 2016, Chinese G-SIBs had an average NPL ratio of 1.75 per cent, 0.65 percentage points lower than the G-SIB average (2.4 per cent) (see Table 2-10). At the end of 2016, the average capital adequacy ratio of Chinese G-SIBs was 14.4 per cent, higher than the capital requirements of 11.5–12 per cent. In the same period, G-SIBs' capital adequacy ratio averaged 17.7 per cent, 3.3 percentage points higher than the average of Chinese G-SIBs. Reasons for the low capital adequacy ratio of Chinese G-SIBs include insufficient financing by other tier 1 and tier 2 capital instruments and a relatively high risk per unit of assets.

Table 2-10: Operating indicators of G-SIBs (2016)

Bank	Net interest margin	Proportion of interest income (%)	Capital adequacy ratio	NPL ratio	ROA	ROE	Equity multiplier
ICBC	2.2	71.8	14.3	1.6	1.2	14.8	12.3
CCB	2.2	74.0	15.3	1.5	1.2	15.4	12.8
ABC	2.3	76.2	13.1	2.4	1.0	14.6	14.6
BOC	1.8	65.3	14.7	1.5	1.1	12.1	11.0
Barclays	1.5	46.5	19.6	1.7	0.2	2.9	14.5
HSBC Holdings	1.7	57.3	20.1	2.1	0.1	0.7	7.0
Standard Chartered	1.7	55.5	21.3	3.7	0.0	−1.0	N/A
Royal Bank of Scotland	1.7	65.6	22.9	3.1	−0.6	−13.6	22.7
UniCredit	1.4	56.6	11.7	12.5	−1.4	−26.4	18.86

Bank	Net interest margin	Proportion of interest income (%)	Capital adequacy ratio	NPL ratio	ROA	ROE	Equity multiplier
Banco Santander	2.8	64.9	14.7	4.1	0.5	6.9	13.8
UBS	0.9	21.5	24.7	0.8	0.3	5.9	19.7
Mitsubishi UFJ Financial Group	0.9	43.9	15.9	1.4	0.3	6.0	20.0
Sumitomo Mitsui Financial Group	1.1	41.5	16.9	1.1	0.4	7.6	19.0
Mizuho Financial Group	0.6	33.8	16.3	1.1	0.3	7.3	24.3
JP Morgan	2.3	48.5	16.4	0.8	1.0	10.0	10.0
Wells Fargo	2.9	55.8	16.1	1.0	1.2	11.8	9.8
Bank of America	2.2	48.1	16.3	0.8	0.8	6.8	8.5
Citigroup	2.8	63.1	19.1	0.9	0.8	6.6	8.3
Goldman Sachs	0.3	6.9	17.8	-	0.8	9.4	11.8
Morgan Stanley	0.7	10.7	22.0	-	0.8	8.1	10.1
ING	1.7	72.5	19.3	2.3	0.5	9.5	19.0
Crédit Agricole	1.6	45.6	14.5	5.4	0.4	8.3	20.8
Société Générale	0.9	34.6	17.9	5.4	0.3	5.6	18.7
Banque Populaire	0.9	55.2	20.1	4.4	0.2	5.9	29.5
Deutsche Bank	1.4	44.8	17.4	1.8	−0.1	−2.7	27.0
Average	2.1	47.8	17.7	2.4	0.5	5.5	11.0

Note: NPL = non-performing loans, ROA = return on assets, ROE = return on equity, ICBC = Industrial and Commercial Bank of China, CCB = China Construction Bank, ABC = Agricultural Bank of China, BOC = Bank of China.
Source: Wind (2017) and Institute of International Finance Research, BOC (2016).

Continuously improving banking regulations

In recent years, China's banking industry has undergone rapid development. The regulatory authorities have constantly adapted to changes in the financial environment and optimised regulatory policies to achieve positive results.

Promoting the implementation of 'Basel III'

In 2013, the Chinese version of Basel III was formally implemented in China's banking sector. Since then, the loss-absorbing capacity of commercial banks has strengthened continuously. At the end of 2016, the level-1 core capital adequacy ratio and capital adequacy ratio of commercial banks were 10.75 per cent and 13.28 per cent respectively. These figures are much higher than the minimum requirements established in Basel III. In addition, the provision of China's banking sector is relatively high compared to other banks. By the end of 2016, the provision coverage ratio of commercial banks was 176.4 per cent, 94.6 percentage points higher than the average of non-Chinese G-SIBs in the same period. The provision-to-loan ratio was 3.08 per cent, 1.15 percentage points higher than the average of non-Chinese G-SIBs. Additionally, the introduction of two liquidity risk measures (the liquidity coverage ratio and net stable funding ratio) improved the loan-to-deposit ratio and resulted in the establishment of a liquidity risk management system that meets Basel III's requirements.

Regulating interbank, asset management and investment business

Since 2013, the regulatory authorities have introduced a series of policies aimed at regulating the development of interbank, asset management and investment businesses. Of these, the stricter policies include the 2014 Documents No. 127 and 140 that target interbank business, the 2016 'Regulation and Supervision of Asset Management Activities of the Commercial Banks (Exposure Draft)', the September 2016 Document No. 42 that targets credit risk, and the 'Notice on Inclusion of Off-balance-sheet Financing into Calculation of General Credit' (issued by the PBC in October 2016) that placed off-balance sheet financing activities in the scope of macroprudential assessment.

Further, since March 2017, the China Banking Regulatory Commission (CBRC), China Insurance Regulatory Commission (CIRC) and other financial regulators have issued a series of documents introducing financial deleveraging. The CBRC issued eight consecutive documents to crack down on 'three violations', 'three arbitrages' and 'four misconducts'. The CIRC issued four documents, including the 'Notice on Further Strengthening the Risk Prevention and Control of the Insurance Industry'. This notice targeted systemic loopholes in eight major fields, including insurance company governance, the use of insurance funds, claims-paying ability, product management, intermediaries and consumer rights protection.

Normalising the development of internet finance

In July 2015, the PBC (together with 10 other ministries) issued the 'Guiding Opinions on Promoting the Healthy Development of Internet Finance' to regulate the development of internet finance. This document clarified the regulatory responsibilities of the 'central bank and three regulatory commissions' in relation to internet finance and gave clear instructions on custody of funds, information security, the nature of business platforms and other related issues. In August 2016, the CBRC issued the 'Interim Measures for the Regulation of Business Activities of P2P Information Intermediaries'. This document established the legal status of peer-to-peer lending and established the regulatory requirements, including the upper limits of business scale and investment directions.

Speeding up the settlement of non-performing loans

To address significant issues related to the quality of bank assets, the regulatory authorities introduced policies to hasten the settlement of NPLs. In 2016, the CBRC issued the 'Notice on the Work of the Creditors' Committee of Banking Financial Institutions' to clarify the nature, purpose and operation mechanisms of the creditors' committee. In October 2016, the State Council issued the 'Guidance on Actively and Steadily Reducing the Leverage Ratio of Enterprises' to provide an overall framework for reducing the leverage ratio of non-financial enterprises. In December 2016, the CBRC issued 'Several Opinions on Properly Addressing Financial Debts in the Process of Capacity Reduction in the Steel and Coal-mining Industries' to strengthen the management of problematic debts in overcapacity industries by supporting the reasonable demand for capital, increasing financial support for mergers and acquisitions and establishing creditors' committees.

Regulating cross-border business

In recent years, the regulatory authorities have introduced a series of policies to regulate and standardise the development of international banking businesses. In March 2016, the CBRC issued the 'Notice on Further Strengthening the Risk Management of Overseas Operation of Banking Financial Institutions'. This document required banking financial institutions to strengthen the risk management of overseas operations, incorporate a country's risks into banks' stress tests and develop contingency plans based on the test results. In January 2017, the CBRC issued the 'Guiding Opinions on Regulating the International Business of Banking Services and Strengthening Risk Prevention and Control'. This document required Chinese banks to regulate their overseas business activities, strengthen anti-money laundering and anti-terrorism financing practices and enhance the service capabilities that support Chinese enterprises' 'going global' efforts.

Future development directions

A comparison of the business indicators of large and medium-sized banks in China and abroad show that China's banking industry should take the following directions in the future.

First, the banking sector should continue to play a leading role in China's financial system for the foreseeable future. In recent years, China's capital market has developed rapidly and direct financing has assumed an increasingly important role in supporting development of the real economy. However, given China's historical traditions, credit environment and legal system, it is unlikely that the dominant position of the country's banking sector will change radically. Thus, bank credit will continue to be the main source of funding for the real economy, even though it may decline as a proportion of funding.

Second, universal banking will be the preferred option. With the acceleration of market-oriented reforms directed at financial factors, such as interest and exchange rates, Chinese banks will move from the traditional business model—which largely depends on deposit and loan business—towards universal banking. In particular, the proportion of deposit and loan business will continue to decline, while the proportion of securities investment and wholesale financing will increase. The proportion of non-interest income will increase among all revenue sources, especially investment income. The contribution of overseas markets to overall profitability will increase, gradually moving towards the average of large global banks (i.e. 40 per cent). Consumer finance will see greater growth, while the contribution of personal business will continue to rise.

Third, the major tasks of banking regulatory reforms should be to strengthen capital, behavioural and functional regulations. Presently, regulatory approaches cannot keep up with development of the banking sector. The current framework must be improved and upgraded. In the future, regulatory authorities should strengthen capital regulations, improve the quantity and quality of banks' capital, and expand the scope of risk-weighted assets and increase measurement accuracy so that these regulatory indicators can fully reflect the real risks. China should also strengthen behavioural regulations, improve the protection of consumer rights and interests, and strengthen on-spot inspection mechanisms to normalise the operations of financial institutions and eliminate irregularities. Additionally, China should strengthen functional regulations, establish and improve regulatory coordination mechanisms, clarify regulatory responsibilities, constantly enhance its regulatory capabilities and allocate regulatory resources according to the systematic importance of financial institutions.

Part 2: China's capital market: Development history and international comparison

Since its reform and opening, China's capital market has developed rapidly. The once relatively minor stock and bond markets are now flourishing and significant sectors and China's market scales are now among the world's largest. However, the degree of market openness is relatively low and numerous structural problems highlight the gap between China's market and mature markets in developed countries. In the future, China will continue to expand the opening of the capital market, increase the proportion of direct financing, and promote market-oriented reform to achieve healthy and stable development of its capital market.

The rapid expansion of China's capital markets brought about by financial reforms

Stock market

The development of China's stock market began relatively late. On 14 November 1986, Shanghai Feilo Acoustics Co. Ltd issued shares publicly. This was the first real stock issue since China's reform and opening and marked the beginning of China's capital market reform. In 1987, the Shenzhen Special Economic Zone Securities Company was established, largely to manage securities trading and transfers and provide securities investment consulting services. It was China's first securities company established after the reform and opening.

Since the 1990s, the infrastructure construction of China's securities market has accelerated significantly. In November 1990, China's first stock exchange, the SSE, was established. The SSE conducts transactions via electronic auctions. All the listed securities can be publicly bid upon through computers. In December of the same year, the Shenzhen Stock Exchange (SZSE) was also launched. Since then, China's securities market has experienced a period of rapid development. In 2004, the SZSE established the Small and Medium Enterprises (SMEs) Board. This board has played an important role in promoting the development of the Growth Enterprises Market (GEM) Board.

After 20 years of concerted effort, China's stock market has developed into a large and flourishing sector. The number of listed companies has increased rapidly and secondary transactions have become increasingly active (see Table 2-11). By the end of 2016, the total number of listed companies in mainland China reached 3,052, 16 times that in 1993. Total market capitalisation reached CN¥50.8 trillion in 2016 (equivalent to 68.3 per cent of the gross domestic product [GDP]), 38.8 percentage points higher than that in 2000 and the second largest in the world. The circulating market value accounted for 52.9 per cent of the total market value. China has also driven the construction of a multilevel capital market and the number of companies listed on the national equities exchange and quotations (NEEQ) system continues to increase. By the end of 2016, the total number of companies listed on the NEEQ system had reached 10,163. Of these, 5,034 were new companies.

Table 2-11: China's stock market (1993–2016)

Year	Number of listed companies	Number of investors (10 thousand)	Market value (100 million yuan)	Circulating market value (100 million yuan)	Transaction amount (100 million yuan)	Amount of domestic equity financing (100 million yuan)
1993	183	835	3,531	832	3,627	-
1995	323	1,294	3,474	938	4,036	-
2005	1381	7,189	32,446	10,638	31,664	338
2010	2063	13,391	265,422	193,110	545,633	8,954
2015	2827	21,478	531,304	417,925	2,550,538	8,295
2016	3052	11,741	508,245	393,266	1,267,262	18,910

Source: Financial Stability Analysis Group of the PBC (2016), National Bureau of Statistics of China (2017) and Wind (2017).

Bond market

China's bond market came into being in 1981 when the government issued treasury bonds. In the following 10 years, the Chinese Government issued a number of bonds, including financial, national construction, special treasury and indexed bonds. The issuing process relied on a combination of political mobilisation and administrative distribution. Corporate bonds were first issued in 1984. In 1993, the PBC began issuing central bank bills to adjust the balance of funds among different regions and financial institutions and to make comprehensive use of the fund transfer function. In 1994, policy-oriented financial bonds appeared with the establishment of three policy banks. During this time, China's bond market largely consisted of treasury bonds, central bank bills, financial bonds and non-financial corporate bonds.

From a transaction perspective, bond transactions were largely conducted in the over-the-counter (OTC) market before moving to the interbank bond market. In 1993, the SSE launched a pilot scheme of government bond futures. In 1994, the SZSE also started bond transactions. Consequently, bond transactions gradually became concentrated in the two exchanges. However, in 1997, a large amount of bank capital flowed into the stock market from various channels. To address this issue, the PBC introduced a requirement that commercial banks conduct repurchase and spot transactions under the National Interbank Funding Centre's trading system. In 2012, due to the continuous development of primary and secondary markets, China established a bond market system consisting of the exchanges and OTC markets, with the interbank market as the mainstay and the exchange market and bank counters as supplementary.

In the last 20 years, China's bond market has shown rapid development in three respects. First, trading volumes have increased significantly and the market structure has changed. China's bond issuance increased to CN¥185,643 trillion in 2016, 574 times that in 1990 (CN¥32.3 billion). Bonds in custody rose from CN¥418.4 billion at the end of 1997 to CN¥63.7 trillion at the end of 2016, a 151-fold increase. Before 2000, both the exchange and OTC markets were active. Since then, the rapid increase of market participants and diversified bond products increased the activity of the interbank bond market until it gradually became the main venue for transactions. Since 2001, the interbank bond market has generally retained more than 70 per cent of the market share. By 2015, it occupied a market share of 76 per cent.

Second, bond products and trading instruments have been enriched. Before 2005, China's bond products mainly comprised government bonds, policy financial bonds, central bank bills and corporate bonds. From 2005, China's interbank market has constantly rolled out innovative products. Notably, it has introduced general financial bonds, commercial bank subprime bonds, mixed capital bonds, asset-backed bonds, short-term financing bills and warrant bonds. Currently, the trading instruments in China's securities market include spot trading, pledged repo, outright repo, bond lending and bond forwards, most of which were developed after 2004.

Table 2-12: China's bond market (1990–2016)

Year	Bond issuance (100 million yuan)	Bond turnover (100 million yuan)	Bond custody by the end of the year (100 million yuan)	Government bonds (100 million yuan)	Central bank bills (100 million yuan)	Financial bonds (100 million yuan)	Non-financial corporate bonds (100 million yuan)
1990	323	-	-	197	-	-	126
1995	1,811	-	-	1,510	-	-	300
2000	4,414	-	16,746	4,657	-	1,645	83
2005	42,182	60.1	73,402	7,042	27,882	7,159	2,047
2010	95,238	64.0	205,108	19,778	46,608	14,122	16,811
2015	144,178	87.6	479,000	59,408	-	102,095	67,205
2016	185,643	127.1	637,000	91,086	-	52,421	82,242

Source: Financial Stability Analysis Group of the PBC (2016) and Wind (2017).

Third, the proportion of government bonds has decreased, while the proportion of corporate bonds has exhibited an inverted U-shape trend (see Table 2-12). Initially, the issuance of treasury bonds accounted for a relatively high proportion of total bond issuance, but this was followed by a downwards trend. In 1990, government bonds accounted for 60.1 per cent of total bond issuance. In 1996, the proportion rose to 87 per cent, but dropped to 18 per cent in 2014. In 1990, corporate bonds accounted for 39 per cent of total bond issuance, but from 1997–2007, the proportion was no more than 10 per cent. Since the GFC in 2008, loose monetary policies, interest rate marketisation and the rapid development of the bond market have caused the amount of non-financial corporate bonds (as a proportion of the total bond issuance) to increase. In 2014, this proportion reached 43 per cent, an increase of 30 percentage points from 2008. Financial bonds initially accounted for a large proportion of total bond issuance (approximately 34 per cent), but from 2002–2010 they experienced an overall decline, falling to 14.5 per cent in 2010. However, in recent years, they have risen as a proportion of total bond issuance once again. In 2015, financial bonds accounted for 39 per cent of total bond issuance, an increase of 24.5 percentage points from 2010.

The international status of China's capital market

The market value of Chinese listed companies is among the world's largest. According to the World Federation of Exchange, as of 2016, the total market value of Chinese listed companies had reached US$7,311.4 billion and China was ranked second in the world after the US (see Figure 2-2). Additionally, the SSE and SZSE are now respectively ranked as the fourth- and sixth-largest world exchanges.

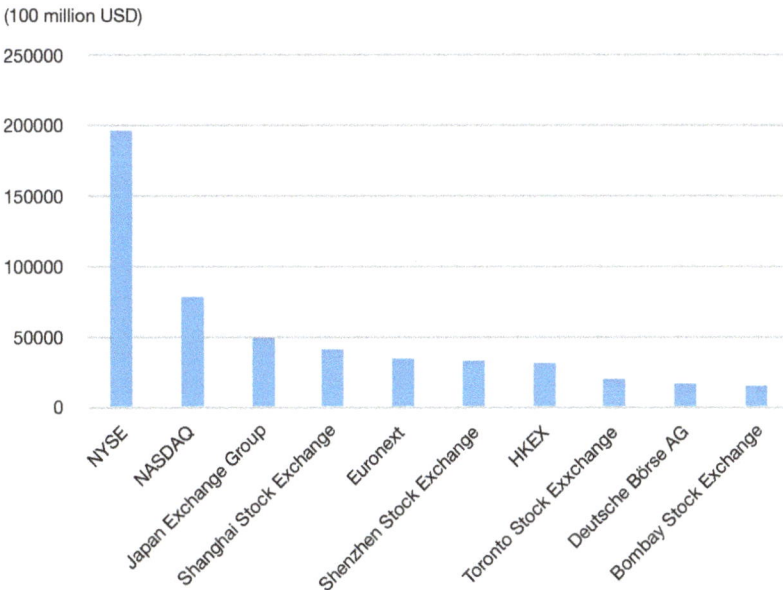

Figure 2-2: Market capitalisation rankings of the world's major stock exchanges at the end of 2016 (US$100 million).

Source: World Federation of Exchanges (2017).

The market capitalisation of China's stock market ranks second in the world (see Table 2-13). In 1995, the total market capitalisation of China's listed companies was US$42.1 billion. This rose to US$7.3 trillion in 2016, a more than 170-fold increase. This figure represents nearly 13.3 per cent of the global total market capitalisation. Notably, in 1995, China held only 0.2 per cent of the global total market capitalisation. At the same time, the total market value of the US, the world's largest stock market, increased 3.8-fold from US$5.3 trillion in 1993 to US$25.1 trillion in 2015. The US's global share rose from 37.5 per cent in 1993 to 40.6 per cent in 2015. The total market capitalisation of Japan's listed companies increased by 68 per cent; however, its global share fell from 20.7 per cent in 1993 to 7.9 per cent in 2015. The United Kingdom (UK) also experienced a decline in market share, from 8.2 per cent in 1993 to 5.2 per cent in 2015.

Table 2-13: Total market capitalisation of listed companies (US$100 million)

Year	US	Eurozone	Japan	China	Global	China's share of global total market capitalisation (%)
1993	52,511	15,920	29,063	-	139,963	0.0
1995	69,520	21,957	35,453	421	175,030	0.2
2005	170,009	62,086	47,529	4,018	406,638	0.9
2010	172,835	64,395	38,278	40,278	514,530	7.8
2015	250,675	61,206	48,949	81,880	617,811	13.3
2016	273,522	62,178	49,553	73,207	648,196	11.3

Source: World Bank (2017).

In relation to bond market size, China ranks behind only the US and Japan. China's bond market value increased 44-fold, from US$202.3 billion in 2000 to US$9.1 trillion in 2016. Over this same period, the US bond market value increased 1.5-fold, from US$14.6 trillion in 2000 to US$35.8 trillion in 2016. Korea's bond market value increased 3.9-fold during this period. Compared to these economies, China's bond market has shown the most rapid development (see Table 2-14).

Table 2-14: International comparison of domestic bond size
(US$100 million)

Country	2000	2005	2010	2016	Growth (2000–2016) (%)
China	2,023	8,992	3,0551	91,786	4,437
US	146,503	2,185,881	293,531	358,223	145
Japan	65,715	90,140	143,392	116,650	78
UK	6,955	18,899	35,380	28,675	312
France	10,376	16,129	25,403	25,630	147
Korea	3,540	7,530	11,490	17,200	386

Source: Bank for International Settlements (2000, 2005, 2010, 2016).

Problems in the development of China's capital market

The degree of foreign capital participation and the openness of China's capital market are limited

China's stock and bond markets implemented different opening policies. In the primary stock market, nonresidents are not yet permitted to issue equity securities in mainland China. Conversely, in the secondary market, Qualified Foreign Institutional Investor (QFII) and RMB Qualified Foreign Institutional Investor mechanisms for foreign institutional investors have been established and the Shanghai–Hong Kong Stock Connect and Shenzhen–Hong Kong Stock Connect have been launched. In the secondary bond market, the interbank market has been opened, such that qualified foreign investors and foreign institutions can enjoy the same standards as domestic institutions when entering the market. However, transactions conducted by the foreign funds that have entered China's market through these methods are relatively small. QFII shares account for less than 1.5 per cent of the A-share market (see Figure 2-3). The Shanghai–Hong Kong Stock Connect and Shenzhen–Hong Kong Stock Connect account for no more than 2 per cent of the total market turnover (see Figure 2-4), and foreign institutions hold less than 2.5 per cent of the treasury bond and financial bond market (see Figure 2.5).

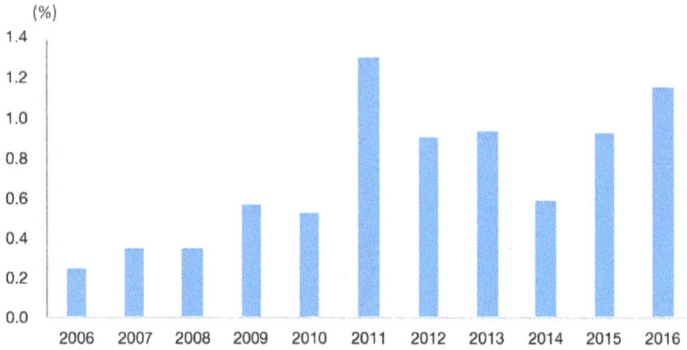

Figure 2-3: The proportion of QFII shareholding in the A-share market (%).
Source: Wind (2017).

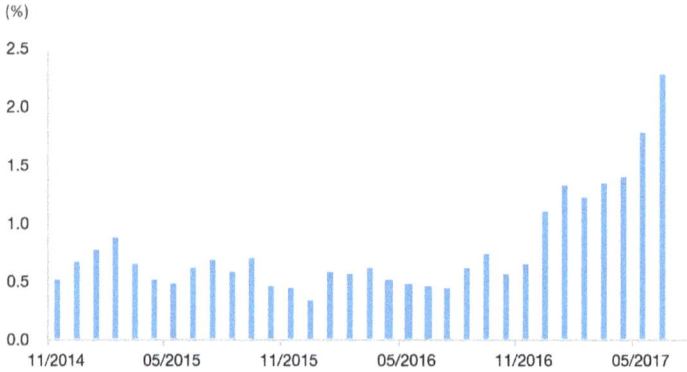

Figure 2-4: The proportion of trade volume via the Shanghai–Hong Kong Stock Connect and Shenzhen–Hong Kong Stock Connect (%).
Source: Wind (2017).

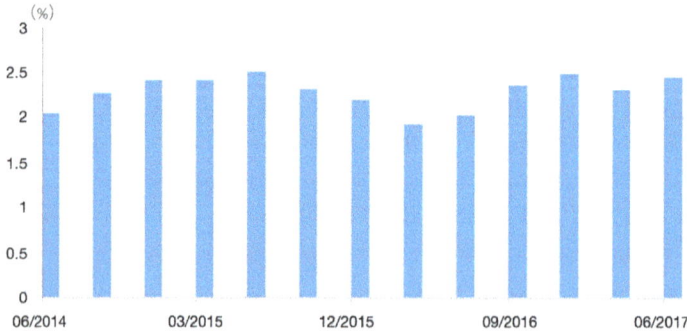

Figure 2-5: Proportion of holdings by foreign institutions in the government bond and financial bond market (%).
Source: Wind (2017).

The depth of China's capital market has increased, but not sufficiently

China's GDP ranks second globally, but its capital market depth and securitisation rates lag behind those of developed countries. In China, the ratio of market capitalisation of listed companies to GDP increased by 20 percentage points from 2011–2016, rising to 65 per cent. China's ratio was slightly higher than the ratios of Germany, Brazil and Mexico, but was below the global average, significantly lower than the ratios of Japan, South Korea and France and less than half that of the US (see Figure 2-6). The ratio of China's private sector domestic bond balance to GDP increased by 15 percentage points from 2011–2016, to 47 per cent. China's ratio was higher than the ratios of Germany, Brazil and Mexico, but lower than the ratios of Japan, South Korea and France and almost half that of the US in 2011 (see Figure 2-7).

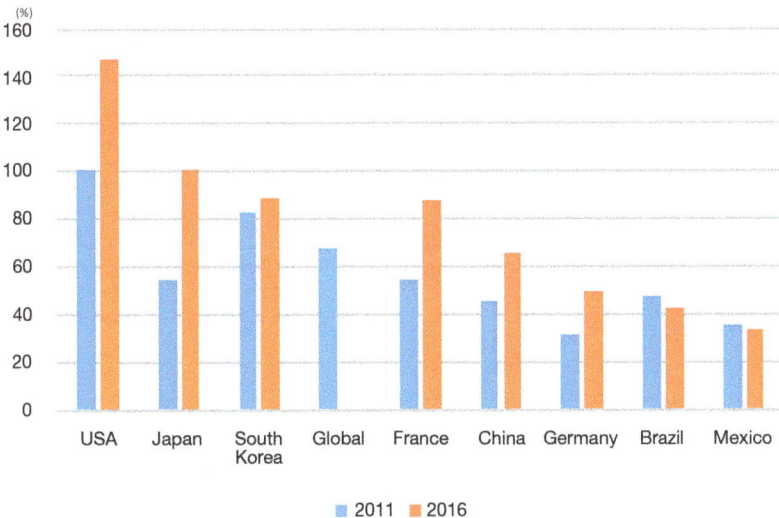

Figure 2-6: International comparison of the ratio of the market capitalisation of listed companies to GDP (%).

Source: Wind (2017) and World Bank (2017).

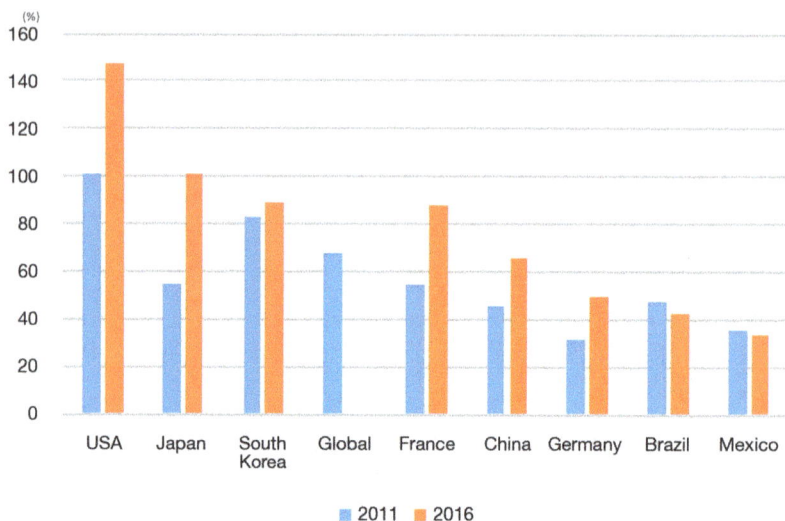

Figure 2-7: International comparison of the ratio of the domestic bond balance of the private sector to GDP (%).
Source: World Bank (2016).

The breadth of China's capital market still lags behind that of advanced economies

China's stock market capitalisation is among the world's largest; however, the breadth and accessibility of China's market is far lower than those of advanced economies. The number of listed companies per million population increased from 1.16 in 2007 to 2.06 in 2015. Despite this, China continues to lag significantly behind other countries (see Figure 2-8). An international comparison reveals that, on average, there are more than 10 listed companies per million population in the US, Japan, the UK and South Korea, and around seven listed companies per million population in Germany and France. Conversely, in developing countries, such as China, Brazil and Mexico, this figure is less than three.

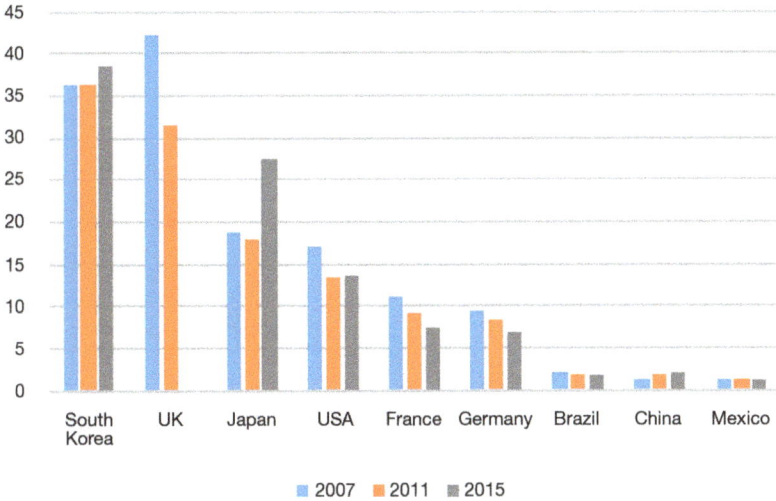

Figure 2-8: International comparison of the number of listed companies per million residents.

Source: World Bank (2016).

Direct financing has developed, but its contribution to total social financing is relatively low

In the US and many other mature markets (as well as some emerging markets), direct financing (e.g. the issuance of shares or corporate bonds) is an important method of corporate financing. Before the GFC, China's direct financing accounted for less than 15 per cent of social financing. However, in recent years, it has undergone rapid development (see Figure 2-9). In 2016, the proportion of direct financing increased to 24 per cent, still relatively low. In terms of structure, the bond market made a significant contribution to social financing, but the contribution of the stock market has been particularly low. In 2016, in sharp contrast to China's world-leading market capitalisation and turnover ratio, equity financing accounted for only 7 per cent of China's social financing.

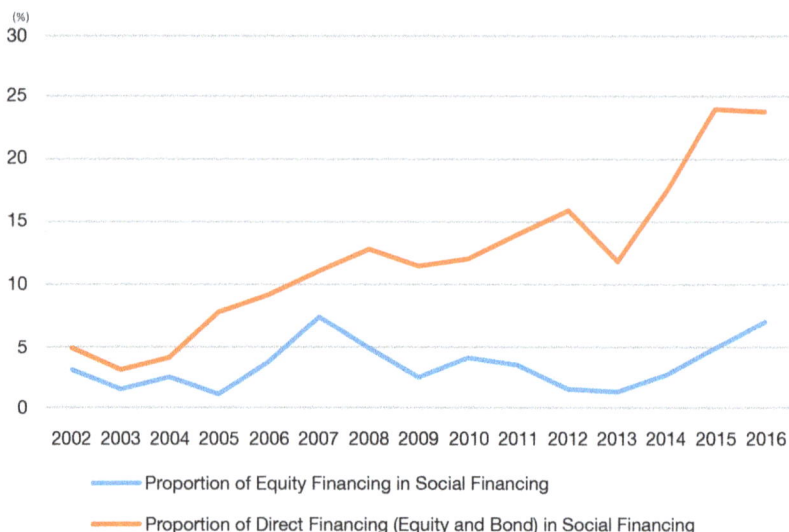

Figure 2-9: Proportion of equity and direct financing in China's social financing.

Source: World Bank (2017) and Financial Stability Analysis Group of the PBC (2017).

The stock market is mainly composed of retail investors and the turnover ratio is comparably high

The Chinese stock market, which comprises of a large number of retail investors, lags significantly behind mature markets. In China's stock market, an overwhelming majority of stock trading accounts are held by individual investors accounts. By the end of 2016, 99.72 per cent of stock trading accounts were held by 'natural person' investors, the majority of these being 'retail investors', while non-natural persons held 0.28 per cent of stock trading accounts (see Figure 2-10). Over 72 per cent of natural person investors hold less than CN¥100,000 of the market value, while retail investors hold more than 43 per cent of the free float market capitalisation of the A-share market (see Figure 2-11). Thus, retail investors have assumed a leading role in China's stock market transactions, creating high turnover ratios.

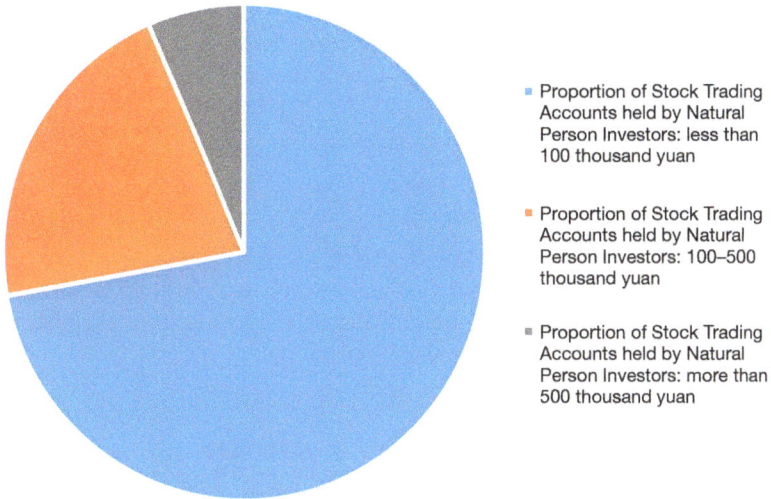

- Proportion of Stock Trading Accounts held by Natural Person Investors: less than 100 thousand yuan

- Proportion of Stock Trading Accounts held by Natural Person Investors: 100–500 thousand yuan

- Proportion of Stock Trading Accounts held by Natural Person Investors: more than 500 thousand yuan

Figure 2-10: Account structure of Chinese investors in 2016 (%).

Source: Wind (2017) and China Securities Depository and Clearing Co. Ltd (2017).

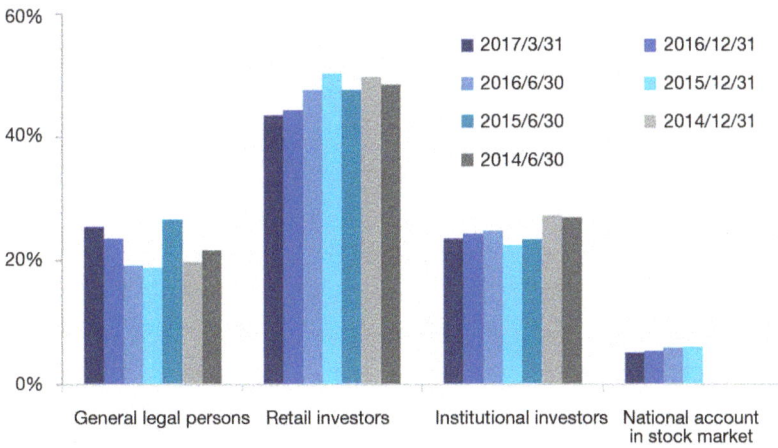

Figure 2-11: Investor structure of free float market capitalisation of A-share market (%).

Source: Haitong Securities (2017).

China's stock market turnover ratio is much higher than that of other markets (see Figure 2-12). In 2016, China's turnover ratios in the Shanghai Composite Index and GEM were more than 500 per cent and 900 per cent respectively. Given the special conditions of China's stock market, this represents more than 1,000 per cent if the calculation is based on free float market capitalisation. The turnover ratio of the Shanghai Composite Index was more than twice that of the S&P 500 Index and FTSE 100 Index, and 180 per cent higher than that of the NASDAQ Index. Further, the turnover ratio of the Nikkei 225 Index was only 200 per cent, and the turnover ratios of South Korea's KRX100 Index and the Hong Kong Hang Seng Index were less than 100 per cent.

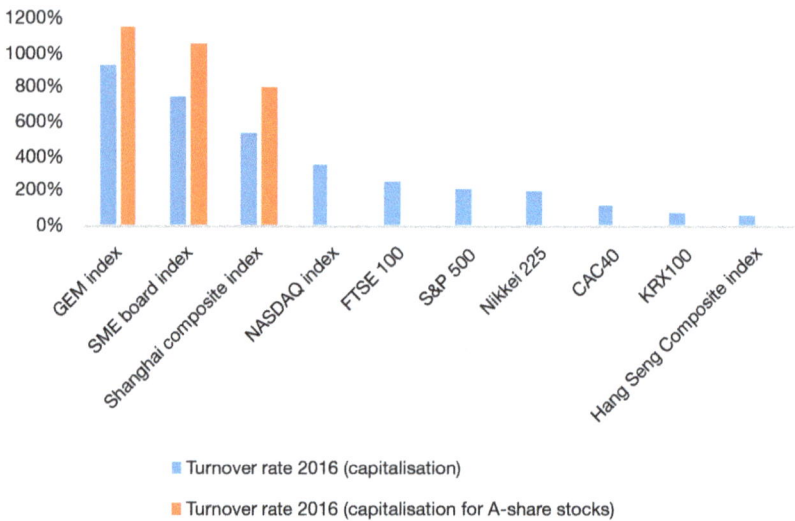

Figure 2-12: International comparison of stock market turnover ratios.
Source: Wind (2017).

Stock market volatility is too high, while the rate of return is too low

The turnover ratio and volatility of China's stock market are considerably higher than those in more mature markets, while the overall low rate of return indicates relatively low transaction efficiency.

A high turnover ratio indicates higher volatility. Similar to Brazil, China's stock market volatility was as high as 27 times (see Figure 2-13). While the number for mature markets with high volatility, such as France, Germany and Japan, was only around 18 times. More mature markets, such as the US and UK, experienced half of the volatility of China's market.

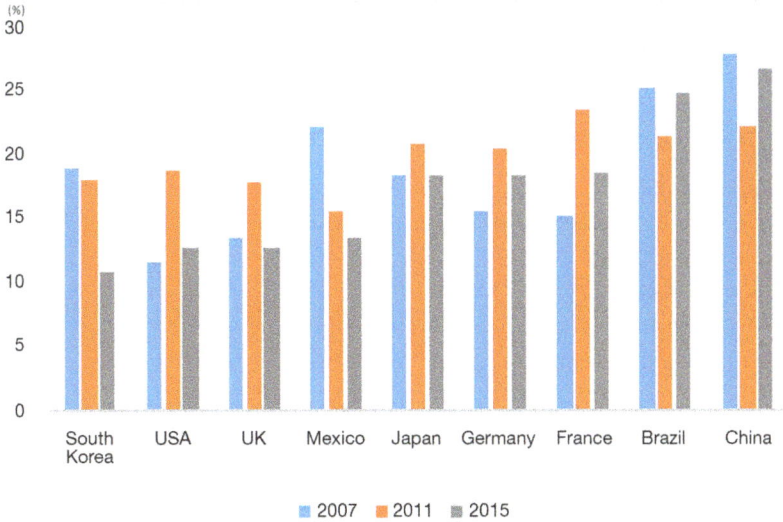

Figure 2-13: International comparison of stock market volatility (%).
Source: World Bank (2016).

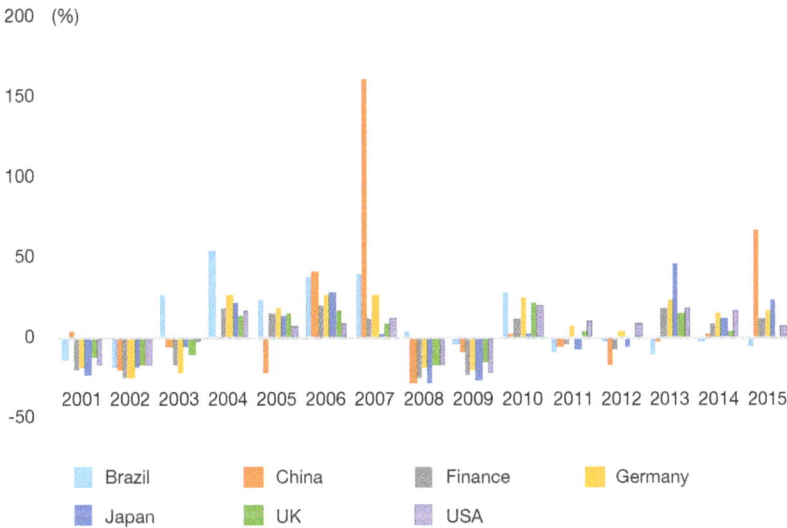

Figure 2-14: International comparison of stock market returns (%).
Source: World Bank (2016).

A market with high volatility and high risks encourages short-term speculation. In an effective financial market, risks can be properly priced and positively correlated with returns. The long-term volatility of China's stock market is higher than that of other markets; however, the rates of return in China's market have been consistently lower than those of other markets over many years (see Figure 2-14). If the opportunities available in the two bull markets of 2006–2007 and 2015 had not been taken, the rate of return would not only have been lower than the international level, but would also have been lower than China's inflation rate for the same period. This has made long-term investment in China's stock market unattractive, but has made short-term speculation attractive.

The structure of government bond investors should be optimised

Despite the rapid development of China's bond market, the major investors are commercial banks. Institutional investors represent key players in China's bond market, including state-owned commercial banks, joint-stock commercial banks, urban commercial banks, insurance companies and AMCs. In the overall bond custody balance, commercial banks hold a considerably high proportion (30 per cent) of government bonds. At the end of 2016, China's commercial banks held 67 per cent of total government bonds; of these, national commercial banks held up to 50 per cent (see Figure 2-15). Conversely, US commercial banks hold less than 4 per cent of US Treasury bonds and 15 per cent of municipal bonds. These percentages are far below those held by China's commercial banks (see Figure 2-16).

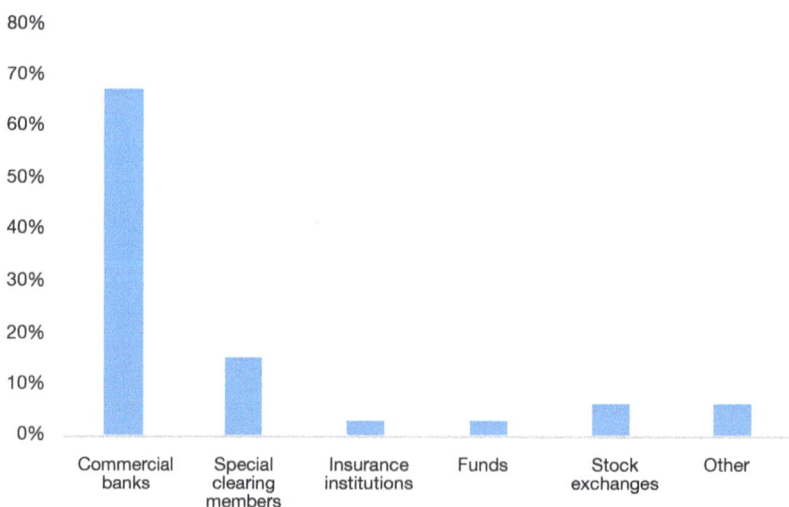

Figure 2-15: Structure of China's government bond holders in 2016.
Source: World Bank (2017) and ChinaBond (2017).

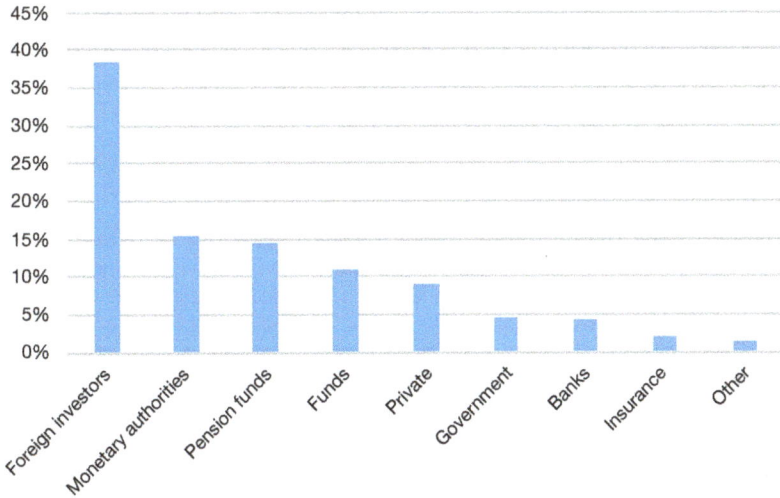

Figure 2-16: Structure of US Treasury bond holders in 2016.
Source: Securities Industry and Financial Markets Association (2017).

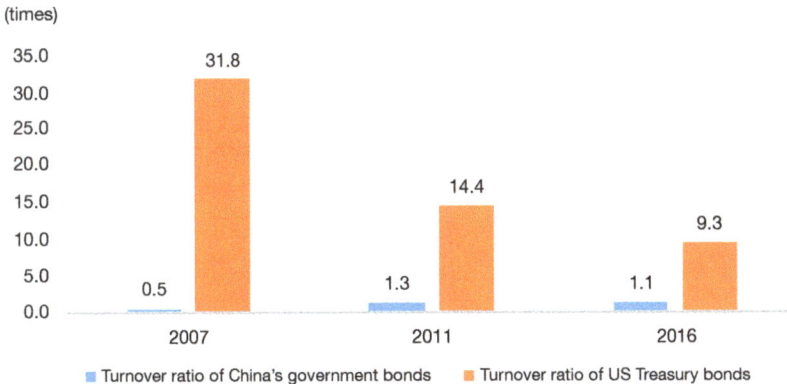

Figure 2-17: Comparison of China and the US government bond turnover ratios (times).
Source: Authors' original based on Wind (2017) and ChinaBond (2017).

An investor structure dominated by commercial banks has resulted in a low turnover ratio of government bonds. Commercial banks hold government bonds to meet risk management needs and regulatory requirements. Thus, they often hold bonds until maturity. Additionally, insurance companies generally hold long-term government bonds and AMCs hold government bonds as part of their portfolios. However, Chinese fund and insurance companies hold less than 10 per cent of total government bonds. All these factors have led to a sustained low turnover ratio in the bond market, especially in relation to government bonds. To some extent, this has restricted the transmission effectiveness of the monetary policy on the financial market. In 2016, China's turnover ratio for government bonds was 1.1, far below the US's turnover ratio of 9.3 (see Figure 2-17).

The status quo of China's capital market regulation

China's capital market was established in the early stage of the economic system transition, when elements of a market economy were introduced while strong administration was maintained. The regulatory system has continued to develop and improve, but, overall, the regulatory mechanisms are not yet perfect and struggle to meet the demands of economic development and reform.

The fragmented regulatory system restricts the sustainable development of the credit bond market

Credit bond regulation in China is conducted by multiple agencies. The National Development and Reform Commission approves the issuance of corporate bonds, the China Securities Regulatory Commission approves the issuance of bonds by listed companies and the National Association of Financial Market Institutional Investors (under the PBC's leadership) registers and approves medium-term notes and short-term financing bills. This fragmented system places significant constraints on the bond market. The market lacks a unified development plan. Additionally, the application scope and effectiveness in relation to the execution of laws and regulations are limited. For example, while the Securities Law applies to bond transactions on the exchanges, it does not apply to the interbank market. Conversely, the interbank market is limited by its self-disciplinary nature and lack of law enforcement authority. Thus, different standards are applied to illegal conduct in the two markets. Finally, the lack of unified regulatory standards and accountability mechanisms creates regulatory arbitrage opportunities in relation to the issuance of different types of bonds.

Two separate bond markets

In general, China's bond market is divided into the interbank and exchange market. In recent years, several attempts have been made to build connections between the two markets, but limited interconnectivity has been achieved. The separation has had a negative effect on bond pricing.

Significant differences exist between the two markets in relation to fund supply and market liquidity. Notably, funding costs in the exchange market are higher than those in the interbank market. Consequently, the bond prices on the exchange market are significantly lower than those on the interbank market. Thus, different prices often exist for the same bond. Additionally, the separation has increased operation costs. Issuers and investors must follow the different regulatory standards of the individual markets, are subject to the regulations of multiple agencies and must manage procedures in two registration systems—all of these increase the transaction costs. Finally, fragmentation of the transaction, clearing, settlement and custody systems affects the efficient and smooth operation of the bond market.

The stock issuing system results in insufficient market-based share pricing

China's A-share market approval system for stock issuance has resulted in abnormal stock pricing behaviours. In the 2015 stock market turmoil, even after the entire market had declined, IPO was still subject to much speculation. From 26 June to 2 July 2015, 25 new shares were issued, all of which saw an increase of more than 40 per cent in their market prices in their first days of listing, and 20 enjoyed an increase of more than 100 per cent in their first five days of listing. The approval system—with its strong administrative characteristics—limits the number of companies able to be listed and the supply of new shares on the market, prolongs the listing cycles and increases listing costs. These strict controls result in generally high stock prices and the high prices and yields of newly issued stocks.

The delisting mechanism has not been fully implemented

In recent years, delisting mechanisms have been continuously improved; however, in practice, the rules have not been implemented strictly. For example, some companies bypass the delisting requirements by manipulating their accounting methods. Consequently, the delisting mechanisms do not fulfil their intended functions. Further, poor-quality enterprises are able to remain in the market, the 'survival of the fittest' rule does not apply in relation to listed companies, and investors' interests are not properly protected. In the absence of an effective delisting mechanism, the capital market lacks a 'purifier' and fails to fulfil its role in eliminating inferior companies.

Future development directions of China's capital market

Under China's '13th Five-Year Plan for Economic and Social Development', development of the capital market includes increasing the proportion of direct financing, promoting equity financing through multiple channels, developing and standardising the bond market, building multilevel financial markets and introducing diversified financial products.

Increasing the proportion of direct financing, particularly equity financing

China used to rely very heavily on credit-led indirect financing. Consequently, economic growth generated incremental debts and caused risks to become excessively concentrated in the banking system. To address this issue, China must now vigorously develop capital markets (such as the stock market), broaden the channels of direct financing for enterprises and optimise social financing structures. Additionally, a path of market-oriented reform must be adopted, and unnecessary administrative interventions must be reduced to stimulate market power and vitality and cultivate commercial credit. Respect for market rules should be enhanced and the investor structure improved to increase stability. Market discipline and risk-sharing mechanisms must be strengthened to further improve the transparency of market operations.

Promoting equity financing through multiple channels

The construction of a multilevel capital market should be accelerated. Simultaneously, the financing functions of the main board, SME Board and GEM Board should be strengthened, reform of the NEEQ system deepened, the regional equity market development standardised and connections within the equity market promoted. Institutional arrangements in relation to market makers, targeted issuance, and mergers and acquisitions should be established and optimised. Financing instruments and transaction types should be enriched and their ability to serve various types of enterprises, including SMEs, improved. China should also actively guide the healthy development of private equity investment and venture capital funds and support the equity financing of innovative and growth-type enterprises.

Developing and standardising the bond market

The development of various fields must first be coordinated. Growing the bond market size will not only increase the proportion of direct financing, but may also increase the leverage ratio. Thus, balance is needed between the development of direct financing and controlling leverage to promote the stable and healthy development of the bond market. Innovative instruments are also necessary. Credit bonds will play an important role in improving underdeveloped areas and optimising supply. SME integrated bonds, private equity bonds and other financing instruments should be developed to broaden corporate financing channels. The proportion of short-term credit bonds should be controlled to avoid moving funds out of the real economy for profit-making from pure financial activities. Finally, institutions should be improved. The custody and settlement infrastructure of the bond market should be properly integrated with specific functions and its responsibilities clearly defined. Further, authorities should drive the unified and coordinated development of the interbank and exchange markets in a steady manner.

Building multilevel financial markets and introducing diversified financial products

The levels of financial markets and the variety of products should be enriched and an innovation-driven strategy adopted. Innovative financial market mechanisms, organisation, products and service models should be promoted and financial market depth and breadth expanded. Effort is required to build a financial market system with a rich variety of products, one that operates efficiently, embodies complete functions, is of considerable scale and adapts to a socialist market economy. Simultaneously, risk prevention must be undertaken in the process of financial innovation. The relationship among innovation, development and risk control needs to be well managed; innovations that seek to circumvent regulations or fail to serve economic development should be avoided.

Part 3: China's insurance industry: Rapid development and improvement of international status

China's insurance industry has one of the longest histories of opening up to the outside world and is one of the fastest growing industries in China's financial sector. Since 1980—due to extensive reforms, opening up and rapid economic development—the insurance industry has become much larger and stronger and has achieved extraordinary progress. This vigorous development has played an important role in protecting residents' properties and lives, enriching their investments, expanding their financing channels and optimising the allocation of their financial resources. The industry's international status has also improved. China's premium income is highly ranked globally, and its insurance depth and density continue to grow, as does the international influence of China's insurance regulations.

China's insurance industry: A leap from 'quantitative change' to 'qualitative change'

Since the resumption of insurance businesses in 1980, China's insurance industry has made great advances, along with rapid economic and social development. It has made a number of achievements.

First, the asset scale of the insurance industry has continued to expand, and insurance density and depth have improved significantly. At the end of 2016, the total assets of China's insurance industry reached CN¥15.12 trillion, approximately 23 times that in 2002 (see Figure 2-18). In 2016, premium income reached CN¥3,096 trillion, 10 times that in 2002. In terms of premium income, China has become the world's third-largest insurance market. In 2015, the national insurance density was CN¥1,770 per person, 7.4 times that in 2002. In 1980, the national insurance density was only CN¥0.47 per person. In 2015, insurance depth increased by 3.59 per cent, an increase of 1.07 percentage points over that in 2002 (see Figure 2-19). In 1980, the insurance depth was 0.1 per cent.

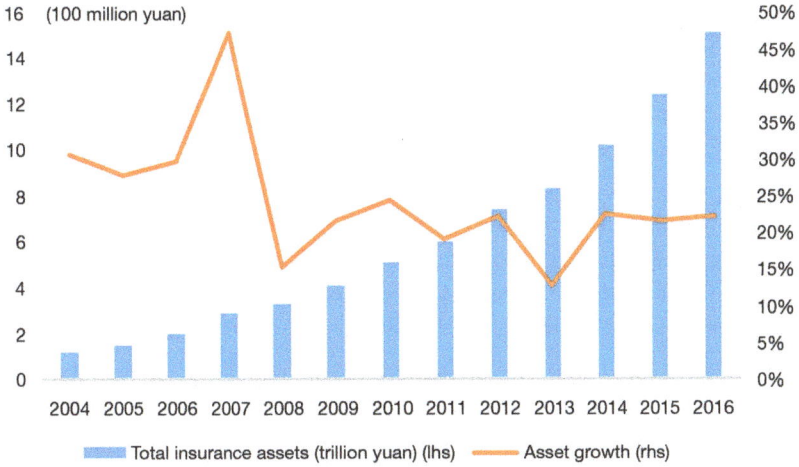

Figure 2-18: Total assets of China's insurance industry and growth trend (2000–2016).

Source: Financial Stability Analysis Group of the PBC (2016).

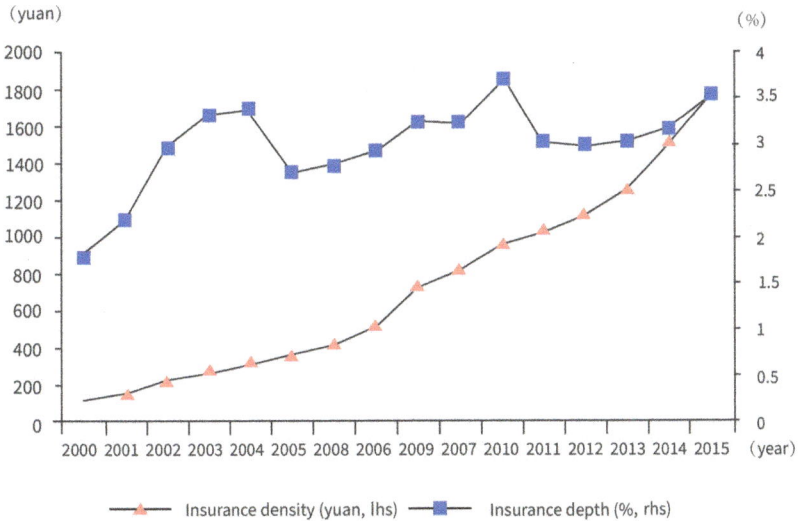

Figure 2-19: China's insurance density and depth (2000–2015).

Source: Compiled based on data from Almanac of China's Finance and Banking (2015).

Second, market participants continue to diversify. By the end of 2016, China had a total of 203 life insurance companies. Notably, only one existed immediately following the resumption of insurance businesses in 1980. Of these 203, 12 were insurance groups, 79 were property insurance companies, 77 were life insurance companies, 22 were insurance AMCs, nine were reinsurance companies and four were other types. Over almost 40 years of development, China's insurance industry has formed a market structure based on fair competition and joint development. The industry encompasses various types of organisations and multiple types of ownership, including state-owned enterprises, joint-stock companies, policy companies (e.g. China Export and Credit Insurance Corporation), professional companies (in health, pensions, agriculture and automobile insurance) and foreign-funded insurance companies.

Third, indemnity and payments by insurance companies have grown rapidly. In 2016, total indemnity and payments by Chinese insurance companies totalled CN¥1,051.289 billion, 10.5 times that in 2004 (see Figure 2-20). Loan guarantee insurance has helped SMEs and individuals obtain CN¥101.56 billion of credit in 2015. Further, short-term export credit insurance has provided nearly US$390 billion (US$416.7 billion in 2016) in risk protection to 63,000 export enterprises (82,200 in 2016). The insurance industry also continues to play out its advantage in long-term investments. In 2015, insurance companies (with registered assets totalling CN¥1.3 trillion) initiated 499 plans to support programs related to debt and equity financing and investment projects. These plans have provided vital funding support to key national projects, including the rebuilding of 'shantytowns' and urbanisation.

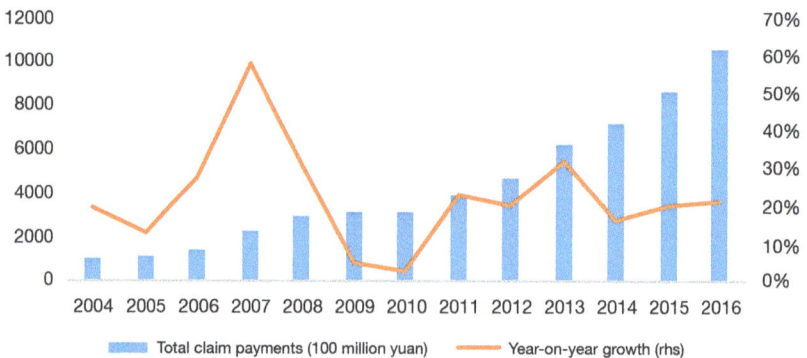

Figure 2-20: Total insurance claim payments in China and growth trends (2004–2016).

Source: Financial Stability Analysis Group of the PBC (2016).

Table 2-15: Utilisation of insurance funds in China

Item	2013 Amount (100 million yuan)	2013 Proportion (%)	2013 Growth (%)	2014 Amount (100 million yuan)	2014 Proportion (%)	2014 Growth (%)	2015 Amount (100 million yuan)	2015 Proportion (%)	2015 Growth (%)
Insurance capital utilisation balance	76,873.4	-	12.15	93,314.4	-	21.39	11,1795.5	-	19.8
Bank deposits	22,640.9	29.5	-	25,310.7	27.1	11.8	24,349.6	21.8	-3.8
Bonds	33,375.4	43.4	-	35,599.7	38.2	6.7	38,446.4	34.4	7.8
Stocks and bond investment funds	7,864.8	10.2	-	10,325.6	11.1	31.3	16,968.9	15.2	64.3
Other investments	12,992.2	16.9	-	22,078.4	23.7	69.9	32,030.4	28.7	14.5

Source: CIRC (2014, 2015, 2016).

Fourth, returns on investments and operational efficiency have improved significantly (see Table 2-15). In 2015, the allocation of insurance funds changed considerably. The ratios of bank deposits and bond investments decreased by 5.3 per cent and 3.8 per cent respectively, while the proportion of securities and other investments (mainly alternative investments) increased by 4.1 per cent and 5 per cent respectively. In 2015, the total yield on insurance fund utilisation reached CN¥780.4 billion, an increase of 45.6 per cent per year. The average yield was 7.56 per cent, the highest since the 2008 GFC. The increase of this yield was mainly driven by investments in stocks.

Fifth, the reform of the insurance industry led to comprehensive breakthroughs. In recent years, entry and exit mechanisms have continued to improve. Comprehensive, professional, regional and group insurance institutions have been developing side by side. Between 2011 and 2015, eight insurance institutions were listed in China or abroad. Innovative forms of insurance companies, such as self-insurance, interactive insurance and online insurance firms, have emerged. A modern, unified, open, coordinated and vibrant market system has emerged. The market is playing a more decisive role in resource allocation. Notably, comprehensive market-oriented reforms have been introduced in relation to life insurance premium pricing, the management of clauses and the premium pricing of commercial auto insurance. Insurance fund utilisation reforms have also been extended, as the allocation of insurance funds has become more diversified.

China's insurance industry began from nothing, but the sector has continued to expand and a market system has now been established. More importantly, behind the quantitative growth, the function, status and nature of China's insurance industry have undergone—and continue to undergo—profound changes.

International status of China's insurance industry

When China began to implement its reform and opening up policy, only one insurance company existed, the People's Insurance Company of China. The insurance industry was small, almost negligible, and had a very low degree of marketisation. After almost 40 years of vigorous development, the international status of China's insurance industry has improved significantly. The income China derives from premiums is one of the largest in the world, and China's insurance depth and density have also significantly improved. An international comparison reveals that the US, Japan and the UK represent the mature insurance markets and have led the world in terms of premium income. China, India, Brazil and Russia are typical emerging insurance markets.

Improvement in the international status of China's insurance industry is observable in the following areas.

First, China's premium income has grown rapidly. In 1995, China's premium income was only US$7.4 billion, a sum 12 per cent of that of the US's premium income of US$624 billion. By 2015, the sum had increased to US$38.65 million, making China the third ranked in the world and one of the fastest growing economies in terms of premium income. In 2015, China's premium income was 29.3 per cent that of the US. This represents an increase of 17 percentage points since 1995. China's share in global premium income also rose to 8.49 per cent in 2015.

Second, insurance density has increased significantly. In 1995, China's insurance density was only US$6.1 per capita while the US's insurance density was US$2,343 per capita (see Table 2-17). By 2015, China's insurance density had reached US$280.7 per capita, a figure 6.8 per cent of that of the US and 45 per cent of the world average.

Third, China's insurance depth has improved greatly. In 1995, China's insurance depth was only 1 per cent, the lowest among many countries (see Table 2-16). By 2015, it had increased to 3.57 per cent. This figure was still significantly lower than that of Japan, the UK, the US and other developed countries (see Table 2-17); however, it also represents a great improvement to China's 1995 insurance depth.

Fourth, the regulatory system continues to improve. An insurance system with Chinese characteristics has been established. Regulation of corporate governance has adopted a new quantitative assessment approach, leading the trend of international regulation. A second-generation regulatory system of insurance companies' claims-paying ability has been established and has had significant effects on the development of the global insurance market and regulatory rules. Multilateral and bilateral international cooperation has also advanced. Notably, China was elected as the presiding chair of the Asian Forum of Insurance Regulators. China also led the passing of the 'Colombo Declaration' and has gained a much stronger voice in informing international insurance regulations.

Table 2-16: Comparison of GDP, premium income and insurance density and depth across selected countries (1995)

Region/Country	GDP (100 million USD)	Premium income (US$100 million)	Insurance density (per capita premiums, USD)	Insurance depth (premiums/ GDP, %)
China (mainland)	7,345	74	6.1	1.00
US	76,641	6,240	2,343.3	8.14
Japan	54,491	6,373	5,080.2	11.69
Germany	25,916	1,551	1,898.3	5.98
France	16,099	1,316	2,210.8	8.18
The Netherlands	4,465	353	2,281.8	7.90
South Korea	5,593	600	1,330.3	10.73
Mexico	3,438	37	39.3	1.08
India	3,666	60	6.3	1.64

Note: China's data excludes data of Hong Kong, Macau and Taiwan.

Source: Insurance density and depth calculated based on GDP and population data from the World Bank and premium income data from Swiss Reinsurance Company Sigma (1998).

Table 2-17: Comparison of GDP, premium income and insurance density and depth across major economies (2015)

Region/ Country	GDP (US$100 million)	Premium income (US$100 million)	Rank	Insurance density (per capita premiums, USD)	Insurance depth (premiums/ GDP, %)
Global	730,497	4,553,785	-	621.2	6.23
US	180,899	1,316,271	1	4,095.8	7.28
China (mainland)	108,114	386,500	3	280.7	3.57
Japan	41,561	449,707	2	3,553.8	10.82
Germany	33,543	213,263	6	2,562.5	6.24
UK	28,491	320,176	4	4,358.5	9.97
France	24,228	230,545	5	3,392.0	9.29
India	20,868	71,776	12	54.7	3.44
Italy	18,147	165,037	7	2,580.5	8.68
Brazil	17,723	69,091	14	332.1	3.90
Korea	13,452	153,620	8	3,034.2	11.42
Russia	12,364	16,801	31	117.1	1.41

Note: China's data excludes data of Hong Kong, Macau and Taiwan.

Source: Swiss Reinsurance Company Sigma (2016).

Problems with the development of China's insurance industry

The development mode is still extensive and the insurance industry is large, but not strong

After nearly 40 years of development, China can be described as an insurance giant, but still not an insurance power. Mainland China's premium income ranks third in the world (following the US and Japan). However, the measure of a country's insurance industry development is not its scale, but its depth (premium income divided by GDP) and density (premium income divided by total population). In 2015, China ranked 40th and 63rd in terms of these two indicators respectively, both below the world average.

A large gap still exists between China's insurance industry and those of developed countries. First, China's insurance coverage remains limited. Many properties in China are not insured. For example, more than 70 per cent of Chinese property insurance covers automobiles. Office buildings and other valuable types of property are less likely to be insured. Similarly, liability insurance is also uncommon. On average, residents in developed countries have more than one life insurance policy per person. In China, life insurance coverage per capita is 0.2. Second, catastrophes are not adequately insured against. Chinese people rarely see the necessity of insurance. Consequently, in the event of earthquakes, floods and other catastrophes, they receive very small amounts of compensation. Third, a wide variety of insurance products exists, but these products are largely homogenous. Fourth, the pricing of insurance products is generally too high. However, in recent years, the CIRC has sought to drive the market-oriented pricing of premiums and, consequently, prices have become more reasonable.

The foundation and environment of China's insurance industry development have undergone profound changes. However, the industry has retained an extensive development mode. Overall, competition in the industry still focuses on business scale and market share. Most companies emphasise expanding scales and establishing more branches, but ignore internal management issues and product and service innovation. Some companies blindly pursue expansion and market share and do not consider the cost effectiveness or legality of their behaviours. This extensive development mode cannot meet the demands of China's increasingly young and well-educated consumer groups. It could even harm the interests of consumers and lose their trust.

The '13th Five-Year Plan for Insurance Industry Development of the People's Republic of China' issued in 2016 stated that effort needs to be made 'to develop China from an insurance giant to an insurance power'. Specifically, the objectives were for China's national insurance premium income to reach CN¥4.5 trillion with an insurance depth of 5 per cent, an insurance density of CN¥3,500 per person and total assets of around CN¥25 trillion by 2020. These objectives were to be achieved by unremitting efforts, but they only represent short-term targets. Long-term effort will be required if China is to become an insurance power.

The risk prevention function of insurance is still weak

Non-life insurance can only hedge against risks, but life insurance can also be an investment instrument. Normally, life insurance products should have a clear risk hedging feature. However, this feature has been weakened in some products that largely serve as investment instruments. The premium income of China's life insurance companies was CN¥2,169.281 billion in 2016. This represents an annual increase of 36.78 per cent. Clients' investment funds and the incremental funds of their independent accounts that are not included in insurance contracts reached CN¥1,279.913 billion. This represents an annual increase of 53.86 per cent, much higher than the growth of the premium income of China's life insurance companies. The data indicate that the investment functions of life insurance products were magnified, but the risk protection function was weakened. Some life insurance products were essentially investment instruments, but had very few risk protection functions.

Compared with other financial products, the advantages of life insurance products lie in their risk protection function and long-term features. This protection function is not offered by other financial products and the long-term nature can smooth the effect of economic cycles for secure returns. When a life insurance product loses its insurance function and changes into a pure investment instrument (so that, in essence, it is no longer an insurance product), it is prone to liquidity risk and likely to cause turmoil in the market. Insurance is essentially a loss-sharing mechanism and must perform a risk prevention function.

In 2016, the CIRC issued the 'Notice on the Issues Concerning the Standardization of Short- and Medium-Term Life Insurance Products', 'Notice on Further Improving the Actuarial System of Life Insurance' and 'Notice on Strengthening the Regulation of Life Insurance Products'. All of these sought to limit the scale of short- and medium-term insurance products, strengthen the protection function of insurance products and guide the industry to fulfil its risk protection responsibilities.

The interests of the insured are not sufficiently protected

There are two ways to maximise an insurance company's profitability. The first is to increase the underwriting profit. To this end, it is necessary to expand underwriting, charge higher premiums and reduce the loss ratio. The second is to increase investment profits. To this end, it is necessary to expand the scale of assets and raise the return on investments. Induced by profits, insurance companies may expand underwriting, increase premium rates, delay indemnity or invest in high-risk projects. Such actions can be deceptive and misleading. Legally, insurance companies and insurance consumers enter contractual relations with equal status. However, in reality, insurance consumers are in a weaker position. Insurance companies decide in advance on the clauses and premium rates that insurance consumers must accept. Insurance companies possess expertise, while insurance consumers generally know very little about insurance. Insurance companies have solid foundations and professional legal teams, while consumers can generally only afford limited legal assistance once involved in disputes with insurance companies. The CIRC should follow the law and operate according to the principles of openness and impartiality when implementing regulations, supervising the insurance industry and maintaining market order. Insurance regulations are intended to protect the lawful rights and interests of the applicants, insured and beneficiaries.

Progress has been made in opening the market, but openness is still at a low level

The openness stipulated under the insurance industry's market access policy is relatively high among financial industries and allows the establishment of wholly foreign-owned insurance companies, foreign insurance company branches and joint-venture insurance companies. However, the actual degree of openness is low. There is only one foreign-owned insurance company in China (AIA Group). Foreign investors are allowed to own a maximum of 50 per cent of joint-venture insurance companies. At the end of 2016, foreign insurance companies from

16 countries and regions had established 57 companies in China, 31 per cent of the total number of insurance companies in China. Of these, 22 were property insurance companies (27 per cent of the total property insurance companies in China), 28 were life insurance companies (36 per cent of the total life insurance companies in China), six were reinsurance companies and one was an asset management company. Simultaneously, the number of province-level branches of joint-venture insurance companies reached 304. As of July 2017, the total assets of foreign insurance companies reached CN¥1,002.25 billion. This figure was only CN¥3 billion when China first entered the World Trade Organization (WTO) in 2001. The market share held by foreign insurance companies has increased in recent years, but remains low. The proportion of premium income of foreign insurance companies has increased from below 1 per cent when China entered the WTO in 2001, to 5.19 per cent by the end of 2016. The proportion of assets held by foreign insurance companies has increased from 4.4 per cent in 2006 to 6.1 per cent in July 2017 (see Figure 2-21).

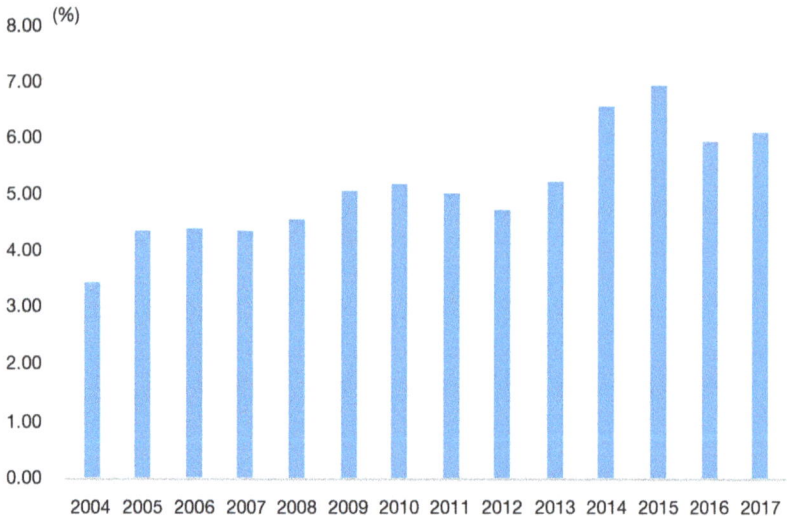

Figure 2-21: Share of insurance assets held by foreign insurance companies in China (%).

Source: Wind (2017) and CIRC (2017).

Regulation of China's insurance industry

Currently, laws relating to the insurance industry are inadequate, and companies have weak internal controls. Further, both information and infrastructure are lacking. In light of these problems, China has adopted a regulatory approach that emphasises the regulation of both market behaviours and the claims-paying ability of insurance companies.

Regulation of insurance institutions

To regulate insurance institutions, reviews of applicant companies' qualifications are undertaken and the market behaviours of insurance companies are monitored. Currently, China is enforcing a strict approval system to manage market access. Requirements for capital adequacy and management qualifications are strictly adhered to when issuing licences. However, as current mechanisms rely on off-site supervision, it is difficult to ensure the integrity of insurance institutions. Consequently, the ongoing supervision of market behaviours is weak.

Regulation of insurance policies and premium rates

Under a strict regulatory model, all policy terms must be examined and approved. Currently, the internal control systems of insurance companies are imperfect and the ability of insurance companies to design policies is limited, as is the public's knowledge of insurance products. If regulations were relaxed, insurance companies could compete on premium rates, distort premium pricing and introduce risks to the market. Thus, it is necessary to implement an approval system in relation to insurance policy terms and premium rates. Specifically, the CIRC should formulate the basic clauses and premium rates for major types of insurance, while non-basic clauses and the premium rates for non-major types of insurance should be set by insurance companies and registered with the CIRC.

Regulation of insurance companies' claim-paying ability

Claim-paying ability refers to the ability of an insurer to fulfil its contractual agreement with an insured person or body and provide economic compensation. It is the key ability of an insurance company. Thus, it has also been subject to regulation in China. As part of a developing trend in international regulations, an increasing number of countries have adopted (or are close to adopting) a regulatory model centred on insurance companies' claim-paying ability. Currently, China uses a minimum claim-paying ability rule. Whether the CIRC intervenes is determined by the variance between the actual claim-paying ability of the insurance company and the established standard. Compliance with this regulation is considered in relation to a number of major financial indicators (e.g. capital adequacy, contribution of a security deposit, contribution to an insurance security fund, contingency reserves and the use of funds). All these indicators affect an insurance company's claim-paying ability, which is not a static factor, but one in constant flux.

Regulation of the use of insurance funds

In response to financial innovation and increases in market competition, the insurance industry now undertakes both underwriting and the investment of insurance funds in their operations. Previously, the insurance industry relied on underwriting alone. However, the investment of insurance funds has become an important pillar of insurance companies' business. Insurance fund investments are regulated in relation to their source and use. Further, quotas are imposed on the amounts that can be invested to ensure the stability and security of investment income, strengthen insurance companies' claim-paying abilities and protect the interests of the insured.

The active use of insurance funds in China began from nothing. Currently, regulations in this area are still lacking and investment returns are low. It is difficult for insurance companies to cover losses from their underwriting businesses with their investment incomes. The regulations largely seek to limit the areas in which funds can be invested and the proportion of funds that can be invested (see Table 2-18).

Table 2-18: Restrictions on the investment of insurance funds in stocks and real estate (%)

Country	Government bond	Corporate bond	Stock	Loan	Real estate	Overseas investment
US	N/A	N/A	20	20	25	10
UK	N/A	N/A	N/A	N/A	N/A	N/A
Japan	N/A	N/A	30	N/A	20	30
China	N/A	30	10	0	5	15

Source: Financial Stability Analysis Group of the PBC (2016).

Future development directions of China's insurance industry

According to the '13th Five-Year Plan for Insurance Industry Development of the People's Republic of China', in the next few years, the basic principles of reform and development will be to liberalise thinking, introduce more initiatives, focus work on key areas, improve reform effectiveness, give full play to institutional advantages, promote structural adjustments and transform the industry's development mode. To achieve these, China should affect the following:

1. Perfect the modern insurance market system. Reform of the market access mechanism must be pursued. An upgrade of the market participant structure, business structure and regional layout should also be promoted. Additionally, the insurance market system should be able to support the real economy and be compatible with financial innovations.

2. Further insurance company reforms. Development of a modern insurance enterprise system should be accelerated. Investments in insurance companies by qualified state-owned capital, private capital and foreign capital should be supported, and the diversification of capital and equity should be encouraged. Additionally, the mixed ownership reform of insurance companies should be promoted.

3. Accelerate development of the reinsurance market. Steps should be taken to improve the reinsurance market system, moderately increase market participants, develop regional centres for reinsurance businesses and increase China's voice and pricing power in the global reinsurance market.

4. Steadily advance development of the intermediary agencies. A multilevel, multicomponent and multiform insurance intermediary service system should be established. Intermediary agencies with unique professional strengths—agencies that are internationally competitive—should be fostered. Small and micro, community, brick-and-mortar insurance agencies should also be established. Diversified insurance sales and the development of an independent individual agent system should also be encouraged.

5. Comprehensively drive the market-oriented pricing of insurance premiums. A comprehensive reform of the clause and premium rate management system for commercial vehicle insurance should be promoted. This should establish a pricing mechanism with a pure industry risk premium as its basis, and in which additional premium rates and adjustment factors are decided by companies.

References

Bank for International Settlements. *Debt securities statistics*. Retrieved from www.bis.org/statistics/secstats.htm?m=6%7C33%7C615

China Banking Regulatory Commission. (2007). *China Banking Regulatory Commission 2006 annual report*. Retrieved from zhuanti.cbrc.gov.cn/subject/subject/nianbao/english/ywqb.pdf

China Banking Regulatory Commission. (2009). *China Banking Regulatory Commission 2008 annual report*. Retrieved from zhuanti.cbrc.gov.cn/subject/subject/nianbao2008/english/zwqb.pdf

China Banking Regulatory Commission. (2011). *China Banking Regulatory Commission 2010 annual report*. Retrieved from zhuanti.cbrc.gov.cn/subject/subject/nianbao2010/english/zwqb.pdf

China Banking Regulatory Commission. (2013). *China Banking Regulatory Commission 2012 annual report*. Retrieved from www.cbrc.gov.cn/chinese/home/docView/5F0858ECD7B442AA8B56365B2992E8B1.html

China Banking Regulatory Commission. (2015). *China Banking Regulatory Commission 2014 annual report*. Retrieved from www.cbrc.gov.cn/chinese/home/docView/7E0CF3C51001425E919F739562C350BA.html

China Banking Regulatory Commission. (2017). *China Banking Regulatory Commission 2016 annual report*. Retrieved from www.cbrc.gov.cn/chinese/home/docView/FDF4A782E9E34140B13ACFFE774FAB1A.html

China Insurance Regulatory Commission. (2014). *Statistics report on insurance sector 2013*. Retrieved from bxjg.circ.gov.cn/web/site0/tab5257/info3901864.htm

China Insurance Regulatory Commission. (2015). *Statistics report on insurance sector 2014*. Retrieved from bxjg.circ.gov.cn/web/site0/tab5257/info3948914.htm

China Insurance Regulatory Commission. (2016). *Statistics report on insurance sector 2015.* Retrieved from bxjg.circ.gov.cn/web/site0/tab5257/info401 4824.htm

China Insurance Regulatory Commission. (2017). *Statistics report on insurance sector 2016.* Retrieved from bxjg.circ.gov.cn/web/site0/tab5257/info406 0001.htm

China Securities Depository and Clearing Co. Ltd. (2017). *China Securities Depository and Clearing Corporation statistical yearbook.* Retrieved from www.chinaclear.cn/zdjs/editor_file/20180824144624273.pdf

ChinaBond. (2017). *Statistics* [database]. Retrieved from www.chinabond.com.cn/ Channel/19012917

Financial Stability Analysis Group of the People's Bank of China. (2016). *China financial stability report 2016.* Beijing: China Financial Publishing House.

Financial Stability Analysis Group of the People's Bank of China. (2017). *China financial stability report 2017.* Beijing: China Financial Publishing House.

Financial Stability Board. (2016). *2016 list of global systemically important banks (G-SIBs).* Retrieved from www.fsb.org/wp-content/uploads/2016-list-of-global-systemically-important-banks-G-SIBs.pdf

Haitong Securities. (2017). *2016 analysis on A-share investors.* Retrieved from finance.stockstar.com/SS2017051000001936.shtml

Institute of International Finance Research, Bank of China. (2016). *2017 global banking outlook report.* Retrieved from wenku.baidu.com/view/ 1c567d780622192e453610661ed9ad51f01d54f1.html

National Bureau of Statistics of China. (2017). *China statistical abstract 2017.* Beijing: China Statistics Press.

People's Bank of China. (2015). *Almanac of China's finance and banking 2015.* Beijing: Author.

Securities Industry and Financial Markets Association. (2017). *US capital markets deck 2016.* Retrieved from www.sifma.org/resources/archive/research/

Swiss Reinsurance Company Sigma. (1998, 25 July). *Swiss re-releases 'Sigma' 4/1998: World insurance in 1996.* Retrieved from www.propertyandcasualty. com/doc/swiss-re-releases-sigma-41998-world-insurance-0001

Swiss Reinsurance Company Sigma. (2016). *Sigma report 3/2016: World insurance in 2015: Steady growth amid regional disparities.* Retrieved from www.swissre. com/institute/research/sigma-research/sigma-2016-03.html

The Banker. *The Banker Database*. Retrieved from www.thebankerdatabase.com

Wind. (2017). *Wind Economic Database*. Retrieved from www.wind.com.cn/ NewSite/edb.html

World Bank. *Open Data* [database]. Retrieved from datacatalog.worldbank.org/

World Federation of Exchanges. *Statistics* [database]. Retrieved from www.world-exchanges.org/our-work/statistics

3

Further Expanding the Opening Up of China's Financial Industry

Zhu Jun,[1] Guo Kai,[2] Ai Ming,[3] Zhao Yue[4] and Bai Xuefei[5]

Introduction

A Communiqué of the Third Plenary Session of the 18th Central Committee of the Communist Party of China (CPC) proposed that the government should 'perfect the financial market system and expand the opening up of the financial industry both domestically and internationally'. The '13th Five-Year Plan' further clarifies the goal of 'promoting two-way opening of the financial industry'. The financial industry is essentially a competitive industry, and only full competition can improve its efficiency and vitality. International practice shows that expanding the opening of the financial industry can enhance the competitiveness of financial institutions and fundamentally prevent and defuse financial risks. Since joining the World Trade Organization (WTO) in 2001, China has made great progress in opening its financial industry. Openness of financial institutions has kept increasing, a multilevel and diversified financial market is taking shape, the degree of two-way openness is constantly expanding, and the institutional environment has improved. However, the openness of China's financial industry is still insufficient. The overall

1 Director-General of the International Department, People's Bank of China (PBC).
2 Deputy Director-General of the International Department, PBC.
3 Staff researcher at the International Department, PBC.
4 Staff researcher at the International Department, PBC.
5 Staff researcher at the International Department, PBC.

market share of foreign financial institutions in China is low, much lower than in major developed economies and most developing countries. There are still many discriminatory provisions in regard to the ownership ratio and business scope of foreign financial institutions. Additionally, the breadth and depth of China's financial market is insufficient and the accounting, audit and taxation systems are underdeveloped, leaving much room for improvement.

China's experience shows that opening up has promoted trade and investment liberalisation, exchange rate liberalisation, relaxation of foreign exchange control and allowed the market to play a more active role. Over the years, the troika reforms—opening of the financial industry, exchange rate liberalisation and relaxation of capital control—have made coordinated progress, creating a favourable financial environment for China's economic growth (Zhou, 2017). A problem with any of these three will affect the entire opening process. Therefore, although the pace of the three reforms may be uneven, they have been moving forward in the same direction. Other chapters discuss the exchange rate and capital flows; this chapter focuses on the opening of the financial industry.

Part 1: Theoretical basis and practical significance of further opening of the financial industry

The opening of the financial industry needs to address two important issues: whether a country should open its financial industry, and how to open it. To answer the first question, we need to have a clear understanding of the nature and position of the financial industry. If the financial industry is a competitive industry, it does not need monopolies and should not impose too many restrictions on investors. The authorities should fully promote market competition and enhance the efficiency and vitality of the financial system through further opening.

The nature and position of financial services industry

In theory, the financial service industry is essentially competitive; therefore, its vitality and competitiveness must be enhanced through competition. George Stigler, the Economics Nobel laureate, proposed three elements that a competitive industry should possess (Stigler, 1983). First, there should be a high number of enterprises within the industry, and the products of the enterprises should be similar and substitutable to a certain extent. Second, collusion among enterprises should be difficult. Third, for new enterprises wishing to enter the industry, the long-term average cost should not be significantly higher than for existing enterprises in the industry.

The financial industry conforms to the above characteristics of a competitive industry. First, there are many financial institutions and the financial services are very similar. For example, China's banking industry had 4,399 corporate financial institutions at the end of 2016 (China Banking Regulatory Commission [CBRC], 2017). Their main financial services included clearing business, credit business, financial transaction, and investment banking—homogenisation is quite apparent. Second, it is difficult for different financial institutions to influence the prices of financial services through collusion. Due to the large number of financial institutions and high similarity of financial products, consumers have greater freedom in choosing financial services and it is difficult for financial institutions to monopolise pricing. Additionally, along with the deepening of financial innovation, the barriers among banking, securities and the insurance industry are gradually being removed. Different businesses overlap and penetrate each other. The competition in financial institutions no longer originates in that industry, which further increases the difficulty of collusion. Third, natural monopoly industries such as water, power and gas often require a significant initial investment in pipelines and other infrastructure, so the sunk costs are relatively high. Many enterprises providing similar services will lead to the duplication and waste of inputs and are not conducive to efficiency improvements in the industry. However, as a service industry, the competitiveness of the financial industry is mainly embodied in the customer relationship, core technology and financial innovation. It is more dependent on limitless investments, rather than a one-off large investment. Therefore, the average operating costs of new financial institutions are not significantly higher than those for current financial institutions. Further, the innovation of products and services provided by a single financial institution also contributes to the development of the entire financial industry, along with improvements in financial efficiency, reducing duplication and waste. Thus, the financial service industry is essentially competitive, and only competition can enhance efficiency and stimulate vitality.

From the practice of China's reform and opening, the introduction of competition has effectively improved operational efficiency in the banking industry. This further confirms the financial services industry's competitive nature. During the 40 years of reform and opening, domestic banks have achieved great improvements in operating efficiency, asset quality and corporate governance through introducing external strategic investors, competitive share reform, initial public offerings and other measures. Simultaneously, more and more financial institutions have begun to 'go global'. They have participated in international competition globally; made substantial improvements in all aspects including risk management, product pricing and anti-money laundering; and have promoted the stable operation of enterprises and the healthy development of the financial market. Conversely, a lack of competition can lead to inefficient practices, resulting in high leverage, low capital, non-performing loans and other phenomena, making the system prone to financial crises. The main reason for the Asian financial crisis was the low efficiency and risk accumulation caused by the lack of competition among financial institutions over a long period.

Compared to competitive industries, the financial services industry also has its own characteristics. First, the asset liability structure of financial institutions is unique, such as the liquidity risk brought about by high leverage and maturity mismatches that are naturally formed. This makes financial institutions vulnerable to competition, which shows a certain level of fragility. Second, the day-to-day operations of financial institutions are susceptible to market sentiment, and public confidence is critical to the soundness of the financial system. Third, financial crises are highly contagious; the problems of a single financial institution may lead to a chain reaction in many financial institutions, and even endanger the stability of the whole financial system. Therefore, the security and stability of the financial industry is essential to the healthy and smooth operation of the economy. A fully competitive financial services industry is premised upon an effective allocation of resources, the basis for effective transmission of monetary policy and a guarantee for the rapid development of financial innovation. Only by building a more competitive financial service system can we effectively maintain financial stability and enable a comprehensive supporting role of finance in the real economy.

Comparison of international and Chinese experiences of opening

Opening to the outside world can promote competition. By introducing advanced management models, technologies and rules, the competitiveness and soundness of the financial system will be improved, and financial risks will be reduced. The entry of foreign financial institutions has compelled domestic financial institutions to achieve greater improvement in product design, market development, business models, management experience and other aspects. Additionally, it creates the need to reform accounting rules and regulatory standards (Zhou, 2017). Market competition can force financial institutions to focus more on key areas such as the capital adequacy ratio, leverage ratio and liquidity risks, and encourage them to guard against risks through self-discipline. Additionally, full competition can reduce the moral hazard associate with 'too big to fail' and better safeguard the bottom line of no systemic financial risks. International experiences also show that financial opening is not the cause of financial risk. On the contrary, opening can reduce and defuse financial risks.

First, expanding opening can introduce advanced management concepts, techniques and rules to promote market competition, improve market efficiency and maintain financial stability (Claessens, 2009; Yeyati & Micco, 2007). An efficient financial system is the fundamental guarantee of financial stability. Taking Turkey as an example, the entry of foreign banks had a positive spill-over effect on its financial system. During the 1980s and 1990s, foreign banks took the lead in using modern budgeting methods in Turkey. An electronic banking office system was introduced and use of the Society for Worldwide Interbank Financial Telecommunications network was pioneered. These advanced systems and technologies were subsequently adopted by many Turkish banks. Financial sector efficiency was improved, along with management standards and budget transparency.

Second, expanding opening is beneficial for risk diversification. Previous financial crises show that concentrated financial risks can have a significant impact, while dispersed risks can be defused more easily. More opening is an important method to spread risk. Opening will bring in more market players and increase competition, meaning risks will be less concentrated and borne by more market participants (Dages, Goldberg & Kinney, 2000). For example, from 1994–1999, Latin American economies were highly dependent on foreign debts, cross-border capital flows fluctuated dramatically, the governments ran long-term deficits and local currencies were seriously overvalued. As a result, serious crises broke out successively in some countries. However, foreign banks were not the trigger of these crises. Instead, they played the role of 'economic stabiliser'. Both before and after the crisis, the non-performing loan ratios of foreign banks in Argentina, Brazil and other Latin American countries were generally lower than those of domestic banks, and the pro-cyclicality and volatility of their lending were also smaller than domestic banks.

Third, a closed financial industry will lead to risk accumulation and threaten financial stability. For example, Mexico forbade foreign banks from entering the domestic market before the late 1980s. During the 1990s, the pace of opening remained slow in Mexico. In 1994, foreign bank loans in Mexico accounted for only 1 per cent of Mexico's total bank loans. Due to lack of competition, the efficiency of domestic banks was very low, risk control was inadequate, moral hazard was serious and potential non-performing loans surged. Faced with rising interest rates globally, the Mexican Government was forced to raise interest rates in 1994. As a result, the interest rate burden of enterprises was increased, loan defaults started to rise, financial risk was highlighted, investor panic grew and the Mexican peso was sold off. The Mexican Government issued large amounts of debt in dollars to maintain the exchange rate. Eventually, the government was overwhelmed by the debt burdens, the peso depreciated sharply, the default rates of bank loans rose dramatically and Mexico was plunged into a full-blown financial crisis. After the crisis, the Mexican Government drew on the lessons learned and gradually allowed foreign financial institutions to enter the domestic market to encourage competition, strengthen market discipline and reduce the risk of financial instability.

Since China joined the WTO, all those areas that have thoroughly opened and actively participated in the global allocation of resources—China's finance, commerce, agriculture, automobile and other industries—have achieved better development, strong competitiveness and high degrees of internationalisation. China has become the world's second-largest economy and the largest exporter. Opening has ushered in extensive reform in China, helped industries to meet international standards, promoted innovation of mechanisms and systems, and expanded the competitiveness and influence of many sectors. Some competitive industries, such as the home appliance industry, developed rapidly after opening. With goods such as colour televisions, refrigerators, washing machines and other large appliances, domestic brands occupy the leading position in China's market and operate as spokespeople for 'Made in China' internationally.

Conversely, industries that lag in opening are developing at a slower pace. More protection and restriction policies can only protect the weak and preserve monopolies. China started its WTO negotiations during the aftermath of the Asian financial crisis, and there were various views on financial opening and financial risks. Compared to other industries, the liberalisation of the financial industry was relatively slow. With the accomplishment of banking reforms and the continuous development of the financial market, the time was right for the financial industry to open. However, the opening process still lagged significantly due to outdated thinking and institutional inertia. After a series of reform, state-owned banks in China have improved in indicators, such as the non-performing loan ratio and capital adequacy ratios, and the four major state-owned banks now rank among the global systemically important banks (see Table 3-1). However, Chinese financial institutions still lag behind in many areas such as fund management and derivatives. The level of financial opening is becoming increasingly incompatible with the development of the real economy and the overall openness. This not only affects the financial industry's competitiveness, but also restricts the internationalisation of the RMB and the 'going global' strategy. Therefore, China needs to further open up the financial services industry, introduce more competition and provide a strong incentive for reform.

Table 3-1: Global systemically important banks (2016)

Grade (Capital requirement)	Bank
5 (3.5%)	–
4 (2.5%)	Citi Group, JP Morgan Chase
3 (2.0%)	Bank of America, BNP Paribas, Deutsche Bank, HSB
2 (1.5%)	Barclays, Credit Suisse, GoldmanSachs, Industrial and Commercial Bank of China, Mitsubishi UFJ FG, Wells Fargo
1 (1.0%)	Agricultural Bank of China, Bank of China, Bank of New York Mellon, China Construction Bank, Groupe BPCE, Credit Agricole, ING Bank, Mizuho FG, Morgan Stanley, Nordea, Royal Bank of Scotland, Banco Santander of Spain, Société Générale, Santander, State Street, Sumitomo Mitsui FG, UBS, Unicredit Group

Note: Classification is determined by the criteria set by the Basel committee.

Source: Bank for International Settlements (2016).

Further opening the financial industry meets China's own need for development

Currently, international and domestic situations have set higher demand for the opening of China's financial industry. Internationally, globalisation faces great challenges due to unbalanced technological development, low productivity growth and increased income inequality. Following Donald Trump's election as president of the United States (US), nationalism, populism and trade protectionism have increased, and an undercurrent of anti-globalisation has surged. The US and other developed economies have taken measures to enhance their competitiveness, such as bringing manufacturing industries home, offering tax cuts and deregulating the financial industry. These policies may set an example for other countries and impact the free trade system and the multilateral rules that have been formed globally over the years. As a result, the global governance system may reach a 'crossroad'. China is a rising power and a beneficiary of globalisation and the current multilateral mechanism. It needs an open and fair environment that protects international trade and investment. If protectionism continues to grow and global trade and investment fade, China's interests will suffer. Therefore, China should send a clear message that it will further open to the outside world; play a leading role in globalisation together with other major countries; ensure free movement of trade, resources, capital, technology and human resources across borders; and better safeguard its interests.

Domestically, China's economic development has entered a 'new normal'. Economic transformation and upgrading have entered a crucial period, and the foundation of financial development is undergoing profound changes. Additionally, the financial industry also has the arduous task of supporting the supply-side structural reform, and potential financial risks cannot be ignored. Therefore, China must further open the financial sector to promote reform, improve the investment environment and market condition, and enhance the soundness of the financial system. Simultaneously, China's comparative advantage is changing and enterprises have accelerated their pace of 'going global'. This places higher requirements on the depth and breadth of the financial system. However, the pace of China's financial institutions entering the global markets is lagging significantly and can barely meet the financial needs of enterprises that are 'going global' (Ministry of Commerce, 2015). Therefore, further opening of the financial sector is required, along with the acceleration of the 'going global' of financial institutions and financial services. A global network must be formed to support the real economy more effectively.

Simultaneously, the low level of openness of China's financial sector has brought criticism from the outside. Some foreign businesses believe that the improvement in China's business environment in recent years is limited and, thus, hope China will further push forward reform, opening and marketisation (American Chamber of Commerce in the People's Republic of China, 2017). For example, they hope that the government further loosens restrictions on market access and business scope for banking, securities, insurance and fund management. It is also hoped that the government increases the transparency, consistency and predictability of foreign exchange policy; treats foreign enterprises fairly; further reduces licensing barriers; strengthens the protection of intellectual property rights; and relaxes or cancels data flow restrictions. The top priority for Chinese authorities is to improve the domestic investment and market environment. One important measure is to further expand the opening of the financial sector.

Opening the financial industry: Pros and cons

First, opening the financial industry can help build a diversified financial system. Theoretically, the entry of foreign financial institutions into the Chinese market promotes competition, expands financial services channels and enhances financial stability (Clarke, Cull, Martinez Peria & Sanchez, 2001; Claessens, Demirguc-Kunt & Huizinga, 2001). Foreign banks, securities and insurance firms have brought new business models to China, which has enriched the Chinese financial system and improved its operational efficiency. China's first township bank was established by a Hong Kong financial institution (Hong Kong and Shanghai Banking Corporation), and unsecured credit loans were launched by Standard Chartered Bank in 2006. Foreign banks also had an earlier interest in green finance, financial technologies, risk pricing and other business. Their technology and concepts have provided valuable reference to Chinese financial institutions. AIA Group entered China in 1990 and brought in the sales agent model. The model was gradually adopted across the country and became an important sales channel for life insurance companies in China. The development of China's securities market also draws on the Western trading system. The trading rules of the London Stock Exchange and Hong Kong Exchanges and Clearing have become important references for the Shanghai Stock Exchange. The entry of more foreign financial institutions could produce economies of scale and attract new businesses and technologies, which helps build China into an international financial centre.

Second, opening the financial industry can better serve the real economy and push forward supply-side structural reforms. The financial sector and the real economy are closely linked and mutually reinforcing. Transformation and upgrading of China's economic structure needs to further boost domestic demand and encourage the development of small and medium-sized enterprises and high-tech enterprises. However, Chinese financial institutions have made relatively slow progress areas such as consumer credit, small and micro loans, and venture capital investment. As a result, there is only a limited number of financial products that truly serve the real economy, and speculation and arbitrage is prevalent. In contrast, foreign financial institutions have rich experience and advantages in corporate governance, credit management and risk pricing. They can serve as good examples for Chinese institutions and help optimise the economic structure.

Third, opening the financial industry can accelerate the opening of the service sector. Currently, the level of openness of China's service industry is below that of the manufacturing industry and significantly lower than the average level of other countries. The level of openness is not in proportion to the contribution of the service industry to economic growth. This has also been criticised by other countries. Presently, countries are working on more comprehensive and higher standards for opening the service industry. China needs to seize the opportunity and be more proactive. The negative impact of opening the financial sector is relatively small and controllable, and the sector is a critical area in which there are plenty of opportunities for China.

Additionally, opening the financial industry can consolidate the reserve currency status of the RMB and promote internationalisation of the RMB. Owning an international reserve currency is important to the long-term development of an economy. After becoming an international reserve currency, the RMB will enjoy institutional rights, and international recognition and attractiveness of bilateral currency swap agreements signed by the People's Bank of China and other central banks and monetary authorities will substantially increase. The RMB becoming an international reserve currency can greatly enhance confidence in the currency at home and abroad, reduce the possibility of economic and financial turmoil, and lessen the spill-over effects of other countries' policies. Simultaneously, the issuer of a reserve currency can have more independent monetary policies and more tools to deal with financial crises, and use the currency more frequently for international transactions and investment. This will enhance the pricing power and voice of the country in trade and investment. To consolidate the RMB's status as a reserve currency and promote its internationalisation, China must make the RMB more 'freely usable', expand the opening of the financial industry, and provide a friendly and convenient environment for investors to conduct RMB business both in China and overseas to enhance China's global attractiveness.

There are concerns that opening will bring risks. For example, opening the financial sector is likely to accelerate cross-border capital flows and bring risks to the country's macroeconomic and financial stability. Additionally, foreign financial institutions have complex products, have a high frequency of transactions and engage extensively in derivatives transactions. Problems in these areas may cause cross-institutional and cross-market risks through liquidity, products and asset price channels. However, with the continuous progress of reform and opening, the flexibility of RMB exchange rate has been enhanced, the convertibility of capital accounts has also made great progress, and the conditions for opening the financial industry are becoming ripe. The aforementioned risks are largely controllable for several reasons.

First, China has made great progress in strengthening financial regulation and preventing risks. In recent years, China has constantly improved the assessment, prevention and early warning of systematic financial risks as well as risk disposal mechanisms. The financial regulation system has been continuously perfected, the effectiveness of regulation has been enhanced, the framework of macroprudential regulation has been well set up, financial infrastructure has been steadily developed, and authorities' ability to guard against financial risks has significantly increased. These measures can effectively safeguard financial security.

Second, in recent years, Chinese financial institutions have rapidly increased their assets and network of branches, and acquired a high market share and a large client base. Foreign financial institutions have no obvious advantages in business scale, networks and client relations. As such, it is difficult for them to pose a threat to the development of Chinese financial institutions.

Third, China has some unique advantages that enable it to resist external shocks. China is already the world's second-largest economy, the world's largest exporter and has the largest foreign exchange reserve in the world. The size of its financial market is also significant. The balance of China's bond market ranks third in the world and second in Asia (see Figure 3-1). Additionally, China has the second-mover advantage. Many developed countries and emerging markets economies have rich experiences with financial opening that China can use as reference.

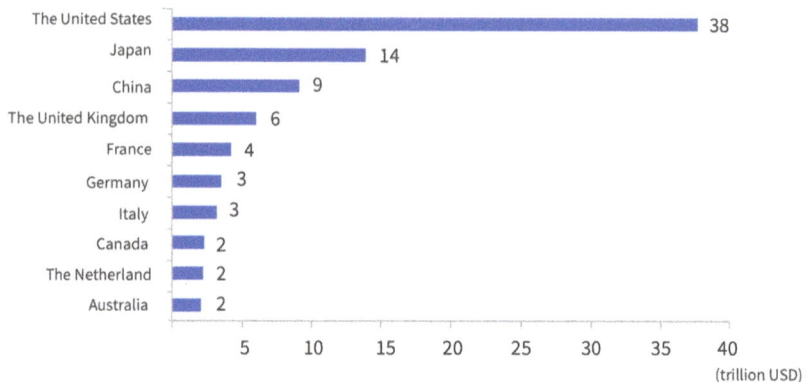

Figure 3-1: International comparison of bond market size (as of September 2016).
Source: Bank for International Settlements (2016).

There are also concerns that further opening of the financial sector might put China's financial security at risk. However, financial security should be secured by sound systems and institutions, rather than discriminatory market access policies. China should safeguard financial security through sound operation and risk management in financial institutions, effective policy tools including a prudential regulation framework, and increasingly effective and transparent financial markets. Only with sound institutions can China maintain public confidence in the financial system and safeguard the bottom line of no systemic financial risks.

Additionally, China can use the national security review mechanism to fend off threats to security, stability and integrity of the financial system. Developed countries have highly open markets where national security review is applied only to a small number of foreign investment applications. China needs to properly balance opening up and national security and use the review rationally. Investigations should be carried out with caution to avoid criticism that China implements protectionism in the name of national security.

Part 2: Progress in opening China's financial sector

In recent years, China has made great progress in opening its financial sector. The openness of financial institutions and financial markets has improved, the pace of financial institutions 'going global' has accelerated, RMB internationalisation has made remarkable achievements, and China's participation in global economic and financial governance has achieved positive results.

Financial institutions and financial markets

The openness of China's financial institutions has improved. Since joining the WTO, the opening of China's financial services industry has constantly deepened. The country launched a series of policies and measures in the banking, securities and insurance industries, and has eased restrictions on the establishment, location and business scope of foreign financial institutions based on a gradual approach. At the end of 2016, there were 39 foreign banks (including financial companies) and 121 branches of foreign banks in China. The assets of foreign banks accounted for 1.3 per cent of the total assets of banking institutions in China (CBRC, 2017). As of March 2017, there were 13 joint-venture securities companies in China, making up 10 per cent of the total securities companies and assets accounting for 4.5 per cent of total assets. At the end of 2016, there were 56 foreign property insurance companies (including wholly-owned and joint ventures) and joint-venture personal insurance companies, accounting for 30.4 per cent of the total property and personal insurance companies in China (see Figure 3-2).

In terms of the opening of the financial market, foreign investors in the bond and interbank bond markets continue to increase. As of February 2017, there were 432 foreign investors in the interbank bond market, including foreign central banks and monetary authorities, sovereign wealth funds, international financial organisations, offshore clearing banks and participating banks, foreign insurance institutions, Qualified Foreign Institutional Investors (QFIIs) and RMB Qualified Foreign Institutional Investors (RQFIIs). This represents a total investment of nearly CN¥800 billion (Zhu, 2017). The varieties of interbank bond investment have been enriched constantly, and the level of development and professionalism of the bond market has been improved. The scope of issuers of Panda bonds has also expanded to include non-financial foreign enterprises, foreign commercial banks, international development institutions and foreign governments. As of the end of 2016, a total of CN¥63.1 billion of Panda bonds were issued (Zhu, 2017). Additionally, the mainland and Hong Kong bond markets have achieved interconnection via the 'Bond Connect'. In the stock market, the Shanghai–Hong Kong Stock Connect and Shenzhen–Hong Kong Stock Connect have been launched successively, greatly improving the two-way opening of capital accounts. China's A-share market was officially included in the MSCI index, which further enhanced the degree of internationalisation.

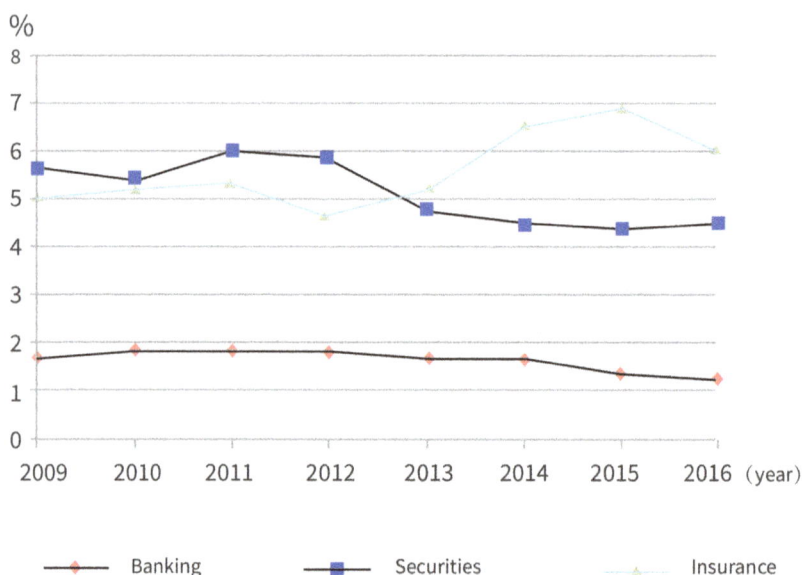

Figure 3-2: The change in proportion of assets of foreign financial institutions in banking, securities and insurance industries in recent years.
Sources: CBRC (2017), China Securities Regulatory Commission (2017) and China Insurance Regulatory Commission (2017).

RMB internationalisation

In recent years, the internationalisation of the RMB has made remarkable progress. In early 1992, China approved small amounts of RMB settlement to meet the demand of trade activities in 13 cities along the borders such as Heihe. After 2002, Vietnam and other neighbouring countries allowed their local currencies and the RMB (or only the RMB) to be used for border trade settlement, which promoted cross-border use of the currency.

In 2004, Hong Kong and Macao launched cross-border RMB business. The business grew rapidly, but the scale remained small. After the 2008 global financial crisis, major international settlement currencies such as the US dollar fluctuated sharply, and the demand for the RMB in cross-border trade settlement by Chinese and foreign enterprises rapidly rose. Given this need, the People's Bank of China conducted pilot programs on cross-border trade settlement in RMB in 2009. In recent years, bilateral currency swap, direct currency trading, RQFII, RMB clearing banks, the RMB cross-border interbank payment system and other institutional arrangements have effectively reduced the exchange rate risk and promoted trade and investment facilitation.

In 2015, the International Monetary Fund (IMF) conducted the special drawing right (SDR) review. The People's Bank of China, along with relevant departments, introduced a number of important measures in relation to opening the bond and foreign exchange markets, improving data transparency and strengthening policy communication. With these efforts, the RMB finally reached the standard of the SDR basket currency. On 30 November 2015, the Executive Board of the IMF decided to include the RMB in the SDR basket, and the IMF affirmed that the RMB was a 'freely usable currency'. The new basket became effective on 1 October 2016. The inclusion of the RMB in the SDR basket greatly increased the attractiveness of the RMB. In September and October 2016, the RMB assets held by the People's Bank of China exceeded US$10 billion. The RMB assets held by international financial organisations and multilateral development institutions and in foreign exchange reserves of various countries also increased. On 31 March 2017, the IMF released its official statistics on the currency composition of official foreign exchange reserves (COFER) in which the RMB was listed separately for the first time. As of the end of 2016, RMB reserves held by COFER-reporting countries were US$84.51 billion (about CN¥582.2 billion), accounting for 1.1 per cent of the total foreign exchange reserves of those countries and further confirming the status of the RMB as a reserve currency (see Figure 3-3).

The aforementioned reform measures also greatly promoted the convertibility of China's capital account. According to the classification of capital account transactions (a total of seven categories and 40 items) by the IMF (2016a), 37 items have achieved convertibility, basic convertibility and partial convertibility in China, accounting for 92.5 per cent of all transaction items.

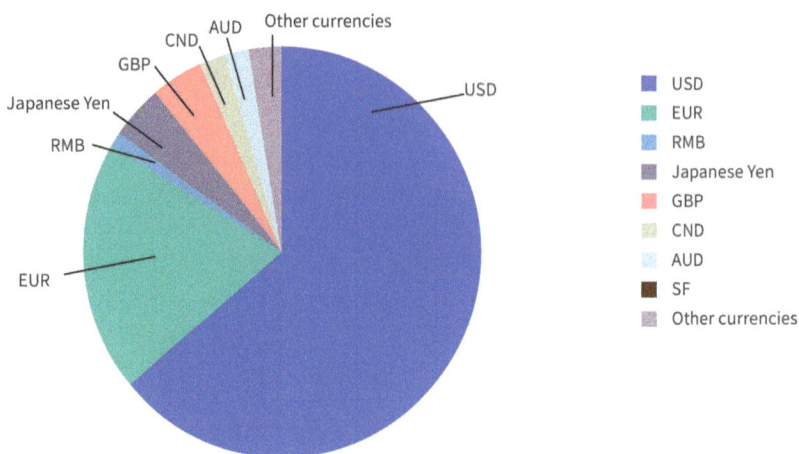

Figure 3-3: Proportion of currencies in foreign exchange reserve assets held by COFER-reporting countries.

Source: IMF (2016a).

Specifically, direct investment has achieved full convertibility, and investment facilitation has been steadily improved. China has adopted registration management for outward direct investment, and eliminated examination of the source of funds of foreign direct investment and approvals for remittance. For the overseas direct investments of banks, China also changed the regulation from administrative approval to filing. In terms of foreign direct investment, China has simplified the regulation process and placed more emphasis on regulation during and after the transactions. Simultaneously, the convertibility of cross-border financing has increased, and most items have achieved basic convertibility. All the items under external debts are also basically convertible. There is no restriction on currency exchange relating to financial credit provided by financial institutions. The proportion limit on commercial credit between residents and nonresidents has been retained, but prior control was abolished. With external debt, only a few necessary authenticity checks remain, and other administrative licensing relating to accounts and currency exchange has been cancelled. Additionally, the convertibility of securities investments has steadily increased. The control over currency exchange relating to cross-border securities trading in the secondary market is relaxed.

Part 3: Problems with China's financial opening process

China's financial industry opening has made some amazing achievements, but many problems remain. The level of openness is below international levels and insufficient to meet the need of economic development, the Belt and Road Initiative, RMB internationalisation and construction of international financial centres.

Financial institutions and financial market

Since China's accession to the WTO, foreign financial institutions have not had as strong a development momentum as expected. Conversely, the assets of foreign financial institutions have remained at a low proportion and have even decreased in recent years. Foreign banks hold around 2 per cent of China's total banking assets, which decreased to 1.29 per cent in 2016. Organisation for Economic Co-operation and Development (OECD) countries' 'average' has declined since the financial crisis but is still above 10 per cent. The average level of the other BRICS countries—Brazil, Russia, India and South Africa—soared to 15.5 per cent in 2009, substantially higher than that of China. The proportion of foreign investment in the insurance industry decreased to 5.6 per cent in 2016 after reaching a peak of 8.9 per cent in 2005; this is well below the 20–30 per cent market share in OECD countries. Additionally, change of ownership occurred in many joint-venture securities firms.

There are a number of causes for the decline of foreign financial institutions. Some multinational financial institutions were greatly affected by the 2008 financial crisis and suffered a decline of profitability. As a result, they shifted business focus to their home countries and reduced business in emerging markets. Financial regulation has also become more stringent after the crisis, cross-border operation costs have risen, and the financial institutions of some developed economies have withdrawn from emerging market economies. China's state-owned bank reform, which began in 2005, attracted a great amount of foreign investment and many foreign banks became strategic investors. With the public listing of Chinese banks, their assets continue to grow. Some foreign banks have chosen to sell the stocks and cash in to realise financial returns.

Additionally, the withdrawal of foreign banks largely reflects that China has a relatively poor environment for business operation. Although it seems that China has a high degree of openness in many sectors, foreign financial institutions in China face more policy barriers, such as restrictions on ownership percentage and business scope.

In terms of shareholding ratio, China is one of the few countries with restrictions on the proportion of foreign ownership in the banking, security and insurance sectors. From an international comparison of the 24 major economies (19 G20 countries including China, as well as Switzerland, Belgium, Luxembourg, Singapore and Chile) (see Tables 3-2, 3-3 and 3-4), most countries have lifted restrictions on the shareholding ratio of foreign and domestic capital in the banking, security and insurance sectors. Countries with requirements for shareholding ratios (the US, Canada, Australia, Mexico, Italy, South Korea and Singapore) treat domestic and foreign ownership equally and have no additional requirements for foreign investors. In some countries, the shareholding ratio is limited only for total foreign investment. For example, Russia has no limit on the shareholding of a single foreign investor; its only requirement is that the total amount of foreign investment does not exceed a certain percentage. Only India and China have discriminative shareholding ratio requirements for foreign ownership, with China's requirements being more stringent.

Table 3-2: Provisions on the proportion of foreign investment in banking sector of major economies

Country	Shareholding ratio	Specific provisions
UK, France, Germany, Switzerland, Belgium, Luxembourg, Japan, Brazil, Argentina, Chile, South Africa, Saudi Arabia	No restrictions on shareholding ratios of domestic and foreign investment.	
Canada	A limit on the proportion of shares held. However, it applies to both domestic and foreign investment.	According to Canada's broad shareholding requirements, for banks with C$12 billion or more in capital, the voting shares and the non-voting shares held by any person or co-actors should not exceed 20% and 30% respectively. For Canadian domestic banks with capital between C$2 billion and C$12 billion, the public holding of voting shares is required to reach 35%. But for those banks with capital of less than C$2 billion, there are no shareholding restrictions.

Country	Shareholding ratio	Specific provisions
Italy	A limit on the proportion of shares held. However, it applies to both domestic and foreign investment.	Domestic or foreign financial institutions cannot hold more than 15% of the shares of banking financial institutions.
Australia	Shareholding by domestic and foreign investors surpassing a certain percentage needs to pass certain regulatory procedures (such as regulatory approval).	Shareholding by a single investor (domestic or foreign) of a financial institution exceeding 15% needs to be approved by the Australian Treasury Department; the Treasury Department authorises the Australian Prudential Regulation Authority the right to approve investment of less than A$1 billion.
US	Shareholding by domestic and foreign investors surpassing a certain percentage needs to pass certain regulatory procedures (such as regulatory approval).	Any company (including foreign banks) acquiring more than 25% of the voting shares in banks or bank holding companies needs to be approved by the Federal Reserve. If a foreign bank has a branch/agent bank, a commercial loan company or subsidiary in the US, the acquisition of more than 5% of the shares of the US bank or bank holding company requires the approval of the Federal Reserve.
Korea	Shareholding by domestic and foreign investors surpassing a certain percentage needs to pass certain regulatory procedures (such as regulatory approval).	Individuals or business entities cannot own or control more than 10% of a national commercial bank's (regional banks, more than 15%) voting shares. In exceptional circumstances, a domestic individual or a business entity may hold 100% of the shares with the approval of the Finance Committee, and a financial institution established under the laws of another country that is an 'internationally recognized financial institution'[1] may owe more than 10% of the shares of commercial banks or bank holding companies established under the laws of the Republic of Korea. However, it should meet additional approval requirements of the Finance Committee.
Singapore	Shareholding by domestic and foreign investors surpassing a certain percentage needs to pass certain regulatory procedures (such as regulatory approval).	For commercial banks, if shareholding by a single or multiple shareholders in a local bank reaches 5%, approval by the Monetary Authority of Singapore is needed. For financial companies, if shareholding by a single or multiple shareholders reaches 5%, 12% or 20% of a financial company, approval by the Monetary Authority of Singapore is needed.

Country	Shareholding ratio	Specific provisions
Indonesia	Shareholding by domestic and foreign investment surpassing a certain percentage needs to pass certain regulatory procedures (such as regulatory approval).	A single domestic or foreign financial institution cannot hold more than 40% of the shares of a bank, a single domestic or foreign non-financial institution cannot hold more than 30% of the shares of a bank, and a domestic or foreign individual investor cannot hold more than 20% of a bank's shares. For shareholdings exceeding the above ratios, approval by the Indonesian central bank is needed.
Mexico	Restrictions for certain banks.	Restrictions on foreign investment in development banking institutions.
Russia	No restriction on shareholding ratio of foreign investors in any single bank. Restrictions on the proportion of foreign investment in the banking system.	The amount of a single bank's foreign investment is not limited, but the amount of foreign investment in the entire banking system is limited. All foreign investment in the Russian banking system cannot exceed 50% (excluding foreign capital entering the Russian system before 2007 and that went into privatisation of Russian banks after Russia's accession to the WTO).
Turkey	Restrictions on the form of establishment.	Foreign investment in Turkish banks must be in the form of a joint venture or a branch and should be approved by the Turkish Banking Authority.
India	Only restrictions on shareholding ratios of foreign investment.	In the first five years, the proportion of shares held by foreign institutions shall not exceed 50% and shall not exceed 74% later.
China	Only restrictions on shareholding ratios of foreign investment.	The proportion of the shares held by a single foreign institution shall not exceed 20%, and the proportion of total foreign investment shall not exceed 25%.

[1] According to Appendix 3 of the Free Trade Agreement between Korea and the United States, 'internationally recognized financial institutions' refers to any financial institution that obtains a rating from an international rating agency that is accepted by a Korean regulator, or that shows it has similar qualifications to Korean regulators via other means.

Source: Regulatory agencies of the countries.

Table 3-3: Provisions on the proportion of foreign investment in the insurance sector of major economies

Country	Shareholding ratio	Specific provisions
US, UK, France, Germany, Italy, Switzerland, Belgium, Luxembourg, Japan, Korea, Saudi Arabia, Brazil, Argentina, Chile, South Africa, Australia, Turkey	No limits on domestic or foreign shareholding.	
Singapore	There is a limit on the proportion of shares held. However, it applies to both domestic and foreign investment.	49% is the cap of shareholding allowed in a life insurance or non-life insurance company, and no foreign investors can be the largest shareholder.
Canada	There is a limit on the proportion of shares held. However, it applies to both domestic and foreign investment.	According to Canada's shareholding requirements, for insurance institutions with capital of more than C$2 billion, voting shares held by the public should reach 35%. But for insurance institutions with capital of less than C$2 billion, there are no shareholding restrictions.
Mexico	Shareholding by domestic and foreign investment surpassing a certain percentage needs to follow specific regulatory procedures (such as regulatory approval).	Generally, foreign ownership should not exceed 49%; if more than 49%, it must be approved by the foreign investment committee.
Russia	No restriction on foreign holding of a single insurance company. Restrictions on the proportion of foreign investment in the insurance system.	Total foreign investment in the Russian insurance system cannot exceed 50%. Foreign capital entering the Russian insurance system before 2007 and foreign capital that went into privatisation of Russian insurance companies after Russia's accession to the WTO are excluded.
Indonesia	Restrictions only on foreign shareholding.	A foreign investor cannot hold more than 80% of the shares.
India	Restrictions only on foreign shareholding.	A foreign investor cannot hold more than 49% of the shares.
China	Restrictions only on foreign shareholding.	Foreign insurance companies that set up joint-venture life insurance business with Chinese companies and enterprises cannot hold more than 50% of the total shares.

Source: Regulatory agencies of the countries.

Table 3-4: Provisions on the proportion of foreign investment in the securities sector of major economies

Country	Shareholding ratio	Specific provisions
US, UK, France, Germany, Italy, Switzerland, Belgium, Luxembourg, Japan, Korea, Singapore, South Africa, Brazil, Argentina, Chile, India, Saudi Arabia, Turkey, Australia, Canada[1]	No limits on domestic or foreign shareholding.	
Mexico	Foreign ownership exceeding certain percentage needs regulatory approval through specific regulatory procedures.	Generally, foreign shareholding of brokerage firms and bonding institutions should not exceed 49%, and if foreign shareholding of institutions that qualify stock and similar exceeds 49%, approval by the foreign investment committee is needed.
Indonesia	Restrictions for shareholding ratio by foreign investment only.	A foreign investor cannot hold more than 49% of the shares.
Russia	Restrictions for shareholding ratio by foreign investment only.	Foreign investment can only enter the securities market as a Russian legal entity. Foreign shareholding of certain types of securities market participants (securities registration company, and special depositary company with bookkeeping capacity through the traders) should not exceed 25% of registered capital.
China	Restrictions for shareholding ratio by foreign investment only.	Foreign shareholding of listed securities companies shall not exceed 25% and the proportion of that of unlisted securities companies shall not exceed 49%.

[1] Canada has no uniform rules on foreign holdings of securities companies. The Canadian provinces make their own rules based on specific needs.

Source: Regulatory agencies of the countries.

A number of historical factors contributed to the imposition of restrictions on foreign holdings of financial institutions. When the reform and opening-up policy was first launched in China, 'super-national treatment' was given to foreign financial institutions and joint ventures by some special economic zones and local governments to attract foreign investment. Preferential tax policy is one example. For example, foreign financial institutions and Sino–foreign joint ventures could enjoy a 15 per cent income tax rate if the initial investment or operating capital exceeded US$10 million and the business was in existence for over 10 years. In contrast, the income tax rate was as high as 33 per cent for Chinese financial institutions. Simultaneously, foreign financial institutions enjoyed favourable treatment in terms of tax base, turnover tax, etc. Because of this, some Chinese financial institutions wanted to 'transform' themselves into joint ventures by introducing foreign capital. According to the 'Sino–Foreign Joint Ventures Law', one requirement for a joint venture is that foreign investment should be no less than 25 per cent. Only when foreign investment reached 25 per cent could a business enjoy the preferential tax treatment.

Since China's accession to the WTO, investment policy has become more standardised. 'Super-national treatment' was gradually abolished, but the 25 per cent requirement has been retained. According to 'Measures for the Implementation of Administrative Licensing of Chinese Commercial Banks' (2003), if combined foreign holdings of a non-listed financial institution reached 25 per cent, the business would be treated as a foreign financial institution. In 2015, regulatory authorities amended the implementation measures to impose more strict restrictions on foreign ownership, stipulating that combined foreign shareholding of a Chinese financial institution should not exceed 25 per cent. This provision has substantially limited the role that foreign investors can play in corporate governance, strategic planning and financial management. Restrictions on business scope and licensing has also restricted the development of foreign-funded financial institutions.

The securities sector

Foreign securities companies can only enter China by setting up joint ventures, and can only conduct limited business such as underwriting, brokerage of foreign stocks and bonds.[6] The Chinese controlling shareholder must be a securities firm. Because a subsidiary cannot compete with its parent company, the business of joint-venture securities companies is seriously restricted. The advanced products and pricing technology of foreign companies cannot be introduced to China, which dampens foreign investors' enthusiasm for doing business in China.

---

6   Securities companies have seven business functions: securities brokering, securities investment consulting, financial consulting related to securities trading and investment activity, securities underwriting and sponsorship, securities dealing, securities asset management, and other securities business.

The banking sector

Branches of foreign banks need to operate in China for at least one year before they can conduct RMB business. There is no such requirement for Chinese banks. This requirement has delayed the development of foreign banks. For example, in 2011, the Silicon Valley Bank received approval to set up a joint-venture bank, SPD Silicon Valley Bank (SSVB). However, due to regulatory restrictions, SSVB could only conduct foreign exchange business until 2015 when it was allowed to engage in RMB business. As the bank's major customers are small and medium-sized technology start-ups that do not have much demand for foreign exchange, SSVB did not experience much growth in China. In 2011, SSVB also entered the UK market and was allowed to conduct pound business immediately. The bank has since provided professional financial services to many British small and medium-sized enterprises, especially technology companies. Even though the operating requirement has been reduced from three years to one year in China, this restriction is still a major impediment to foreign banks at their initial stage of development in China.

Foreign banks that intend to establish branches in China must have significant amounts of assets. Foreign banks establishing subsidiaries and joint-venture banks in China must have total assets of no less than US$10 billion the year before application. Foreign banks that intend to set up branches in China must have no less than US$20 billion.[7] Neighbouring countries and countries along the 'Belt and Road' find it difficult to meet such requirements. International experience shows that most countries do not have requirements regarding total assets for foreign banks intending to establish subsidiaries or branches; rather, emphasis is given to regulatory and compliance factors.

In terms of the number of licences, even big foreign banks can only acquire up to two licences each year, and the two licences are usually for different regions. Although this approach has been gradually abolished, foreign banks are no longer enthusiastic about investing in China. Therefore, China has missed the best opportunity to attract foreign banks.

---

7   The total asset requirement was abolished in October 2019.

The insurance sector

The regulator has been slow to approve the establishment of branches of foreign insurance companies in China. Fewer than two new licences are granted each year for qualified joint-venture life insurance companies. Strict licence approvals and the small quota have distorted the business plans of foreign insurance companies and restricted their ability to serve the Chinese market.

An international comparison shows that the openness of China's financial industry is still low. According to the Services Trade Restrictiveness Index (STRI),[8] as of 2016, Latvia's banking industry had the highest degree of openness (0.12), while China's banking industry ranked 41st among the 44 countries surveyed (including all the OECD countries and nine emerging economies[9]) with an STRI of 0.41, just above Brazil, India and Indonesia (OECD, 2016a) (see Figure 3-4). The STRI of China's insurance industry was 0.46 (Korea had the highest degree of openness at 0.11), ranking 42nd among the 44 countries surveyed, only above India and Indonesia (OECD, 2016b) (see Figure 3-5).

Simultaneously, the depth of China's financial market is insufficient. The opening of the securities markets is not conducted in a systemic manner, but via a 'channelised' mode, whereby foreign institutional investors invest in the domestic market through QFII and RQFII schemes, domestic institutional investors invest in the international market through QDII and RQDII, and domestic individual investors invest abroad through the Shanghai–Hong Kong Stock Connect and Shenzhen–Hong Kong Stock Connect. But outside these channels, the domestic market is disconnected from the international market. The 'channelised' opening mode is a very primitive approach with heavy administrative intervention and a low degree of openness.

---

8   The STRI measures market access, competition and regulatory transparency and represents the degree of openness. The higher the STRI, the lower the degree of openness.
9   The nine emerging economies are Brazil, China, Colombia, Costa Rica, India, Indonesia, Lithuania, Russia and South Africa.

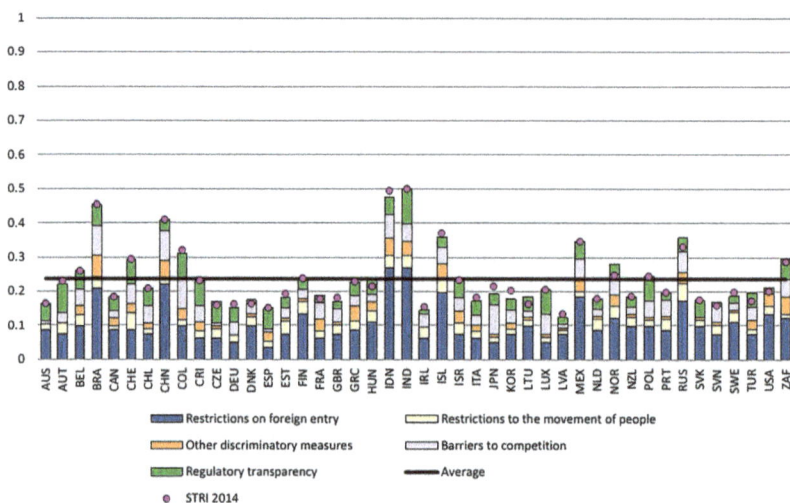

Figure 3-4: Degree of openness of the banking sector (2016).

Note: Blue represents foreign capital restrictions, yellow represents labour mobility restrictions, orange represents other discriminatory measures, purple represents competition restrictions, green represents regulatory transparency, the black horizontal line represents the average, and the purple dot represents data in 2014.

Source: OECD (2016a).

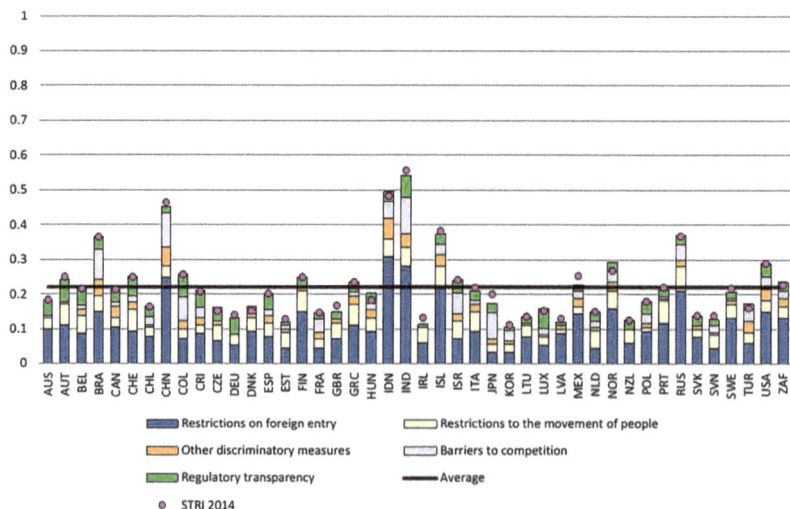

Figure 3-5: Degree of openness of the insurance sector (2016).

Note: Blue represents foreign capital restrictions, yellow represents labour mobility restrictions, orange represents other discriminatory measures, purple represents competition restrictions, green represents regulatory transparency, the black horizontal line represents average, and the purple dot represents data in 2014.

Source: OECD (2016b).

Bond market convenience has yet to be improved; some of the provisions and procedures are tedious, opaque and unfriendly to market participants. First, foreign investors cannot transfer their positions among different accounts (such as QFII account, RQFII account and interbank bond market investment account), which affects the efficiency of use of their funds. Second, investors in China's interbank bond market are required to open accounts with the central custody institution, while internationally investors can open accounts with custody institutions at various levels, which offers higher efficiency, lower transaction costs, flexible market-based transactions, and convenient and efficient clearing. Third, foreign institutions can participate in bond underwriting, but cannot be the lead underwriter. This has caused the business of foreign institutions to shrink, making it more difficult for them to meet the business qualification requirements and compete with domestic financial institutions. Fourth, non-central bank foreign investors can only sign the NAFMII (National Association of Financial Market Institutional Investors) Derivative Master Agreement, which differs from the commonly used ISDA Agreement and increases the legal costs of foreign investors. Fifth, the exchange bond market is more blocked than the interbank bond market, with a lower level of openness. Currently foreign investors can only invest in the exchange market through the QFII and RQFII channels.

Additionally, China's accounting, auditing and taxation systems are not yet aligned with international standards (discussed at length in Chapter 5).

Convertibility of the capital account

Despite significant progresses in China's capital account liberalisation in recent years, openness remains low compared to developed economies and many emerging market economies. An international comparison shows that China's capital account convertibility is low among the G20 countries. According to IMF's measure of capital account convertibility based on the countries' capital control provisions, China's capital account convertibility is ranked the second lowest, only higher than that of India.[10]

---

10   The compilation of capital account convertibility is based on the IMF's (2016a) 'Annual report on exchange arrangements and exchange restrictions'. This was prepared by authorities in each country, describing in detail the seven categories and 40 items of the capital account. Based on the report, the number of convertible items or the weighted average index can be calculated, such as the Chinn-Ito index and Quinn index. The Chinn-Ito index focuses on whether there are multiple exchange rates, whether the current account and the capital account are regulated, and whether there are controls on remittance of funds. The Quinn index not only measures the presence of controls, but also assesses the degrees of regulations.

The Chinn-Ito index, Quinn index and other indices of capital account convertibility have shown that the convertibility of China's capital accounts is not only far below that of the major developed economies, but also lower than the average level of emerging market economies (see Figure 3-6). Some indices focused on laws and regulations and may underestimate the actual degree of convertibility; however, there is much China could do to improve capital account convertibility.

Quinn index

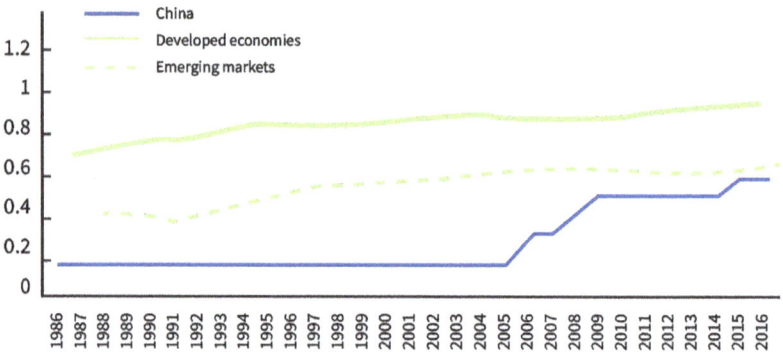

Chinn-Ito index

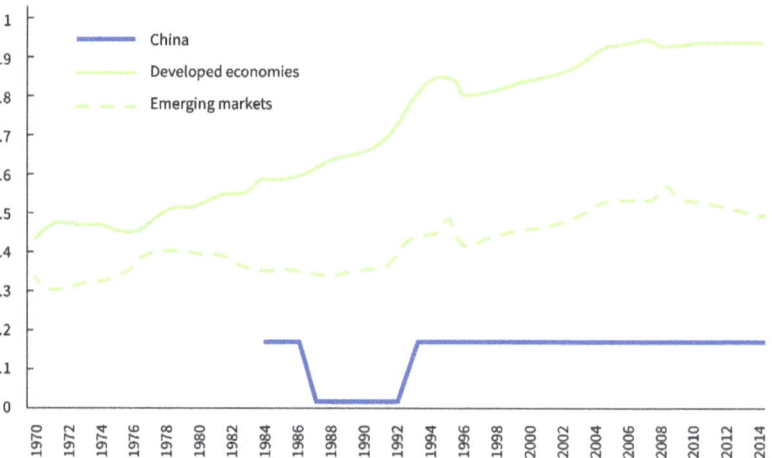

Figure 3-6: International comparison of capital account convertibility.
Source: IMF (2016a).

Part 4: Proposals on further opening the financial sector

China should consider both national conditions and international best practices; proactively expand the opening of its financial sector; adopt a more transparent approach that aligns with international practices; treat domestic and foreign financial institutions equally; and improve regulatory rules, accounting standards and other systems.

Principles for opening the financial sector

Principle I: continue to promote the 'troika'—opening the financial sector, improving the exchange rate regime and reducing capital controls—in a coordinated fashion.

China is already deeply integrated into the global economic and financial system. China should continue to push forward the opening of the financial sector, market-oriented reform of the exchange rate regime and liberalisation of capital controls in a coordinated manner. Expanding financial opening will help China better use both domestic and international markets and resources, optimise resource allocation and enhance the competitiveness of the financial system. Improving the exchange rate mechanism could enable the authorities to better regulate cross-border capital flows and enhance macroeconomic flexibility. Reducing capital controls helps stabilise market expectations and attract more foreign capital. Coordinated progress of the troika provides momentum for China's sustained and healthy development.

Principle II: opening the financial sector with pre-established national treatment and the negative list system as the core approach.

The financial industry is a competitive industry and should operate on market principles. Financial institutions should be allowed to make their own decisions and innovate. In terms of market access, competitive industries usually implement the negative list system, which allows market players to equally enter all the areas not specified in the list. This system helps all types of market players to form clear expectations and ensures that they compete fairly.

The implementation of pre-established national treatment and the negative list has become common practice internationally, and China has made it clear it will also adopt the approach. Currently, more than 100 countries employ this model including many developing and emerging market economies. China is the only BRICS country and one of only two G20 countries (the other being Saudi Arabia) that has not implemented this model. The third plenary session of the 18th CPC Central Committee decided to explore the use of this approach under which China has conducted negotiations on the Sino–US bilateral investment agreement and Sino–Europe bilateral investment agreement. Free trade zones in Shanghai, Guangdong, Tianjin and Fujian are applying the model that will be applied nationwide in the future. The negative list approach is in line with China's financial reform and opening policy and will facilitate China to better participate in global economic and financial governance.

Currently, the negative list of the financial industry is rather long (The State Council, 2017). Therefore, the primary task is to shorten the list and replace market access restrictions with prudential supervision. The negative list still contains restrictions on shareholding percentage, shareholder qualifications and business scope of foreign financial institutions (The State Council, 2017). These discriminatory restrictions reduce the enthusiasm of foreign investors and make it difficult for them to leverage advantages in corporate governance, credit management and risk pricing. Therefore, China should shorten the negative list, eliminate unreasonable access and qualification restrictions, and carry out prudential regulation to provide proper incentives to foreign financial institutions and enhance the competitiveness of Chinese financial institutions.

Principle III: promote opening of the financial sector in an orderly manner and effectively prevent risks.

Over the past four decades, the overall openness of China's financial sector has been low. One reason is that there were varied opinions over the relationship between financial crises and the admission of foreign financial institutions when China negotiated its WTO accession. Thus, while other industries have greatly increased their level of openness, the financial sector has opened slowly. It is relatively easy to control risks when openness is low. However, the situation has changed, and China needs to learn how to effectively control risks while further opening the financial sector. This requires China to strengthen financial regulation;

draw lessons from global regulators; and improve capital, behaviour and functional regulation to ensure that its regulatory capability is compatible with the level of openness.

Generally speaking, in the short term, equal treatment of foreign and domestic financial institutions should be applied to remove restrictions on the equity cap, form of incorporation and business scope of foreign financial institutions. Regarding custody model and underwriting qualifications, the standards and requirements that are unfriendly to foreign investors should be re-examined. Additionally, accounting and auditing standards need to align with international standards to facilitate overseas investors. In the medium to long term, China should pay more attention to market cultivation and product innovation; develop an open and inclusive financial market that is in line with international standards; and create a fair, transparent and predictable business and legal environment. Simultaneously, China should further promote RMB internationalisation and achieve capital account convertibility in an orderly fashion.

In the short term, China should remove policy constraints and release the vitality of financial institutions and the financial market

Equal treatment of foreign and domestic financial institutions should be applied to remove restrictions on the equity cap, form of incorporation, business scope and number of licences of foreign financial institutions to create a fair and equitable environment for foreign institutions. The following are recommended:

- Apply equal treatment of domestic and foreign financial institutions; reduce restrictions on foreign ownership of banking, securities and insurance firms; and allow wholly foreign-owned securities companies and life insurance companies.

- Further action could include eliminating the requirement on the total assets of shareholders of foreign banks, the minimum years of operation for foreign banks to conduct RMB business, and the requirement that at least one Chinese shareholder of a joint-venture securities companies must be a securities firm.

- Do not limit the number of licences granted to joint-venture life insurance companies. Grant regional operation licences to wholly-owned foreign life insurance companies and speed up the issuance of licences to facilitate the business of those institutions.

Regarding the bond market, the following are suggested:

- Streamline the transfer process between various bond accounts to improve the efficiency of fund utilisation.
- Introduce multi-tiered custody and gear up to international practice, establishing a multi-tiered custody model and a nominal holder account.
- Give foreign banks special treatment in granting some business licences based on their overall capability and scale, including their global networks and expertise in specific products and business areas.
- Align with international standards and allow foreign investors to independently choose between the NAFMII and ISDA master agreements.

Chapter 6 contains recommendations for financial infrastructure and institutions.

In the medium term, China should improve the institutional environment and promote deep integration of domestic and foreign capital markets

In terms of the stock market, China should improve the Shanghai–Hong Kong Stock Connect and Shenzhen–Hong Kong Stock Connect and explore connecting domestic and foreign capital markets via the Shanghai–London Stock Connect and Shanghai–Singapore Stock Connect to achieve full opening of the market. This will help mobilise global capital to serve China's economy, expand the investor base, attract more experienced and professional institutional investors that are committed to long-term investment, reduce market disturbance caused by the great number of retail investors and curb speculation.

In terms of taxation, China should clarify tax rules relating to foreign institutional investors in the interbank bond market as soon as possible. Preferential policies should be adopted at certain times to bring down tax rates to relatively low levels globally to attract more foreign institutions to invest in China's market.

In the medium to long term, China should further promote RMB internationalisation and achieve convertibility of the capital account in an orderly manner

The inclusion of the RMB in the SDR has brought China many practical benefits. China should seize the opportunity to strengthen the RMB's status as an international reserve currency and further promote its internationalisation. The following are recommended:

- Consolidate the RMB's status in the payment and denomination of international trade and finance; support the international reserve function of the RMB; promote the use of the RMB in the pricing and settlement of large commodity transactions; raise the degree of convenience of cross-border RMB payment of non-bank payment institutions; support cross-border, e-commerce, RMB-denominated settlement; and fully liberalise the personal current account cross-border RMB settlement business.

- Promote the development of markets for direct exchange of the RMB and other currencies to support cross-border RMB settlement business, continue currency cooperation with the monetary authorities of other countries, and support the inclusion of the RMB in the reserves of foreign central banks.

- Support the healthy development of offshore RMB markets, expand the channels for offshore RMB to flow back, and establish a virtuous circle between the two markets.

Achieve capital account convertibility in an orderly manner

At present, China is not far from achieving capital account convertibility. The following three reforms are vital (Zhou, 2015). First, relax the control on overseas investment of domestic individual investors and introduce Qualified Domestic Individual Investor (QDII2) scheme. Second, amend the 'Foreign Exchange Management Regulations' based on the 'negative list + national treatment' approach. Third, while pushing forward a registration-based initial public offering system, allow a small number of high-quality foreign companies to issue shares in China based on existing policy and domestic market situations. A great deal of preparation has already been conducted for these reforms, and relevant programs have been carefully designed. China should introduce the reform measures at an appropriate time.

Use comprehensive measures to better deal with capital flow shocks

The IMF (2016b) pointed out that countries should mainly rely on macroeconomic policies to cope with cross-border capital flow shocks. This can include increasing the flexibility of the exchange rates, curbing excessive fluctuations in the foreign exchange market, adjusting monetary and fiscal policies, establishing a more inclusive financial system, developing deep and well-regulated financial markets, and avoiding the use of capital control measures. Therefore, China should accelerate the pace of domestic reform, further improve the macroeconomic policy framework, and improve the resilience of the economic and financial system against capital flow shocks. Simultaneously, China should accelerate the reform of state-owned enterprises, reduce the distortion of price signals caused by soft budget constraints, improve the efficiency of resource allocation and enhance financial system soundness.

References

American Chamber of Commerce in the People's Republic of China. (2017). *China businesses climate survey report*. Retrieved from www.amchamchina.org/policy-advocacy/business-climate-survey/2017-business-climate-survey

Bank for International Settlements. (2016). *2016 list of global systemically important banks (G-SIBs)*. Retrieved from www.fsb.org/wp-content/uploads/2016-list-of-global-systemically-important-banks-G-SIBs.pdf

China Banking Regulatory Commission. (2017). *China Banking Regulatory Commission 2016 annual report*. Beijing: China Financial Publishing House.

China Insurance Regulatory Commission. (2017). *China Insurance Regulatory Commission 2017 annual report*. Beijing: China Financial Publishing House.

China Securities Regulatory Commission. (2017). *China Securities Regulatory Commission 2016 annual report*. Beijing: China Financial Publishing House.

Claessens, S. (2009). Competition in the financial sector: Overview of competition policies. *The World Bank Research Observer, 4*(1), 83–119.

Claessens, S., Demirguc-Kunt, A. & Huizinga, H. (2001). How does foreign entry affect domestic banking markets? *Journal of Banking & Finance, 25*(5), 891–911.

Clarke, G., Cull, R., Martinez Peria, M. S. & Sanchez, S. (2001). *Foreign bank entry: Experience, implication for developing economies, and agenda for further research* (Working Paper Series No. 2698). World Bank.

Dages, B. G., Goldberg, L. S. & Kinney, D. (2000). Foreign and domestic bank participation in emerging markets: Lessons from Mexico and Argentina. *Federal Reserve Bank of New York Economic Policy Review, 6*(3), 17–36.

International Monetary Fund (IMF). (2016a). *Annual report on exchange arrangements and exchange restrictions.* Washington, DC: Author.

International Monetary Fund (IMF). (2016b, November). *Capital flows - review of experience with the institutional view.* Washington, DC: Author.

Ministry of Commerce. (2015). *China's financial institutions entering the global markets has lagged significantly.* Retrieved from finance.sina.com.cn/360desktop/china/20151213/130724005042.shtml

Organisation for Economic Co-operation and Development. (2016a). *Services Trade Restrictiveness Index: Commercial banking.* Retrieved from stats.oecd.org/Index.aspx?DataSetCode=STRI

Organisation for Economic Co-operation and Development. (2016b). *Services Trade Restrictiveness Index: Insurance.* Retrieved from stats.oecd.org/Index.aspx?DataSetCode=STRI

Stigler, G. (1983). *The organization of industry.* Chicago, IL: R. D. Irwin. (Original work published 1968)

The State Council. (2017). *The special administrative measures (negative list) for foreign investment access in pilot free trade zones (2017 edition).* Retrieved from www.gov.cn/zhengce/content/2017-06/16/content_5202973.htm

Yeyati, E. L. & Micco, A. (2007). Concentration and foreign penetration in Latin American banking sectors: Impact on competition and risk. *Journal of Banking and Finance, 31*(6), 1633–1647.

Zhou, X. (2015). Zhou Xiaochuan: Capital market will become more open. *Sina.* Retrieved from finance.sina.com.cn/hy/20150322/144621777756.shtml

Zhou, X. (2017). Zhou Xiaochuan talks about the RMB joining the SDR basket: The historical progress of the opening-up process. *Caijing.* Retrieved from dy.163.com/v2/article/detail/D0CPA4S70519DFFQ.html

Zhu, J. (2017). Director of the International Department of the Central Bank: Experiences of opening up the Chinese financial sector. *Ifeng.* Retrieved from forex.hexun.com/2017-10-06/191123337.html

4

RMB Exchange Rate: Moving Towards a Floating Regime

Zhang Bin[1]

Introduction

The RMB exchange rate formation mechanism has undergone frequent adjustments since the 1980s, with the transition from a double-track exchange rate system to a single exchange rate system, a de facto fixed regime (pegged to the USD) during the financial crisis, as well as many attempts in normal periods to reform the exchange rate regime so that it can respond to market changes.

The major challenge is that the exchange rate does not respond adequately to changes in market supply and demand. When the exchange rate deviates from economic fundamentals, expectation for one-way currency fluctuation and large-scale capital flow follow. Authorities are then forced to intervene in the foreign exchange market. This affects the independence and effectiveness of monetary policy and also jeopardises domestic economic stability. Additionally, regular intervention in the foreign exchange market has negative effects on economic upgrading, RMB internationalisation and outbound investment.

Since the beginning of 2017, supply and demand in the foreign exchange market have been more balanced, and the time is right for further reform. International experience suggests that reducing intervention in the foreign

---

1   Senior Fellow at the China Finance 40 Forum.

exchange market will not lead to a large depreciation of the RMB, given China's economic fundamentals. Two strategies can be used to introduce a floating exchange rate regime: free-floating regime, and allowing a wide band for the RMB exchange rate fluctuation against a basket of currencies. The latter could well be a transition plan towards a free-floating regime.

Part 1: History and current situation of the RMB exchange rate regime reform

Since the launch of reforms and the opening policy, the RMB exchange rate regime has undergone frequent changes, switching from a double-track exchange rate system to a single rate system during early 1980s and mid-1990s. After the mid-1990s, the Chinese monetary authorities experimented with the managed floating regime and the de facto USD-pegged regime, and attempted many reforms under the managed floating exchange rate regime. Currently, the authorities are still driving the RMB exchange rate through measures such as guidance of the central parity, the daily floating band, market intervention and capital controls. The RMB central parity formation mechanism has been adjusted to take into account multiple factors including foreign exchange supply and demand, exchange rate stability against a basket of currencies and the counter-cyclical factor. Clearly, the exchange rate of the RMB against the USD is a dollar-pegged regime with a slope rate (reflecting market supply and demand and the counter-cyclical factor) and a stochastic volatility variable (reflecting basket currency exchange rate movements). This chapter briefly reviews the evolvement of the RMB exchange rate regime since the 1980s while focusing on analysis of the current regime.

History of the RMB exchange rate regime reform

First stage: from 1981–1984, China adopted a dual exchange rate system with an official exchange rate and an exchange rate for trade settlement.

Objectives: to promote exports and increase foreign exchange earnings.

Measures: based on the 'Regulations Concerning a Number of Issues on Vigorously Boosting Foreign Trade and Foreign Currency Earnings' enacted by the State Council in 1979, on 1 January 1981, the government introduced the exchange rate for trade settlement in addition to the official exchange rate. First, the trade settlement exchange rate was applied to exports. Based on 1978 data, the average cost of US$1 in export revenue was 2.56 RMB; after adding a profit of 10 per cent, the settlement exchange rate was set at 2.8 RMB. Second, the official exchange rate was applied to imports. US$1 was exchanged for 1.5 RMB in July 1980, based on a weighted average exchange rate against a basket of currencies.

Second stage: from 1985–1993, China adopted a dual rate system with an official exchange rate and a foreign exchange market exchange rate.

Objectives: to establish a more reasonable exchange rate level through market mechanisms, improve the efficiency of foreign exchange utilisation and compensate for the loss of foreign trade enterprises.

Measures: first, foreign exchange swap centres had been established throughout the country since March 1988. The exchange rate in the foreign exchange swap markets was liberalised to balance the supply and demand of foreign exchange and compensate for the loss of foreign trade enterprises. In September 1988, an open foreign exchange swap market was pioneered in Shanghai. The open bidding mechanism was introduced in foreign exchange swaps, and the foreign exchange swap price was allowed to float within a certain range according to supply and demand in the open market. Second, the official exchange rate underwent several significant devaluations, and gradually came closer to the foreign exchange swap market exchange rate. With gradual liberalisation of the exchange rate in the foreign exchange swap market, the share of foreign exchange transactions at official exchange rate gradually decreased.

Third stage: from 1994–1996, China unified the exchange rates and adopted a managed floating exchange rate regime.

Objective: to establish a more reasonable exchange rate level through the market mechanism.

Measures: on 29 December 1993, the People's Bank of China (PBC) issued the 'Public Announcement on Further Reforming the Foreign Exchange Administration System', declaring a major reform to take effect on 1 January 1994. Several important measures were undertaken. First, the official exchange rate of the RMB and the swap market exchange rate were unified. Second, the foreign exchange retention system was abolished, a system of foreign exchange surrender and purchase through banks was implemented, and the RMB achieved convertibility under the current account. Third, mandatory foreign exchange planning was cancelled; users with valid import documents were allowed to purchase foreign currencies from designated banks. Fourth, any form of pricing and settlement in foreign currencies domestically was also cancelled. The circulation of foreign currencies within the territory and foreign exchange transactions outside of designated financial institutions were prohibited. Additionally, the issuance and circulation of Foreign Exchange Certificates was terminated. Finally, the interbank foreign exchange market was established and a nationwide unified market for foreign exchange transactions was formed.

The fourth stage: from 1997–2005, China adopted a de facto USD-pegged regime for the RMB exchange rate.

Objective: to reduce the risk of exchange rate fluctuations and maintain macroeconomic stability.

Measures: the RMB was pegged to the USD at a fixed exchange rate. During the 1997 Asian financial crisis, east Asian countries devalued their currencies successively, while the Chinese Government adopted a policy of stabilising the RMB exchange rate. The RMB exchange rate against the USD was kept stable at 8.27, and the exchange rate was virtually pegged to the USD until July 2005.

The fifth stage: from mid-2005 to mid-2008, China adopted a managed floating exchange rate regime similar to the crawling peg system.

Objective: to reduce external imbalances and international pressure.

Measures: on 21 July 2005, the PBC issued the 'Public Announcement on Reforming the RMB Exchange Rate Regime', declaring the adoption of a managed floating exchange rate regime based on market supply and demand with reference to a basket of currencies. The RMB was no longer singularly pegged to the USD. The PBC announced the central parity of the RMB exchange rate to guide market participants and intervened to maintain the RMB market price close to the central parity. The monetary authority maintained control over the trajectory of the RMB exchange rate. During this period, the RMB exchange rate fluctuated very slightly against the USD and gained a gradual appreciation. As such, the exchange rate regime was also regarded as a soft peg to the USD.

The sixth stage: from mid-2008 to 19 June 2010, China moved back to a de facto USD-pegged regime.

Objective: to reduce the risk of exchange rate fluctuations and promote macroeconomic stability.

Measures: the 2008 global financial crisis had a serious impact on the real economy. Consequently, the RMB exchange rate was returned to a USD-pegged regime.

The seventh stage: from 19 June 2010 to the present, China has tried various forms of managed floating exchange rate regimes.

Objective: to explore a more market-oriented exchange rate regime.

Measures: China adopted a managed floating exchange rate regime in various forms. On 19 June 2010, a spokesperson from the PBC announced measures to 'further promote the reform of the RMB exchange rate regime, and enhance the flexibility of RMB exchange rate', sending signals to the market about restarting RMB exchange rate reform. The spot daily fluctuation range of the RMB/USD exchange rate was expanded from 0.5 per cent to 1 per cent in April 2012, and then from 1 per cent to 2 per cent in March 2014. Since then, the market has gradually played a more important role in the RMB exchange rate formation.

On 11 August 2015, the monetary authority decided to improve the formation mechanism of the RMB's central parity against the USD. The core reform was to require market makers to refer to the closing rate in the interbank foreign exchange market on the previous day and report the central parity to the China Foreign Exchange Trade System (CFETS) daily before the market opened. This adjustment kept the central parity of the RMB/USD exchange rate close to the previous day's closing rate, instead of being set daily by the monetary authority to meet management goals. By doing this, the monetary authority abandoned years of guiding market expectations through the central parity of the exchange rate, giving way to market supply and demand determining the exchange rate. After the reform, market supply and demand played a larger role in exchange rate determination, and the RMB depreciated by nearly 2 per cent (the threshold of daily fluctuation) for two consecutive days.

On 13 August 2015, the monetary authority believed that the RMB exchange rate had moved to a reasonable and balanced level, so the government took a series of measures (mostly foreign exchange market intervention) to stabilise the exchange rate. After that, the monetary authority made a series of adjustments in the exchange rate regime, including reintroducing the central parity formation mechanism, adopting a transparent formula for central parity and introducing the counter-cyclical factor.

Supply and demand, basket of currencies and the counter-cyclical factor

The RMB exchange rate regime after May 2017 had three characteristics.

First, the monetary authority played a dominant role in the level of the RMB exchange rate. The monetary authority dominated the RMB exchange rate through three key measures: central parity, the daily floating band and intervention in the foreign exchange market. The central parity of the RMB exchange rate can send the market a message about the monetary authority's desired exchange rate level, guiding market expectations of the rate. The daily floating band limits exchange rate fluctuations. Foreign exchange market intervention (mainly referring to the sale and purchase of foreign currencies in the market, as well as other measures affecting supply and demand in the foreign exchange market) can absorb excess supply or demand, given the central parity of the RMB exchange rate and the floating band. For example, assuming the RMB/ USD central parity is 6.5, with 2 per cent daily floating band limit, the range of exchange rate is 6.5±0.13. If the market equilibrium price is out of the above range, the monetary authority must intervene in the market by buying or selling excess supply or demand.

Second, market supply and demand, the basket of currencies and the counter-cyclical factor determine exchange rate movements. In the RMB exchange rate regime reform of 21 July 2005, China adopted a managed floating exchange rate regime based on market supply and demand with reference to a basket of currencies. In 2016, the monetary authority further clarified the specific role of the above two aspects in forming the central parity of the exchange rate. This was explained clearly in 'China Monetary Policy Report Quarter One, 2016':

For example, if the previous day's central parity rate of RMB/USD was 6.5000, closed at RMB6.4950, and the changes in the currency basket indicated the RMB had to appreciate by 100 basis points, the central parity quote from the market makers would be 6.4850, an appreciation of 150 basis points, where 50 basis points reflect the changes in market demand and supply and the other 100 basis points reflect the changes in the currency basket. Likewise, changes in the central parity of the RMB to the USD not only represent changes in the currency basket, but also indicate the market demand and supply situation. The central parity formation mechanism is more clearly characterized as based on market demand and supply and adjusted with reference to the currency basket.

In May 2017, the 'counter-cyclical factor' was introduced to the pricing model for central parity of the RMB against the USD.

Under the new formula, 'the change of central parity rate' = 'the closing rate on the previous trading day – the central parity rate on the previous trading day' + 'the exchange rate movements needed to maintain RMB exchange rate stability against the basket of currencies + the counter-cyclical factor'. The 'China Monetary Policy Report Quarter Two, 2017' explained the counter-cyclical factor as follows:

> To calculate the counter-cyclical factor, one begins by excluding the impact of the currency basket changes from the difference between the previous day's closing rate and the central parity. After that the exchange-rate movements mainly reflect market supply and demand. Then one adjusts counter-cyclical coefficient to get 'counter-cyclical factor'. The coefficient is set by the quoting banks on their own based on changes in the economic fundamentals and the extent of pro-cyclicality in the foreign exchange market.

Third, the monetary authority alleviates the pressure of supply and demand in foreign exchange markets with capital controls. When it is difficult for exchange rate movements to automatically adjust supply and demand in the market, the greater the market pressure and the harder it is for interventions to maintain the RMB exchange rate within the target range. Massive intervention in the foreign exchange market, whether buying or selling, will lead to changes in the RMB's base money supply, putting pressure on China's macroeconomic stability. The monetary authority is faced with the dilemma of stabilising exchange rates and maintaining monetary policy independence. Capital controls are the key means to mitigate this conflict.

China has been facing continuous pressure of capital outflow and RMB depreciation since mid-2014, so capital controls have been strengthened. The government has not placed new restrictions on capital flows, but instead has implemented the existing measures of capital controls more strictly, along with strengthening capital flow authenticity checks. In practice, many companies report that availability of foreign currencies and the convenience of foreign exchange transactions have been affected.

In terms of formula, the RMB/USD exchange rate is a USD-pegged regime with a slope and a stochastic fluctuation of basket currency. The three items in the central parity formula—'the closing rate on the previous trading day – the central parity rate on the previous trading day' + 'the exchange rate movements needed to maintain the stability of the RMB exchange rate against the basket of currencies' + 'the counter-cyclical factor'—correspond to the peg with slope, stochastic fluctuation and the correction of the slope of the peg, respectively.

The first item is 'the closing rate on the previous trading day – the central parity rate on the previous trading day'. Considering that the monetary authority buys or sells foreign currencies and that the closing rate is also affected by intervention in the foreign exchange market, the first item only partly reflects market supply and demand.

To maintain relative stability of the RMB/USD exchange rate, the monetary authority's intervention in the foreign exchange market has to change over time as the need for intervention fluctuates. During 2015 and 2016, China faced great pressure to intervene, and the monetary authority was forced to spend a large amount of foreign exchange reserves, which decreased from US$3.81 trillion in early 2015 to US$3.01 trillion by the end of 2016. From 2017, the pressure of supply falling short of demand in the foreign exchange market eased, and the foreign exchange market intervention required for the gradual change of the exchange rate has been reduced substantially. In addition, the foreign exchange reserve has even rebounded slightly due to the valuation effect.

The second item is 'the exchange rate movements needed to maintain the stability of the RMB exchange rate against the basket of currencies'. For example, three currencies—the USD, euro and JPY—exist in the basket, and their weights are 0.5, 0.3 and 0.2 respectively. If BSK is the exchange rate against the basket (basket rate), then the following formula can be constructed:

BSK = 0.5*USD/RMB + 0.3*euro/RMB + 0.2*JPY/RMB
= USD/RMB (0.5 + 0.3*euro/USD + 0.2*JPY/USD)

'The exchange rate movements needed to maintain the stability of the RMB exchange rate against the basket of currencies' refers to the changes in the USD/RMB exchange rate required to keep the BSK constant, given the changes in the euro/USD and JPY/USD exchange rates. In practice, the basket covers more currencies,[2] and the above is just an example. We can conclude that exchange rate adjustments depend on the exchange rate changes of other currencies in the basket against the USD, which has nothing to do with the domestic economy and supply and demand in the foreign exchange market.

The exchange rates of the USD against other major currencies in the basket, such as the euro, JPY, Australian dollar and British pound, are all under a floating regime and fluctuate randomly. This ensures that the exchange rate movement of the RMB against the USD is random, maintaining a fixed basket rate. The exchange rate against the basket essentially introduces the stochastic fluctuation for the exchange rate of the RMB against the USD.

The third item is the counter-cyclical factor. According to the official explanation, the counter-cyclical factor adds a counter-cyclical coefficient to market supply and demand (i.e. 'the closing rate on the previous trading day – the central parity on the previous trading day'). This coefficient determines to what extent the factor of 'the closing rate on the previous trading day – the central parity on the previous trading day' will be reflected in the central parity on the current trading day.

If the coefficient is equal to –1, 'the closing rate on the previous trading day – the central parity on the previous trading day' will be completely offset. This will not affect central parity on the next trading day. The slope of change in the RMB exchange rate caused by market supply and demand is 0, so the RMB exchange rate regime will be a fixed RMB/USD peg plus the exchange rate movements required to maintain basket rate stability.

---

2   For the latest currencies in the basket and their weights, see Appendix 4-1.

If the coefficient is equal to 0, 'the closing rate on the previous trading day – the central parity on the previous trading day' and 'the exchange rate movements needed to maintain the stability of the RMB exchange rate against the basket of currencies' will jointly determine central parity on the next trading day. Therefore, the RMB exchange rate regime will be a USD peg with the slope plus the exchange rate movements required to maintain basket rate stability.

If the coefficient is between 0 and 1, 'the closing rate on the previous trading day – the central parity on the previous trading day' and 'the exchange rate movements needed to maintain the stability of the RMB exchange rate against the basket of currencies' will jointly determine the central parity of the next trading day. The RMB exchange rate regime will be a USD peg with the slope (the slope is smaller than the slope when the counter-cyclical coefficient is equal to 0) plus the exchange rate movements required to maintain basket rate stability.

Through simple regressions,[3] we can test the effect of various factors on the RMB central parity rate. We take the daily change of the central parity ('D(MID)') as the dependent variable, 'the closing rate on the previous trading day – the central parity on the previous trading day' and 'the exchange rate movements of the RMB/USD needed to maintain the stability of the exchange rate of the basket of currencies' as two independent variables. The sample period is from 5 April 2016 to 8 August 2017. The coefficients of the two independent variables in the regression are 0.96 and 0.5 respectively. Together, they explain 72 per cent of the central parity rate movement.

The residual term has shown a systematic downward deviation since 2017. The part that cannot be explained by the model is no longer subject to random distribution, but concerns appreciation of the RMB against the USD. A possible reason for this is that the influence coefficient of 'the closing rate on the previous trading day – the central parity on the previous trading day' on central parity has changed due to the introduction of the counter-cyclical factor. Through testing, 19 January 2017 was determined as the breakpoint. We conducted the same regression on the two subsamples before and after the breakpoint (i.e. from 5 April 2016 to 19 January 2017 versus from 20 January 2017 to 8 August 2017) (see Tables A4-3 and A4-4 in Appendix 4-2). The results showed that

---

3   For the regression equation, see Appendix 4-2.

the coefficients of the two independent variables are 1.13 and 0.46 in the previous sample, and 0.77 and 0.54 in the latter sample. The effect of 'the closing rate on the previous trading day – the central parity on the previous trading day' on the central parity of the RMB exchange rate was a significant decline.

Part 2: Challenges facing the RMB exchange rate regime

To properly identify the challenges faced by the RMB exchange rate regime, we must first determine an appropriate evaluative framework. The exchange rate is one of the most important prices in an open economy. It affects all aspects of the economy, and evaluations of the regime can vary from different subjects and perspectives. According to Frankel (1999), '[n]o single currency regime is right for all countries or at all times'. This is not to say that a country can choose any kind of exchange rate regime; rather, a country should determine the optimal exchange rate regime based on its specific national circumstances and timing.

From the perspective of macroeconomic management, evaluation of the exchange rate regime should be based on three criteria. First, is it conducive to macroeconomic stability? Second, is it conducive to the adjustment of economic structures and sustainable economic growth? Third, can it assist China's long-term goal of capital account liberalisation and RMB internationalisation? The first is the traditional criterion found in most mainstream literature, while the latter two are tailored to China's development level and policy environment.

A macroeconomic stability perspective

For a long time, the independence of China's monetary policy has been constrained by the exchange rate policy. For most of 2003–2014, the monetary authorities constantly and significantly intervened in the foreign exchange market to maintain the exchange rate target. This resulted in substantial increases of base money. The growth of base money was more than required to maintain price stability, which seriously affected monetary policy independence. The monetary authority had to offset the effect of excessive base money by issuing central bank bills, raising the reserve ratio of commercial banks, etc. Even so, these operations could not completely offset the effect, as the volume of interventions was significant and changes were without restraints. Additionally, continuous interventions led to expectations of RMB appreciation and influenced asset prices, which were difficult to address with quantitative measures. The authority had to balance target conflicts between interest rate policy, whose goal was to serve domestic macroeconomic stability, and exchange rate policy targets. When conflicts arose, the former was compromised for the latter.

After mid-2014, expectations of RMB appreciation turned into depreciation, and the monetary authority faced reversed pressures. Intervention in the foreign exchange market moved from buying to selling foreign currencies, and the amount of base money was reduced. The monetary authority had to find new ways to offset the effect, but a perfect outcome remained difficult to achieve. Interest rate policy was again compromised. See Box 4-1 for details.

Box 4-1: Large capital outflows and RMB depreciation expectations from 2014–2016

This box explains why the RMB faced continuous depreciation expectations and why capital outflows increased substantially from late 2014 to the end of 2016.

1. Predetermined conditions—a sharp increase in external debts and currency mismatch risks

According to Zhang and Xu (2012, p. 7) and Zhang and He (2012), since the expansion of the RMB trade settlement for imports and exports and the further promotion of RMB internationalisation, carry trades profiting from the one-way appreciation expectations of the RMB and the spread between Chinese and US interest rates had increased significantly. As a result, China began to accumulate external debts quickly. Based on the data of Dealogic, Bank for International Settlements and the PBC, Yi and Ports (2016) found that the external debts of Chinese enterprises witnessed substantial increases between 2012 and 2014. The growth of external debts was highly correlated with arbitraging spreads. The indebted enterprises were mainly from the oil and gas, real estate and other sectors. Miao and Rao's (2016) similar findings suggested that the factors (such as the changes in spreads between domestic and foreign interest rates and the credit constraints imposed by macro-regulation authorities on overcapacity industries, including real estate and the iron and steel industry) stimulated the enterprises' borrowing abroad. During the one to two years prior to the second half of 2014, Chinese enterprises had increased their external debts by a large amount. A considerable portion of these enterprises did not have enough foreign exchange earnings to match their external debts. An important motivation of external debt accumulation is to capture the interest rate spread and gain from a one-way appreciation of the RMB. This paved the way for the deleveraging of massive external debts thereafter.

2. Shocks—the divergence of economic trends and monetary conditions in China and the US

Many factors could have impacts on foreign exchange market, among which monetary and credit policies are of higher market concern and greater significance. Around the second half of 2014, the monetary policy environment at home and abroad changed significantly. While the US Federal Reserve was discussing the possibility of raising interest rates, China's domestic monetary policy conditions were relaxed to some extent. Interest rates in the domestic interbank market had been declining generally since the end of 2013, decreasing from 4.78 per cent in the fourth quarter of 2013 to 2.49 per cent in the fourth quarter of 2016. During this period, interest rates experienced a brief rebound in the first quarter of 2015, but this did not change the downward trend that had begun in the fourth quarter of 2013. Since that quarter, the interest rate spread between China and the US was also largely dominated by changes in interest rates in China's interbank market. The spread of change between China and the US markets and the direction of capital flows aligned with expectations.

A high correlation exists between interest rate spreads between China and the US and China's cross-border capital flows. In simple terms, interest rate spreads drive capital flows. More precisely, changes in the economic fundamentals of China and the US drive capital flows, and changes in interest rate spreads reflect comprehensive information on the changes in fundamentals and policy responses. After mid-2014, cyclical industries in China continued on a downward trend, and also had to address overcapacity in the process of economic restructuring. Enterprises' investment returns were low, while the monetary authority adopted a loose monetary policy to boost economic growth. Domestic enterprises generally had relatively ample liquidity and low capital costs, but were troubled by the lack of suitable investment projects. In contrast, the US economic recovery was successful during the same period; enterprises' profits increased and the stock market hit record highs. With distinctly different changes in the economic fundamentals of the two countries, an outflow of capital was expected.

3. Response measures—phased depreciation under the principles of supply and demand, basket of currencies and stability

As previously discussed, the formation of the RMB/USD central parity considers two factors: market demand and supply, and stability against a basket of currencies.

As a result of these two factors combining, when the USD is strong against other currencies in the basket, the RMB depreciates against the USD. When the USD is weak, the RMB is stable against the USD, which leads to a gradual and phased depreciation of the RMB against the USD. From February to April 2016, a weaker USD should have led to an appreciation of the RMB against the USD. A shortage of foreign exchange supply should have led to a depreciation of the RMB against the USD. With the two factors combined, the RMB exchange rate was relatively stable in relation to the USD. After October 2016, the USD strengthened. While these two factors both require depreciation of the RMB, the RMB cannot depreciate too much under the principle of maintaining the stability of the RMB exchange rate.

4. Vortex—the vicious circle of RMB depreciation (due to the exchange rate regime) and capital outflow

Under different exchange rate regimes, the net effects of shocks on short-term capital flows vary widely. In a floating exchange rate regime, capital flow pressure caused by internal or external shocks will lead to exchange rate adjustment. Therefore, the relative prices of domestic and foreign financial assets will change, so the floating exchange rate spontaneously stabilises capital inflow or outflow. In a fixed exchange rate regime, capital flows caused by internal or external shocks will put pressure on the exchange rate. The monetary authorities have to use foreign exchange reserves or adjust interest rates. Therefore, the relative prices of domestic and foreign financial assets will change, so capital flows will be stabilised and the fixed exchange rate level maintained.

Under the current RMB exchange rate regime, exchange rate changes cannot stabilise short-term capital flows, but instead create a cycle where capital outflows and RMB depreciation reinforce each other. The specific logic is as follows: internal or external shocks lead to the situation of demand exceeding supply in the foreign exchange market → under the current RMB exchange rate regime, the RMB shows periodic depreciation → the periodic depreciation of the RMB reinforces the depreciation expectations of the RMB → the depreciation expectation of the RMB stimulates a new round of capital outflow → capital outflows exacerbate the problem of demand exceeding supply in the foreign exchange market (see Figure 4-1).

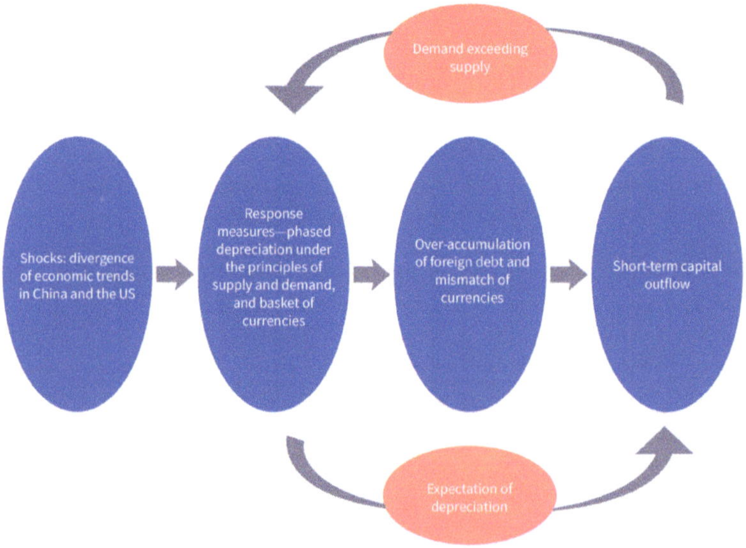

Figure 4-1: The circle of RMB phased depreciation and short-term capital flows.

Source: Author's original.

The monetary authority saw the problems with the exchange rate regime and took measures to modify the central parity formation mechanism. The authority began to consider introducing a counter-cyclical factor into the RMB central parity formation mechanism. The main purpose of this was to offset pro-cyclical fluctuations driven by market sentiment and alleviate the 'herd effect' in the foreign exchange market.

After introducing the counter-cyclical factor, expectations of a one-way movement of the RMB exchange rate should have weakened and capital flow pressure should have eased. However, the exchange rate still cannot reflect market supply and demand or economic fundamentals. It remains difficult to break expectations of a one-way movement of the RMB. The independence of the monetary authority and macroeconomic stability still face challenges. After introducing the counter-cyclical factor, the impact of 'the closing rate – the central parity on the previous trading day' on the central parity decreased. If we do not consider the exchange rate against a basket of currencies, changes in the RMB/USD exchange rate will be minimal or even negligible (i.e. changes could be completely offset by the counter-cyclical factor). The introduction of the RMB exchange rate against a basket of currencies simply adds a stochastic volatility item to the RMB/USD exchange rate.

Compared to the former mechanism with no counter-cyclical factor, the current mechanism has lowered expectations of one-way exchange rate movement and eased the pressure of capital flows. However, this mechanism is essentially similar to a fixed exchange rate regime and the exchange rate does not fully respond to supply and demand in the market. Once economic fundamentals change, if the exchange rate does not respond to this, the aforementioned problems will return. The monetary authority will still need to intervene substantially in the market to maintain the exchange rate target level.

A structural adjustment perspective

To evaluate the exchange rate regime, mainstream literature adopts a macroeconomic stability perspective and generally does not consider an economic structure perspective. But this latter perspective is necessary for China's circumstances. The mainstream literature does not consider this perspective because the monetary authorities cannot control the real exchange rate no matter what type of exchange rate regime is adopted. Under a fixed regime, the nominal exchange rate will not change. However, the price will change when shocks occur, so the real exchange rate will eventually be adjusted according to the economic fundamentals. Under a floating regime, adjustment of the nominal exchange rate will lead to an adjustment of the real exchange rate. In China, intervention in the foreign exchange market has resulted in excess base money, which in turn has pushed up the price level. The monetary authority then uses many policy instruments, including central bank bills, raising the reserve ratio, capital control and credit control, to offset the impact. In this way, the authority has a strong influence on both the nominal exchange rate and price level. Because of these practices, the real exchange rate cannot adjust fully in the short term. If the monetary authority only intervenes temporarily and the intervention offsets the influence of the base money increase fully, distortion of the real exchange rate will gradually be corrected. However, if the intervention remains for an extended period, distortion of the real exchange rate will be long-lasting and resource allocation will also be seriously distorted.

In an unpublished paper, Mao and Zhang (n.d.) introduced capital account control and foreign exchange market intervention to the intertemporal general equilibrium model and explained the mechanism by which continuous interventions in the foreign exchange market influence resource allocation along with the various outcomes. The model assumes that the government's goal is to stabilise the nominal exchange rate. When external demand is high, technology advancement of domestic trade sector is fast, the level of the target exchange rate is low and more intervention will be required to stabilise the nominal exchange rate. The model also assumes that the capital account is balanced under capital control measures and that the scale of market intervention equals the current account balance. Based on these assumptions, the findings are as follows: 1) a current account surplus instigated by massive interventions in the foreign currency market raises real interest rates, which in turn curbs domestic investment; 2) market intervention can stimulate the industrial sector, but it suppresses non-industrial sectors and, as a result, the industrial sector will grow larger relative to the non-industrial sector, causing imbalance within the economic structure (internal imbalance); and 3) domestic consumption is restrained, leading to a rise in both the aggregate savings ratio and private sector savings ratio. This is how continuous purchase of foreign currencies could influence the real economy; the sale of foreign exchange works in the opposite direction.

This model shows that market intervention does affect resource allocation in the real economy and can lead to external and internal imbalances. Simulation analysis shows the effect is significant.

A financial opening up perspective

This perspective is unique to China and is not discussed in mainstream literature. As a large developing country, China still faces many problems of reforms and institutional improvement. The reforms relate to many fields and cannot be undertaken simultaneously but implemented in an orderly manner. The sequence of reform of the exchange rate regime is a key issue.

The current exchange rate regime is not conducive to RMB internationalisation. Further liberalisation of the capital account is needed to promote RMB internationalisation. If the monetary authority frequently intervenes in the market and the RMB is constantly faced with expectations of one-way movement, the relaxation of capital controls will lead to excessive capital flows and threaten economic stability. Control measures will need to be tightened again. During 2010 and 2013, expectations of RMB appreciation were high, and RMB trade settlement was liberalised. Large profits were made through carry trades between the onshore and offshore markets, and overseas RMB deposits increased rapidly. The carry trades boosted capital inflows, the monetary authority was forced to take measures to maintain exchange rate stability and economic stability was threatened. Further, as result of frequent interventions and a failure of market clearing, expectations of RMB depreciation during 2014 and 2016 were high. Then, overseas RMB deposits decreased rapidly and capital inflow turned into capital outflow, again threatening economic stability. During this process, the offshore RMB market experienced great volatility and the monetary authority had to intervene in the offshore market and impose stricter capital controls. However, these measures slowed the development of the offshore RMB market and the pace of RMB internationalisation.

The current exchange rate regime is also a drag on overseas direct investments. If the exchange rate mechanism cannot remove expectations of a one-way RMB movement, overseas direct investments by Chinese enterprises will be hindered. If a persistent expectation of RMB appreciation exists, overseas investment will face additional exchange rate risks and enterprises will choose to delay investment. Conversely, if a persistent expectation of RMB depreciation exists, enterprises will have a strong motivation to invest overseas. In that case, the authorities will tighten capital controls to restrict capital outflow, so enterprises will still have to postpone their investments.

Part 3: Moving towards a floating exchange rate regime

The floating exchange rate regime has become the choice of a growing number of countries. Many developed economies, and all large economies except China, use this regime. An increasing number of emerging market economies have also adopted the regime over the past 20 years. According to Rey (2015), in today's highly integrated global financial market, monetary policy independence might not be fully realisable under a floating regime. Former International Monetary Fund (IMF) Chief Economist Maurice Obstfeld (2015) noted that, compared with other exchange rate regimes, although the floating regime cannot fully protect the independence of monetary policy, it can cushion the shock effectively and provide more space for domestic monetary policy. Under the floating regime, shocks from capital flows can cause the exchange rate to adjust and change the relative prices of domestic and foreign financial assets. Therefore, the floating exchange rate can automatically stabilise capital flow.

A consensus between the government and academia already exists that the ultimate goal of RMB exchange rate regime reform is to adopt a floating regime. However, widespread concerns remain that the transition will cause drastic volatility of the exchange rate and hurt the real economy. Many emerging market economies were forced to abandon the managed exchange rate regime and move to a floating regime after losing the ability to intervene effectively in the market. This was an involuntary choice for those economies in crisis situations. The following discussion is on whether China can actively introduce a floating regime as soon as possible.

In the medium and long term, adopting a floating regime is conducive to macroeconomic stability. It can improve resource allocation and promote RMB internationalisation and opening of the financial market. Putting these benefits aside, this part discusses concerns over the adoption of a floating regime. The focus is on whether the RMB will depreciate substantially if the currency floats freely, the impact of currency depreciation on the economy and specific approaches to achieve a floating regime.

The changing trend of capital flows

Currently, short-term capital outflow is relatively large, but has steadily decreased. This change is due to the following situations.

First, since mid-2016, changes in net external debts have turned capital outflows to inflows. There are several reasons for this: 1) the scale of China's external debts is not large relative to the size of the economy. The external debts of enterprises have decreased by more than US$300 billion over the past two years, and the need to further reduce external debts has decreased; 2) local government financing platforms and state-owned enterprises have increased their external debts; 3) interest rates in the domestic interbank market have increased slightly since mid-2016. Financial regulation has also tightened, making it more difficult for enterprises to raise capital in the domestic market, and enterprises are more willing to take on external debts; and 4) the size of existing external debts in China is relatively small compared to the size of its economy, and there is a great potential for overseas investors to hold more RMB assets. For these reasons, external debts should increase naturally.

Second, the motivation to hold overseas assets is weakening because: 1) many enterprises engaged in international trade significantly increased their holdings of the USD in the past two years to avoid the RMB's depreciation. Now that the expectation of RMB depreciation has weakened and the cost of holding the USD is high, these enterprises are less willing to increase their holdings of the USD; 2) higher interest rates in the domestic market and tighter financial regulations have discouraged enterprises from increasing overseas assets. Yields on wealth management products in the household sector have recently risen significantly, while the opportunity cost of holding USD assets has increased; and 3) control of foreign exchange has been tightened and illegal overseas investments are subject to stricter controls.

Third, the size of China's current account surplus and foreign direct investment is large, and the return on China's financial assets is comparable to that of US assets. A floating exchange rate will lead to an expectation of two-way fluctuations in the currency. If there is no expectation of RMB depreciation, the rate of return on Chinese financial assets, including safe assets such as government bonds, will not be lower than the yields on US Treasury bonds. Therefore, net foreign assets will not be expected to increase and neither will net foreign liabilities be expected to decrease.

Even so, it is difficult to estimate the degree of RMB depreciation that would occur after adopting a floating exchange rate regime. International experiences may shed some light on this issue.

Abandoning intervention would not lead to sharp currency depreciation

Here, a 'large depreciation' is defined as an annual depreciation of more than 15 per cent, and below are tallied the cases of 'large depreciation' in the IMF's database since the end of the Bretton Woods system in 1971. In subsequent years, a sample of 27 developed countries accumulated 72 cases of large depreciation, while 25 less developed countries saw 85 cases. Altogether, there are 157 cases of large depreciation from 52 sample countries.

Most of the large depreciations occurred in a situation of inflation or trade deficits. Of the 157 cases, the countries in 148 cases had high inflation or trade deficits or both. Only nine cases occurred in the context of low inflation and trade surplus. Table 4-1 shows these nine cases and their backgrounds, which can be divided into several categories: 1) export-oriented economies suffered severe external crises, South Korea (2008–2009) and Malta (1993); 2) governments guided the devaluation with a substantial relaxation of monetary conditions, Sweden (2009) and Japan (2013); 3) monetary system reform, Denmark (2000) and Switzerland (1997); 4) currencies were overvalued during the previous period, Japan (1996) and the Netherlands (1997); and 5) excessive credit and external debts, Indonesia (2001).

These international experiences show that the foreign exchange market is not as ineffective as some argue. Most large depreciations have occurred only when serious problems existed in the economic fundamentals, when the monetary system or monetary policy changed suddenly, or when the country suffered from a severe external crisis. Currently, China's economy is growing at a medium rate with low inflation and a large trade surplus, no serious external economic crisis exists, the overall risk of the domestic financial system is manageable, and external debts have reduced. According to international experiences, the probability of large depreciation in this context is very low.

Table 4-1: Cases of large depreciation

Country	Year	Depreciation (%)	Background
Developed countries			
Denmark	2000	47.84	Introduction of the euro
Japan	1996	15.65	Substantial appreciation during the previous period (appreciated 56.8% in the previous two years)
Japan	2013	22.31	Abenomics, printing money aggressively
Malta	1993	19.87	Europe's economic crisis
The Netherlands	1997	15.74	Pegged to the deutschmark; depreciation of the deutschmark led to the depreciation of the Netherlands guilder
Sweden	2009	16.12	The monetary authority guided depreciation by reducing interest rates
Switzerland	1997	17.42	The gold content of each Swiss franc was decreased from 40% to 25%
Less developed countries			
Indonesia	2001	21.84	Banking crisis and debt crisis
South Korea	2008–2009	37.41	2008 global financial crisis

Source: IMF database.

The advantages of deprecation to the real economy outweigh the disadvantages

In theory, in regard to the relationship between depreciation, economic growth and price, the conclusion is that depreciation will usually increase aggregate demand, increase economic growth and raise price levels. But what is the reality? According to the above sample, the economic growth rate in a depreciating year was higher than that of the previous year in 41 cases, and lower in 95 cases. The inflation rate in the depreciating year was higher than that of the previous year in 75 cases, and lower in 52 cases. On the surface, a large depreciation was accompanied by a decline in economic growth and a rise in inflation. However, this is not a causal relationship. The large depreciation itself is a result, and the driving forces behind it are often economic downturn and upward inflation. Instead of depreciation leading to slower economic growth and higher inflation, the same negative factors instigate depreciation, declining economic growth and rising inflation.

We should examine the relationship of depreciation to economic growth and inflation, after controlling for the effects of other common factors. Economies without high inflation and trade deficits before depreciation did not suffer from the effects of serious negative shocks, so the changes in their economic growth and inflation might reflect the impact of depreciation. Out of nine cases with low inflation and a trade surplus, the economic growth rate of six in the year of depreciation was higher than that of the previous year. Three were lower than the previous year, Malta (1993), Sweden (2009) and South Korea (2008–2009). Even in these three cases, it is difficult to blame depreciation for the decline in economic growth, because the countries suffered severe external economic crises in the year of depreciation. These external crises may have been the common factor behind the depreciation and the slowing of economic growth. The inflation rate rose in most of the nine cases, but not much further. Only Indonesia (2001) experienced an increase in inflation. This was due to low supply elasticity in Indonesia caused by its relatively single and backward economic structure. This created upward pressure on prices when demand rose sharply.

Yu, Zhang and Zhang (2016) studied the negative effects that a large depreciation might instigate based on international experiences. They found that, in addition to inflationary pressures, excessive external debts, debt crises under the background of serious currency mismatches and even banking and sovereign debt crises could occur. After discussing the overall scale, distribution pattern of industries and recent progress of China's external liabilities, they concluded that the risk of depreciation through external debt channels was set within a limited range. The scale of short-term debts in China was limited and had decreased sharply in the past, and the profitability of cyclical industries such as real estate, steel, coal and other industries that borrowed more money from abroad had improved significantly since 2016. As such, these industries' ability to resist risk was enhanced.

Two alternative floating exchange rate strategies

One strategy is to adopt a free-floating exchange rate regime like the US, the European Union or many other developed countries. This does not mean that monetary authorities have completely abandoned intervention in the foreign exchange market. Monetary authorities can intervene in extreme cases, but intervention should not become the norm.

We can also consider a similar regime in which the RMB exchange rate floats within a wide band, taking into consideration that many policymakers and scholars in China have little confidence in the free-floating exchange rate regime and are concerned that unexpected problems will arise during the transition period despite the advantages of such a regime.

Another strategy is to adopt a regime in which the RMB exchange rate can fluctuate in a wide band. This strategy allows the RMB to float against a basket of currencies and simultaneously introduces a wide band for the annual fluctuation of currency. For example, the index of the RMB against the currency basket is 100 today. In the next year, the index could float freely within the bands of 100±7.5 per cent and will convert to basket peg automatically if it hits the upper or lower limit. The central rate should not be adjusted too frequently.

However, there is arbitrariness about the annual floating range of ±7.5 per cent. The choice of 7.5 per cent is mainly based on the following two aspects. First, if the band is too small, the space left to the market will not be enough. In this situation, the market cannot really play its role of adjusting supply and demand and the monetary authority has to consume more foreign exchange reserves. Second, if the band is too wide, the exchange rate may be too volatile to be accepted by people in China. We can also widen the band to 15 per cent on the basis of the European exchange rate regime experience. The wider the band is, the closer the RMB is to the floating exchange rate, and more reserve ammunition is at the central bank's disposal to spare in guarding the lower limit.

There is no daily central parity and daily floating band in this strategy. The RMB exchange rate against the USD depends on the choice of fluctuation band and the change in the USD exchange rate against other currencies in the basket. The RMB is likely to appreciate or depreciate against the USD. Krugman (1991) found that if the monetary authorities had sufficient market credibility and the exchange rate level did not seriously deviate from the fundamentals, the market exchange rate would fluctuate within the band. Even if the currency faced a greater pressure of depreciation or appreciation, the exchange rate would fluctuate somewhat close to the lower or upper band, with the credibility of monetary authorities guaranteed by ample foreign exchange reserves.

Compared with the current exchange rate regime, this strategy has the following advantages. First, the market forces of supply and demand are fully released and the risk of assuming RMB depreciation increases. Second, it can minimise the consumption of foreign exchange reserves. Third, the relatively stable basket rate is conducive to the stability of foreign trade. Finally, the RMB exchange rate regime can convert spontaneously to a two-way floating regime at any time with changes in the market environment.

Compared with the completely free-floating exchange rate regime, this strategy is a compromised choice. If the band is not wide enough, the independence of monetary policy will still be limited, and the monetary authority will need to consume foreign exchange reserves. However, this strategy avoids the effect of excessive exchange rate depreciation on the economy and combines the benefits of both short-term macroeconomic stability and floating exchange rates. With the widening of the fluctuation band, the difference between this strategy and the free-floating regime will disappear.

There are some important provisos in the transition from a peg regime to a floating exchange rate regime. First, the monetary authority must tolerate abnormal fluctuations of the foreign exchange market after introducing a floating exchange rate. It should not easily intervene in the market, as non-intervention except for in extreme cases is related to the credibility of the monetary authority and market expectations. Second, the transparency and analysis of foreign exchange–related data should be strengthened and all kinds of panic statements eliminated with facts and logic. Third, it must be ensured that financial institutions have ample foreign exchange liquidity, and international coordination and communication must be strengthened. As depreciation of the RMB has an even greater impact on some small trading partners than it does on China, multilateral and bilateral agreements should be used to reduce the impact of exchange rate reform on the international market. Fourth, appropriate capital control should be maintained. This is particularly important during the transition period of exchange rate regime reform.

References

Frankel, J. A. (1999). *No single currency regime is right for all countries or at all times* (Working Paper No. 7338). National Bureau of Economic Research.

Krugman, P. R. (1991). Target zones and exchange rate dynamics. *Quarterly Journal of Economics, 106*(3), 669–682.

Mao, R. & Zhang, B. (n.d.). *Intervention in the foreign exchange market, internal imbalance and external imbalance* (Unpublished paper).

Miao, Y. & Rao, C. (2016). *Assessing external debt by the Chinese corporate sector: An update* (Working Paper). China Finance 40 Forum.

Obstfeld, M. (2015). *Trilemmas and trade-offs: Living with financial globalization* (Working Paper No. 480). Bank for International Settlements.

Rey, H. (2015, May). *Dilemma not trilemma: The global financial cycle and monetary policy independence* (Working Paper No. 21162). National Bureau of Economic Research.

Yi, H. & Ports, R. (2017). *Your dollar, our problem? Evidence from dollar bond issuance by Chinese non-financial firms* (Working Paper). Centre for Economic Policy Research.

Yu, Y., Zhang, B. & Zhang, M. (2016). A new proposal for the yuan exchange rate regime: Floating against a basket of currencies within a wide band. *International Economic Review, 2016*(1), 9–19.

Zhang, B. & Xu, Q. (2013). RMB's internationalisation under the system of limited exchange rate and capital account control. In B. Zhang & X. Qiyuan (Eds), *China and the World* (pp. 237–253). Netherlands: Brill.

Zhang, M. & He, F. (2012). Study on arbitraging between offshore and onshore RMB market in the process of RMB internationalization. *Studies of International Finance, 10*, 47–54.

Appendix 4-1: Latest currency composition and weights in the CFETS basket

The CFETS RMB exchange rate index refers to the CFETS's basket of currencies, including all foreign currencies traded against the RMB in the CFETS. The weights of the sample currencies are calculated by the trade-weighted method after considering transit trade. The base period is 31 December 2014, and the index of the base period is 100 points. On 1 January 2017, the CFETS basket added 11 currencies, increasing the number of currencies in the CFETS basket to 24 (see Table A4-1).

Table A4-1: CFETS's currency basket

Currency	Weight
USD	0.2240
EUR	0.1634
JPY	0.1153
HKD	0.0428
GBP	0.0316
AUD	0.0440
NZD	0.0044
SGD	0.0321
CHF	0.0171
CAD	0.0215
MYR	0.0375
RUB	0.0263
THB	0.0291
ZAR	0.0178
KRW	0.1077
AED	0.0187
SAR	0.0199
HUF	0.0031
PLN	0.0066
DKK	0.0040
SEK	0.0052
NOK	0.0027
TRY	0.0083
MXN	0.0169

Appendix 4-2: Central parity rate and its independent variables

The dependent variable is the change in the central parity rate, D(MID). The independent variables are 'the closing price on the previous trading day – the central parity rate on the previous trading day', CLOSE(–1) – MID(–1), and 'the exchange rate movements needed to maintain the stability of the RMB exchange rate against the basket of currencies', D(BSK) (see Table A4-2 and Figure A4-1).

Table A4-2: Changes in central parity rate: Regression equation with all the samples

Dependent variable: D(MID)				
Sample: 4/05/2016 to 8/08/2017				
Observations: 330 after adjustments				
Variable	Coefficient	SE	t-statistic	Prob.
CLOSE(–1) – MID(–1)	0.959534	0.043452	22.08242	0.0000
D(BSK)	0.498339	0.028272	17.62631	0.0000
C	–0.002882	0.000482	–5.978667	0.0000
R-squared	0.718572	Mean dependent variable		0.000788
Adjusted R-squared	0.716851	SD dependent variable		0.015434
SE of regression	0.008213	Akaike information criterion		–6.757225
Sum squared residual	0.022056	Schwarz criterion		–6.722688
Log likelihood	1117.942	Hannan–Quinn criterion		–6.743448
F-statistic	417.4660	Durbin Watson statistic		2.102728
Prob(F-statistic)	0.000000			

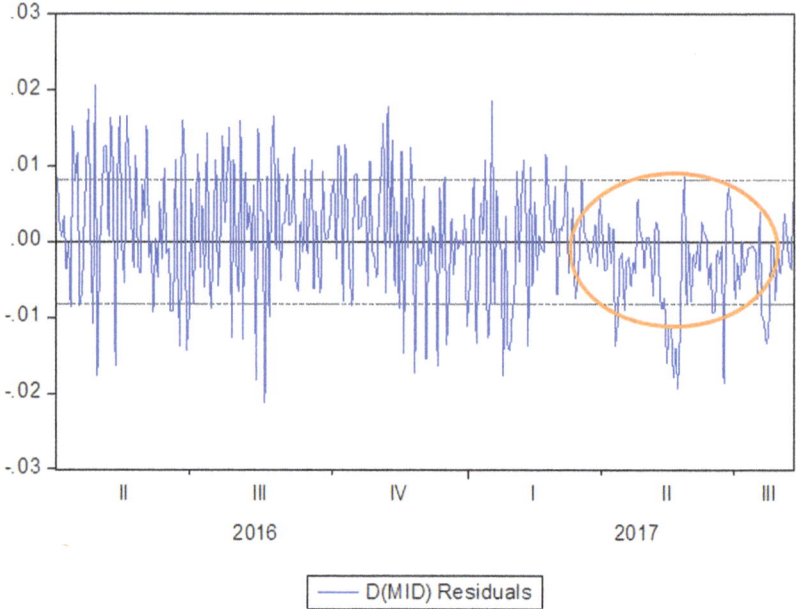

Figure A4-1: Residual term of the regression equation with all samples.
Source: Authors' original.

Table A4-3. Regression equation with the samples before the breakpoint

Dependent variable: D(MID)				
Sample (adjusted): 4/05/2016 to 1/19/2017				
Observations: 197 after adjustments				
Variable	Coefficient	SE	t-statistic	Prob.
C	−0.001625	0.000638	−2.544542	0.0117
CLOSE(−1) − MID(−1)	1.127450	0.058927	19.13298	0.0000
D(BSK01)	0.455855	0.034447	13.23341	0.0000
R-squared	0.755179	Mean dependent variable		0.002022
Adjusted R-squared	0.752655	SD dependent variable		0.017435
SE of regression	0.008671	Akaike information criterion		−6.642570
Sum squared residual	0.014586	Schwarz criterion		−6.592572
Log likelihood	657.2931	Hannan–Quinn criterion		−6.622330
F-statistic	299.2072	Durbin Watson statistic		2.229122
Prob(F-statistic)	0.000000			

Table A4-4: Regression equation with the samples after the breakpoint

Dependent variable: D(MID)				
Sample: 1/20/2017 to 8/08/2017				
Observations: 133				
Variable	Coefficient	SE	t-statistic	Prob.
C	−0.004173	0.000614	−6.797155	0.0000
CLOSE(−1)-MID				
(−1)	0.766417	0.053334	14.37004	0.0000
D(BSK01)	0.543422	0.043856	12.39113	0.0000
R-squared	0.728125	Mean dependent variable		−0.001041
Adjusted R-squared	0.723942	SD dependent variable		0.011693
SE of regression	0.006144	Akaike information criterion		−7.324501
Sum squared residual	0.004907	Schwarz criterion		−7.259306
Log likelihood	490.0793	Hannan–Quinn criterion		−7.298008
F-statistic	174.0805	Durbin Watson statistic		2.058797
Prob(F-statistic)	0.000000			

5

China's Cross-Border Capital Flow Management

Guan Tao,[1] Zhang Antian,[2] Xie Yaxuan,[3]
Gao Zheng[4] and Ma Yun[5]

Since the global financial crisis, China has accelerated the process of capital account liberalisation and RMB internationalisation. Financial openness has increased significantly. However, over the past few years, China has used both market intervention and capital flow management measures to deal with the shocks resulting from intense capital outflow. In the future, China should properly separate macro-management and micro-regulation, and establish a dual-pillar cross-border capital flow management framework. Additionally, capital flow management, especially capital control, should only be temporary measures used to buy time for other reforms.

---

1   Senior fellow at China Finance 40 Forum (CF40).
2   Research associate at CF40.
3   Chief Macroeconomic Analyst, Merchant Securities.
4   Deputy Division-Director of the General Office, State Administration of Foreign Exchange.
5   Division-Director of the General Office, State Administration of Foreign Exchange.

Part 1: Increasing impact of cross-border capital flows

China's balance of payments is changing from 'twin surpluses' to 'one surplus, one deficit'

Since the exchange rate unification reforms in 1994 through to 2013, China's current account and capital account both had surpluses (i.e. 'twin surpluses' until 2013), except in 1998 and 2012 (see Figure 5-1). Since the second quarter of 2014, China's balance of payments has changed to the pattern of current account surplus and capital account deficit (see Figure 5-2).

($100 million)

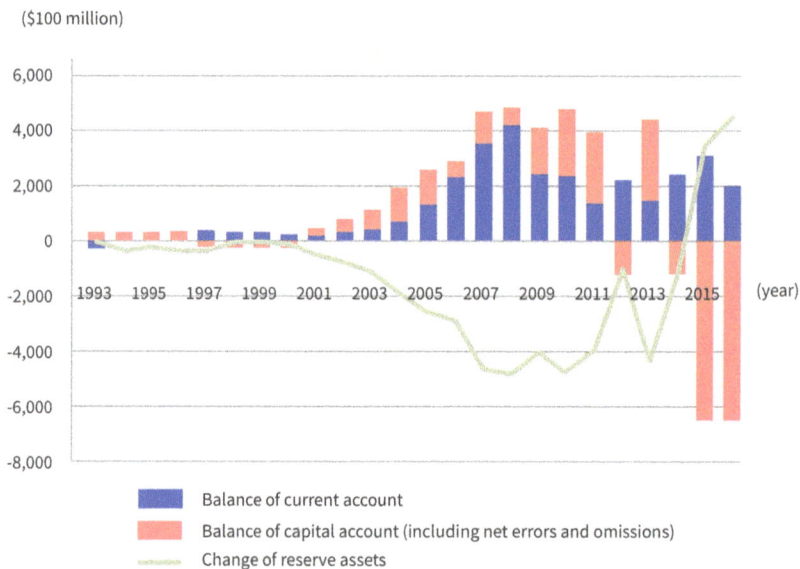

Figure 5-1: China's long-lasting balance of payments 'twin surpluses' (US$100 million).

Source: State Administration of Foreign Exchange (SAFE) (2015) and CF40 (2017).

($100 million)

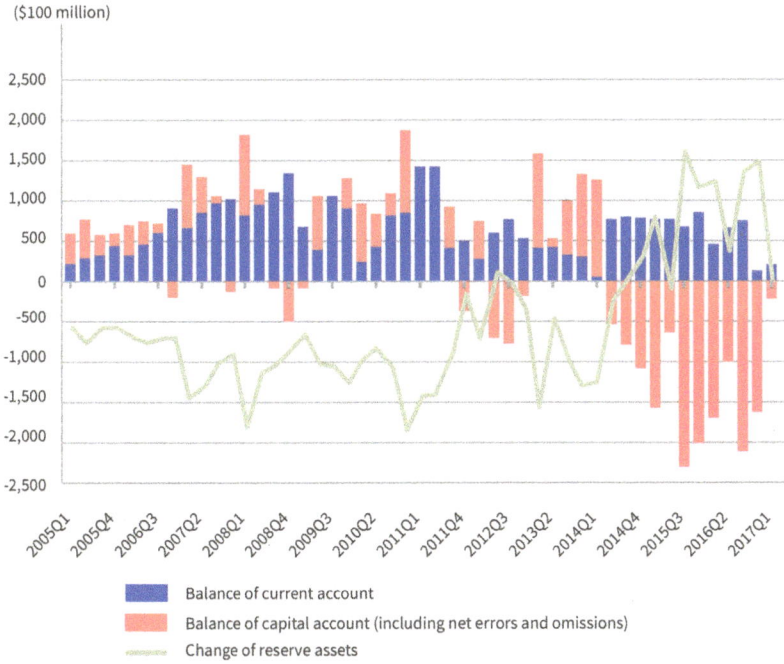

Figure 5-2: Large capital inflows changing into concentrated outflows (US$100 million).
Source: SAFE (2017) and CF40 (2017).

In theory, a country's current account should mirror its capital account; that is, a surplus in the current account is mirrored in the deficit of the capital account (such as in Japan and Germany) or a deficit in the current account is mirrored in the surplus of the capital account (such as in the United States [US] and United Kingdom [UK]). A country's international payments should be generally balanced. China's sustained 'twin surpluses' is a form of external economic imbalance. Ideally, the more trade surplus, the larger the capital outflows. However, a capital account deficit does not mean that the RMB exchange rate must depreciate, just as a trade deficit cannot explain or predict depreciation of the USD. Neither can capital inflows be used to explain or predict appreciation of the USD.

Capital flows have gradually replaced current account transactions as the main items determining balance of payments conditions

China's current account has been in surplus since 1993. After joining the World Trade Organization, the scale of China's current account surplus kept increasing and played a dominant role in the balance of payments surplus. The ratio of current account surplus to gross domestic product (GDP) peaked at 9.9 per cent in 2007. After the global financial crisis (GFC) in 2008, the ratio of current account balance to GDP began to decrease. It has remained within ±4 per cent of the internationally accepted reasonable range since 2010. The current level is about 2 per cent (see Figure 5-3).

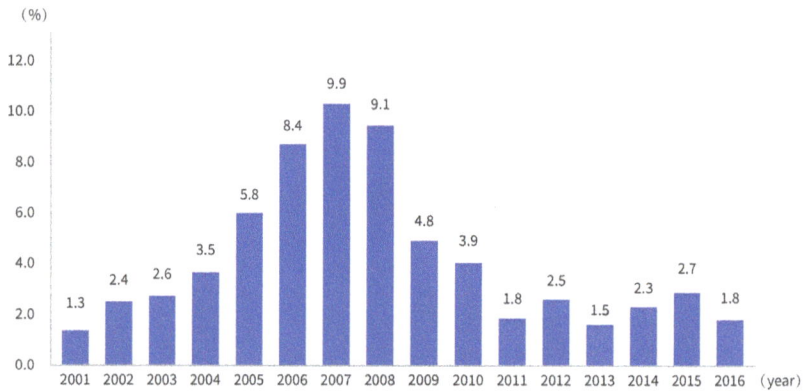

Figure 5-3: China's current account surplus to GDP ratio gradually moving into the range of basic balance (%).
Source: SAFE (2016), National Bureau of Statistics (2016) and CF40 (2016).

Conversely, the proportion of capital account transactions in China's balance of payments increased. These transactions began to dominate against a backdrop of abundant liquidity and low interest rates in developed economies and the rapid growth of China's economy in the post-GFC era. Specifically, between 2005 and 2009, the average contributions of current account surplus and capital account surplus (including net errors and omissions, the same as below) to the growth of China's foreign exchange reserve were 72 per cent and 28 per cent respectively. In 2010, 2011 and 2013, these were 40 per cent and 60 per cent respectively (excluding 2012, due to net capital outflows in that year; see Figure 5-4).

(%)

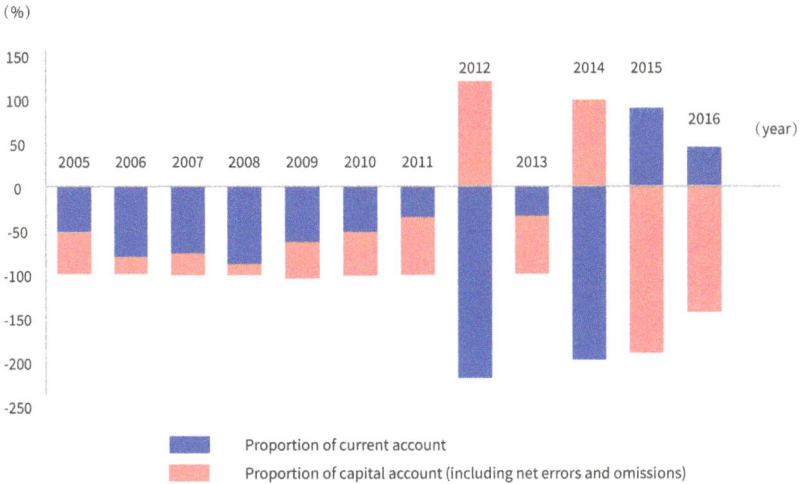

Figure 5-4: The increasing impact of cross-border capital flows on China's balance of payments (%).

Note: The proportions in the graph are the ratios of current account and capital account balances to the change in foreign exchange reserve (excluding the valuation effect).

Source: SAFE (2016) and CF40 (2016).

Since the second quarter of 2014, China's current account has remained in surplus, but the capital account has moved from net inflows to net outflows (see Figure 5-2). After the '8.11' exchange rate reform in 2015,[6] a trend of capital outflows became increasingly apparent. In 2015, the capital account deficit was US$647.5 billion. Foreign exchange reserve decreased by US$342.3 billion, even though the current account surplus amounted to US$304.2 billion. In 2016, the balance of payments remained in significant deficit: the current account surplus was US$196.4 billion and the capital account deficit was US$639.7 billion. Foreign exchange reserve decreased by US$448.7 billion, US$106.6 billion more than the 2015 drop (see Figure 5-1).

---

6   On 11 August 2015, the People's Bank of China (PBC) announced an adjustment of its RMB central parity system. Daily central parity quotes should be based on the previous day's closing rate of the interbank foreign exchange rate market, supply and demand, and price movements of major currencies. The PBC decided to make its exchange rate regime more competitive and market oriented, leading to a depreciation of more than 4 per cent in the same month.

A net capital outflow larger than the current account surplus has become the main cause of the decline in foreign exchange reserves and the main factor influencing the balance of payments situation. The RMB exchange rate is no longer a commodity price determined by the trade balance, but is an asset price driven by capital flows. A major difference between an asset price and a commodity price is that the asset price is prone to overshooting relative to the equilibrium exchange rate level.

Short-term capital flows constitute the main part of current capital outflows

In theory, short-term capital flows are usually measured by portfolio investments, other investments and net errors and omissions in the balance of payments (i.e. non–foreign direct investment capital flows). The sum of the current account and direct investment balances constitutes the basic balance of international payments. This is the main factor affecting the balance of international payments. Empirical analysis shows that as China's economy becomes more open, the impacts of short-term cross-border capital flows on macroeconomic and financial stability are increasingly significant (Li, Wang, Liu & Hao, 2016). Since the exchange rate reform in 2005, several aspects of China's cross-border capital flows have changed. These are discussed below.

Regarding the impact of short-term capital flows on all cross-border capital flows, 13 of the 24 quarters from the beginning of 2005 to the end of 2010 experienced net outflows of short-term capital. Only five quarters experienced net outflows for the entire capital account, all with simultaneous net outflows of short-term capital. Additionally, 17 of the 24 quarters from the beginning of 2011 to the end of 2016 experienced net outflows of short-term capital, while 15 experienced net outflows for the entire capital account, along with simultaneous net outflows of short-term capital (see Figure 5-5). This occurred because the net outflow of short-term capital exceeded the direct investment surplus, such that the capital account ended up with net outflows.

From the beginning of 2005 to the end of 2013, the RMB exchange rate faced sustained pressure of one-way appreciation; substantial net inflows of international capital existed and foreign exchange reserves increased significantly during these years. However, since 2011, China's cross-border capital flows have revealed two-way fluctuation patterns. During the fourth quarter of 2011 and the second and third quarters 2012 (which were affected by the European and US sovereign debt crises), market risk-aversion sentiment increased, RMB depreciation expectations were heightened, carry trade transactions began unwinding, and short-term capital left China. After this, short-term capital inflows and RMB exchange rate appreciation pressure once again became evident. Consequently, when discussing capital flow conditions and exchange rate pressures from 2011 to 2013, it is important to identify the specific period.

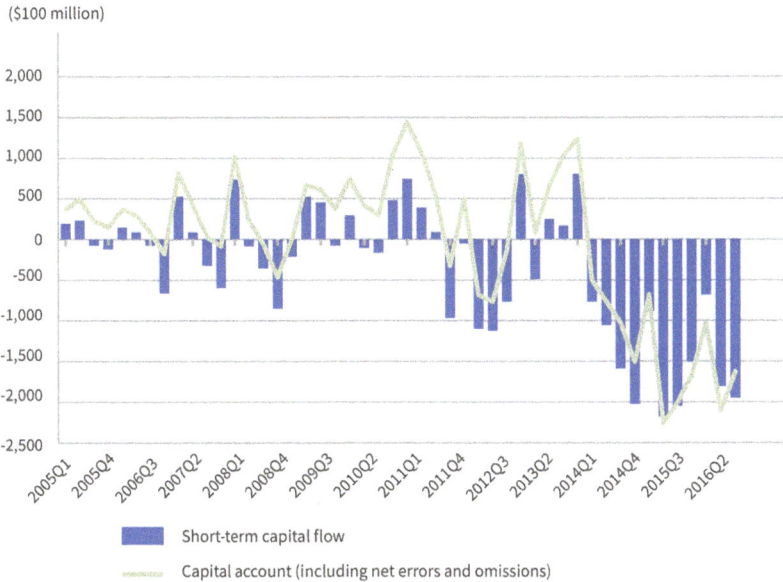

Figure 5-5: The change from cross-border capital inflows to concentrated outflows (US$100 million).

Source: SAFE (2016) and CF40 and (2016).

Short-term capital flows have also had a more significant effect on the balance of international payments. In the 24 quarters from the beginning of 2005 to the end of 2010, short-term capital flows never exceeded the basic balance. However, short-term capital flows exceeded the basic balance in 13 of the 24 quarters from 2011 to 2016 (see Figure 5-6). Especially after 2014, short-term capital exhibited a pattern of sustained net outflows. As seen from annual data, the ratio of net short-term capital outflows to the basic balance in 2014 was –69 per cent, reaching –192 per cent and –396 per cent in 2015 and 2016 respectively. A net short-term capital outflow exceeding the surplus of basic balance is the main reason behind the decrease of foreign exchange reserves and the currency depreciation.

($100 million) (%)

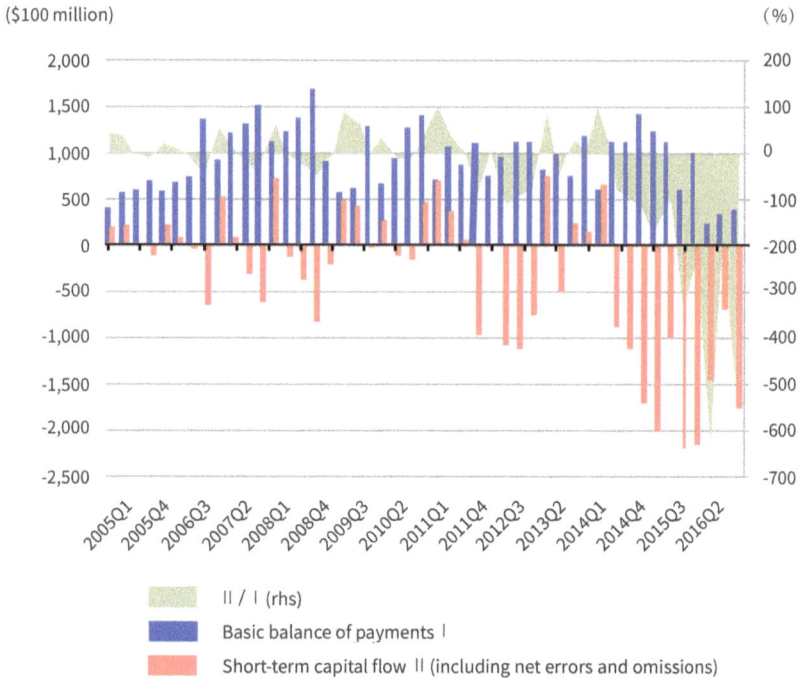

Figure 5-6: China's foreign exchange market entering a state of multiple equilibria (US$100 million; %).
Source: SAFE (2016) and CF40 (2016).

Short-term capital flows are likely to be influenced by changes in market sentiments and deviate from the fundamentals; this has led to a state of multiple equilibria[7] in the domestic foreign exchange market. The multiple equilibria means that capital may flow in or out, and the RMB may appreciate or depreciate, given the economic fundamentals of stable trade surplus, positive economic growth and abundant foreign exchange reserves. This is the restraint faced by China's authorities; that is, regardless of whether the RMB exchange rate is at a reasonable equilibrium level, the market exchange rate cannot automatically stabilise at that level. When the market is generally more bullish, it will

---

7   As discussed by Obstfeld (1994, 1996) and Krugman (1999), there is a multiple equilibria state in the foreign exchange market that goes beyond fundamentals and is determined by market expectations. Obstfeld argued that government and market behaviour can be understood by dynamic game models in the context of stable macroeconomic fundamentals. As the government's objective equation contains multiple policy objectives, the game process will be affected by different market expectations and result in multiple equilibria. Krugman also recognised the existence of such multiple equilibria and analysed the 1997 Asian financial crisis based on the model of the corporate balance sheet.

choose to believe in positive news. Then, the exchange rate may move above the equilibrium level and, thus, the currency becomes overvalued. When the market is generally bearish, it will choose to believe negative news. And the exchange rate may drop below the equilibrium level and, thus, the currency becomes undervalued.

Asset diversification is an important channel for China's capital outflows

The capital account consists of assets and liabilities. The assets are external investments, including outward direct investment (ODI), portfolio investment (such as Qualified Domestic Institutional Investor [QDII], the Shanghai–Hong Kong Stock Connect and the Shenzhen–Hong Kong Stock Connect) and other investment (such as external loans and export accounts receivables). The liabilities are the use of foreign capital, including inward direct investment, portfolio investment (such as Qualified Foreign Institutional Investor [QFII], RMB Qualified Foreign Institutional Investor [RQFII], the Shanghai–Hong Kong Stock Connect and the Shenzhen–Hong Kong Stock Connect) and other investment (such as external borrowings, deferred payments for imports and foreign holdings of RMB assets).

Continuous net outflows have been evident from the asset side since early 2005, except for two quarters. Specifically, before the second quarter of 2014, these outflows included the overseas use of policy funds, such as the establishment of sovereign wealth funds, use of entrusted loans and foreign exchange swaps to support overseas acquisitions. After the second quarter of 2014, with the changes in the market environment, domestic entities increased their overseas investments. In the 11 quarters up to the end of 2016, the asset side has always maintained net outflows (see Figure 5-7).

Net inflows were evident from the liability side from the beginning of 2005 to the first quarter of 2014, except for two quarters. During the 11 quarters with continuous capital outflows under the capital and financial account (from the second quarter of 2014 to the fourth quarter of 2016), only four quarters had net outflows from the liability side due to repayment of external debt, leaving all other quarters with net inflows (see Figure 5-7). In particular, since the second quarter of 2016, the liability side has again seen net inflows, as domestic institutions resumed borrowing from overseas and foreign entities increased holdings of RMB assets.

($100 million)

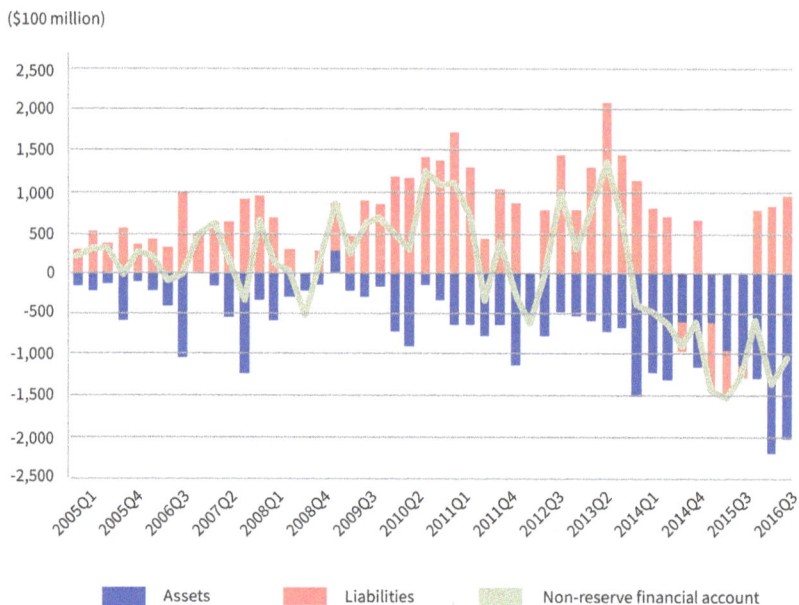

Figure 5-7: 'Increase of foreign exchange holdings by households' is the main driving force behind China's capital outflows (US$100 million).
Source: SAFE (2016) and CF40 (2016).

In terms of annual data, China's external assets increased by US$462.9 billion, US$333.5 billion and US$661.1 billion in 2014, 2015 and 2016 respectively. External liabilities changed by US$411.5 billion, –US$101 billion and US$244.1 billion respectively. This shows that the pressure of capital outflow from the liability side was released; the current pressure of capital outflows is mainly due to demand for foreign exchange assets or an increase of foreign asset allocation by domestic institutions and households. Under this circumstance, stabilising domestic entities' confidence in RMB assets is vital to the stability of cross-border capital flows.

Part 2: International community has softened the stance on cross-border capital flow management

The International Monetary Fund on management of cross-border capital flows

Changes in the International Monetary Fund's position

Since the establishment of the Bretton Woods system, the international community's attitude towards capital flows has undergone a historical cycle from 'control' to 'relaxation' to 'pro-control'. This change is closely related to the specific economic environment, trends in economic thinking and attitudes of important countries to capital controls (see Table 5-1).

Table 5-1: Three stages of capital controls

Historical period	Government's idea	Economic thinking	US's attitude	IMF's attitude
Bretton Woods system	Embedded liberalism	Impossible trinity	Relaxed attitude towards capital controls	Support capital controls
1970–2000	Neoliberalism	New classical	Against capital controls	Indifferent to capital controls
2008 global financial crisis	Variant of liberalism	Macroprudential management	Allows capital controls in some cases	Supports capital controls

Source: International Monetary Fund (IMF) (2001) and CF40 (2017).

In the first stage, the IMF supported capital control. There were four main reasons for this. The first reason concerns the impact of mainstream economic thinking. Under the Bretton Woods system, embedded liberalism was the mainstream concept applied to economic activity. This approach emphasised domestic interventions within multilateral frameworks (Ruggie, 1981).

The second reason concerns the economic mission for the specific period. The 1950s saw the post–World War II recovery of the international monetary system. Countries' major economic objectives were to promote full employment and balance of international payments. Imposing controls on capital flows was an inevitable choice to achieve these goals quickly (Gilpin, 2003).

The third reason concerns the implementation of a fixed exchange rate system under the Bretton Woods system. According to the impossible trinity theory, independence of monetary policy cannot be achieved without placing capital controls under a fixed exchange rate regime (Krugman, 1995). To ensure implementation of a fixed exchange rate system, an economy must control cross-border capital flows.

The fourth reason concerns ideas about international capital flows. During this period, the IMF argued that the chaos in international capital markets prior to World War II was due to unregulated capital flows. Throughout this stage, the IMF's attitude towards capital control was directly reflected in its policymaking. For example, the IMF's *Articles of Agreement* only gave it the right to conduct surveillance over a member's current account convertibility; Article VI allowed IMF member states to exercise appropriate controls under certain conditions.

In the second stage (until the 1970s), the IMF's attitude towards capital controls loosened and the IMF began to think that cross-border capital flows should not be regulated. There were three reasons behind this change. First, changes in economic thinking. During this period, neoliberalism replaced embedded liberalism as the guiding principle of economic activity. Neoliberalism emphasises the market's role and seeks to reduce government intervention in the market.

Second, a new mission for economic governance. After achieving the two goals of full employment and balance of international payments, economies began to pursue greater interests—namely, 'promoting free trade, free capital flows, and free entry into the global market by multinational corporations'. Under this principle, countries gradually relaxed capital controls, and some developed and developing countries began to promote capital account liberalisation (Corker & Tseng, 1991).

Third, the position of the US. As the world's top economic power, the US's position has always had great influence on the IMF and other international organisations. During this period, the US opposed capital controls. The IMF was influenced by this attitude and began promoting capital account liberalisation.

During this period, the IMF made many efforts to promote cross-border capital flows. In 1978, it completed a second revision of the *Articles of Agreement*; Article IV clearly stated that the IMF would facilitate capital exchange among countries (Kose, Prasad, Rogoff & Wei, 2010). In 1997, the IMF's Interim Committee proposed to promote the liberalisation of capital flows as one of the IMF's mandates, and would require that member states (unless approved by the IMF) not impose restrictions on any type of cross-border capital flows. However, due to the outbreak of the 1997 Asian financial crisis, many key members were reluctant to relinquish control of cross-border capital flows, and the proposal was laid aside.

In the third stage, repeated financial crises made the IMF reconsider capital control measures. There were four reasons for this. First, the outbreak of the 1997 Asian financial crisis and the 2007 US subprime mortgage crisis led to a re-examination of capital flows. According to an IMF (2011) report, economic regulators, countries and regions began to realise that capital flows were posing serious challenges to global economic stability. The crucial reason for this was the lack of a global framework for managing and overseeing global capital flows.

Second, successful developing countries (such as China, India and Brazil) were reluctant to liberalise their capital accounts. They had imposed temporary or permanent capital controls, but all had achieved strong economic growth. These countries' success forced others to reconsider whether abandoning capital flow management was an inevitable choice for economic development.

Third, changes in economic thinking prompted reassessment of capital control measures. Neoclassical thinking was overly confident about the market, while it had been proved that the market could also cause economic instability. This approach was gradually replaced by the idea of macroprudential management, which emphasises the need for the government to regulate the economy.

The fourth reason concerns the empirical study of capital flows. The IMF's research team conducted a study on the 2008 GFC (IMF, 2009). The team determined that the more debt capital and direct financial investment inflows grew in a country, the worse its economy performed in the GFC. This indicated the high risks associated with these two types of capital flows. Regarding capital controls, the empirical results revealed that countries with regulations generally performed better than countries without them.

During this stage, the IMF first proposed establishing a unified framework for managing capital movements in 2005. Additionally, it elaborated a specific framework for cross-border capital flow management in the 2009

Global Financial Stability Report (Masciandaro, Nieto & Quintyn, 2009). However, this change in the IMF's attitude did not extend to supporting implementation of capital controls with no restraints. Instead, the IMF still emphasised that capital flow management measures should not affect trade-related capital flows. The third clause of the IMF's *Articles of Agreement* Article VI states:

> members may exercise such controls as are necessary to regulate international capital movements, but no member may exercise these controls in a manner which will restrict payments for current transactions or which will unduly delay transfers of funds in settlement of commitments.

The IMF hoped to establish a unified capital flow management model, but it experienced much resistance. Developing countries did not want the IMF to intervene in their capital flow management, and developed economies still had doubts about capital controls, believing that the cost of maintaining capital controls was too high. This meant that the IMF's position towards capital flow management had to become more flexible. Simultaneously, the IMF also deliberately revised the relevant terminology. 'Liberalisation of capital flows' replaced 'capital account liberalisation', and 'capital flow management measures' replaced 'capital controls'. The former change eliminated unpleasant memories associated with a particular vocabulary in developing countries, while the latter alleviated (to a certain extent) the concerns of developed economies regarding capital controls.

Current account convertibility and cross-border capital flow management

Cross-border capital flow management is related to both capital account convertibility and current account convertibility. Current account refers to payments between countries that are not asset transfers such as those for goods, services and unilateral transfers. According to the IMF's *Articles of Agreement* Article VIII, current account convertibility has the following three meanings: 1) 'no member shall, without the approval of the Fund, impose restrictions on the making of payments and transfers for current international transactions'; 2) 'No member shall engage in ... any discriminatory currency arrangements or multiple currency practices'; 3) 'Each member shall buy balances of its currency held by another member'. On 1 December 1996, China accepted the obligations stated in Article VIII and achieved current account convertibility.

According to the relevant provisions, current account convertibility only covers the outflow of funds; no requirements exist pertaining to the inflow of funds. As long as there are no direct restrictions on the acquisition or use of foreign exchange for external payments in current transactions, no violation of the convertibility commitment exists. In many developing countries, even after they become 'Article VIII countries', governments still take certain capital flow management measures. These commonly include restrictions on settlement methods, authenticity checks and registration requirements for statistical monitoring and analysis.

From the perspective of China's capital flow management operation, neither the previous mandatory repatriation and surrender nor the current stringent authenticity checks for current account payments violate IMF rules. Current account convertibility and capital flow management are non-exclusive concepts. It is reasonable and necessary to conduct capital flow management under the condition of current account convertibility.

Capital controls and macroprudential management

According to the IMF, capital controls, macroprudential regulatory policies and macroeconomic policies together constitute the policy framework for managing capital flows (Coats, 2009). The IMF suggests using different tools for the various circumstances of capital flows. First, when capital flows affect the economy through macroeconomic channels, macroeconomic policy should be used to reduce the impact of capital flows. Second, when capital flows affect the economy through financial channels, macroprudential regulation or capital controls should be considered.

Regarding the difference between capital controls and macroprudential regulatory policies, an IMF working paper (Korinek & Sandri, 2015) provides some approaches.

First, targets of the two types of policies are different. Macroprudential policies and capital controls both address the rapid flows of capital through financial channels, but they affect capital flows in different ways. Macroprudential regulation focuses on the source of funds, restricts the borrowing ability of domestic entities and regulates borrowers and lenders. But it does not differentiate loans from overseas banks from those from domestic banks. The policy will increase the financing cost of domestic borrowers and restricts excessive borrowing by domestic entities. On the other hand, capital control measures identify the real 'international' capital and impose quantity control (such as restrictions on transaction volume) or price control (such as tax). This will create interest rate differentials between the international market and the domestic market.

Second, the timing of implementation can differ. In an open economy, a sudden stop of capital flows could cause currency devaluation and, subsequently, capital outflows. If capital controls are strengthened, domestic entities will reduce lending to international agents due to rising costs. On the other hand, if macroprudential regulations are strengthened, the cost of speculation will increase. Macroprudential policies can be used to combat asset price speculation and prevent the accumulation of financial risks, and are forward looking. Capital controls can break the vicious cycle of capital outflow and currency devaluation, and can be used as a last defence against cross-border capital flow. Macroprudential regulatory tools are summarised in Table 5-2.

Table 5-2: Macroprudential regulatory tools

Types of tools	Name	Brief description
Tobin tax	Unremunerated reserve requirement	Demand a certain share of capital inflows to be deposited in a bank for a certain period without interest
	Withholding tax	Withhold a proportion of the capital borrowed by residents from overseas
	Foreign exchange tax/ financial transaction tax	Transaction tax on foreign exchange transactions
	Capital gains tax/income tax	Tax on gains of nonresident entities in domestic securities markets
	Repatriation tax	Tax on the principal when nonresidents withdraw their investment
	Macroprudential stability levy	Tax on financial institutions' external debt based on maturities
Foreign exchange open position limits		Prevent over-borrowing through spot, forward and derivatives markets for foreign exchange loans
Window guidance that is not administrative measures	Authenticity check	Demand documents proving the authenticity of external payment or transfer; non-restrictive measure
	Restriction on settlement methods	Specify payment forms or payment channels
	Registration for the purpose of statistical monitoring and analysis	Not for the purpose of restricting payment; non-restrictive measure

Source: Compiled by the study group of CF40.

It is not reasonable to define the distinction between capital control measures and macroprudential regulations based on the traditional perspective of whether the policy tool has a direct (quantitative tools) or indirect (price-based tools) impact. For example, quantitative restrictions, which are generally considered capital controls, can also be used for macroprudential regulation. More generally, the difference between macroprudential regulations and capital controls can be attributed to different motives during formulation and implementation.

Macroprudential regulation and the Tobin tax

In practice, both explicit and implicit taxation exists for cross-border capital flows. Explicit taxes include the Tobin tax, income tax and withholding tax, while implicit taxes include the unremunerated reserve requirement (URR).

In the narrow sense, the Tobin tax refers to a tax on all foreign exchange transactions. It can reduce short-term capital flows and alleviate exchange rate instability. However, the Tobin tax cannot differentiate between 'disruptive transactions' and 'normal transactions'. As such, in the long term, it will affect capital inflows. Therefore, a 'two-tier Tobin tax' structure has been proposed. Here, while all financial flows are taxed at a low rate, abnormal capital flows are allotted a temporary and punitive higher tax rate.

In the broader sense, the Tobin tax refers to all the tools that increase the costs of cross-border capital flows, including the aforementioned income tax, withholding tax, repatriation tax and URR. In particular, income tax refers to a tax on gains of nonresidents' holdings of domestic asset; it aims to curb certain capital flows. For example, most countries and regions impose a tax on gains of nonresidents' investment in domestic securities. Withholding tax refers to a tax that withholds a proportion of funds upon receipts; it normally targets the overseas borrowings of domestic agents. Repatriation tax is a tax on the principal of cross-border investment to be repatriated; the tax rate is inversely related to the length of domestic habitation. This seeks to combat 'hot' money. URR requires a certain proportion of cross-border investment to be deposited in a central bank without interest accrued. It can freeze part of the capital and, thus, increase liquidity cost indirectly.

Implementation of the Tobin tax generally has the following effects. First, it curbs short-term capital flows and maintains exchange rate stability. Second, it increases the independence of monetary policy—in theory, the Tobin tax can effectively block the channel between domestic and international markets and create more room for monetary policy implementation. Third, it increases government revenue.

Notably, while the Tobin tax and macroprudential regulatory instruments are common tools for cross-border capital flow management, the regulatory objectives for implementing the Tobin tax and macroprudential regulation are not exactly the same. The Tobin tax's objective is to limit the flow of capital and influence the size and structure of capital flows. Prudential management tools are mainly used to prevent the accumulation of financial risks and to stabilise financial systems, whether the risk originates domestically or internationally.

Notably, from the date of initiation, the Tobin tax was of little concern to the international community. Instead, the IMF and other international organisations changed their views on the Tobin tax many times, much as they had on capital flows. The Tobin tax was first proposed in the early 1970s, when the Bretton Woods system had nearly fallen apart. All economies were faced with the problem of how to promote international capital flows effectively. The famous US economist James Tobin first proposed throwing 'some sand in the well-greased wheels of international finance' (Tobin, 1998). Unfortunately, because the international community and the IMF were tolerant and optimistic regarding cross-border capital flows, such management measures received minimal attention, and the Tobin tax was not discussed at length.

In the early 1990s, successive financial crises exposed the risks of unregulated capital flows to the international financial system and economies. The IMF began to change its attitude towards capital controls and proposed building a cross-border capital flow management framework. The Tobin tax was recommended by some economists, including Tobin, and was once again raised publicly. With Tobin's death and relative stability in the international financial market at the start of the new century, the Tobin tax once again fell from view.

It was not until the outbreak of the 2008 GFC that the Tobin tax once again received wide attention. It was generally accepted by European countries and, inspired by the notion, Germany, France and 11 other European

Union (EU) member states even began to advocate financial transaction taxes on stock, bonds and derivatives transactions. Although the EU initiative to levy a financial transaction tax in 2014 suffered setbacks, a consensus has existed in European thinking and practice regarding the Tobin tax and its upgraded version. Each of the three resurgences of this tax have been related to a financial crisis at a specific time. Thus, it can be said that adopting the Tobin tax is a reaction to financial crises.

International experience and assessment of the effectiveness of cross-border capital flow management

Some cross-border capital flow management policies and measures are shown in Table 5-3.

Table 5-3: Cross-border capital flow management in some countries

Country	Period	Purpose	Measures	Specific policies
Chile	1991–1998	Control inflows	URR	The proportion to the size of inflow was 20% (with differing application times); it was then raised to 30% (1 year)
Columbia	1993–1998	Control inflows	URR	The application time was set at 18 months; the coverage was then extended to trade credit
Columbia	2007–2008	Control inflows	Prudential regulation	The proportion to inflow was set at 40% (6 months), then raised to 50%
Brazil	1993–1997	Control inflows	Tax	Tax on capital inflow
Brazil	2008	Control inflows	Tax	Capital inflow tax was gradually raised from 1.5% to 6%
Brazil	2011	Control inflows	Prudential regulation	Non-interest-bearing reserves with the central bank for banks' borrowing in USD above certain limits
Malaysia	1994	Control inflows	Prudential regulation	Upper limit on bank's net liabilities, non-interest-bearing deposit rules
Malaysia	1998	Control outflows	Administrative regulation	12 months minimum holding period for nonresident purchase of Malaysian stocks

Country	Period	Purpose	Measures	Specific policies
Thailand	1995–1996	Control inflows	URR	URR was applied to nonresident baht accounts
Thailand	2006	Control inflows	URR	URR rate of 30% (1 year) was applied to foreign currency settlement by financial institutions
Thailand	2010	Control inflows	Tax	15% withholding tax on capital gains and interest income on foreign held domestic bonds
Croatia	2004–2008	Control inflows	Prudential regulation	Prudential marginal reserve requirement for banks' foreign financing
Russia	2004	Control inflows	URR	Different URR, for example, 3% (1 year) for foreign loans and 20% (1 year) for transactions of government bonds
Iceland	2008	Control outflows	Administrative regulation	Compulsory requirement on remittance of foreign exchange income by exporters, restrictions on financial derivatives trading in the domestic market
Ukraine	2008	Control outflows	Administrative regulation	5 waiting days for nonresidents to convert hryvnia into foreign currency
Korea	2011	Control inflows	Tax	14% withholding tax on interest and transfer payment on foreign held domestic bonds
Indonesia	2011	Control inflows	URR	URR (6 months) was gradually raised from 1% to 8%
Israel	2011	Control inflows	Prudential regulation	10% reserve requirement for foreign exchange swap and forward transactions of banks and nonresidents
Cyprus	2013	Control outflows	Administrative regulation	€300 limit on residents' withdrawal of cash; partial restriction on remittance of funds overseas by importers

Note: URR = unremunerated reserve requirement.

Source: IMF (2016a) and CF40 (2017).

Success case 1: Malaysia's response to capital outflows in 1998

In the 1970s and 1980s, Malaysia accelerated the liberalisation of the capital account. This increased potential macroeconomic and financial risks, including insufficient foreign exchange reserves, increased financial system vulnerability and disequilibrium in the real exchange rate. Malaysia implemented controls on capital inflows in 1994, which resulted in positive outcomes over a short period, preventing excessive capital inflows and eliminating economic bubbles. However, the control measures did not improve capital flow structure effectively. Thus, when Malaysia experienced political turmoil in 1998, many investors developed a pessimistic outlook on Malaysia's future. Exposure to potential macroeconomic risks led to the rapid withdrawal of foreign capital, which eventually resulted in a sharp increase in exchange rate volatility.

The government immediately launched a new round of capital controls, which included a ban on all offshore trading of the ringgit and a 12-month waiting period before nonresidents could convert the proceeds from selling domestic securities to foreign currency.

After implementing these controls, Malaysia's exchange rate remained stable and foreign exchange reserves increased. Restrictions on capital flows provided policy space within which the Malaysian Government stabilised the exchange rate, accumulated foreign exchange reserves and reduced interest rates to revive the domestic economy.

Malaysia's success in cross-border capital flow management was due to two reasons. First, Malaysia had previously implemented cross-border capital flow management and, thus, had practical experience. Foreign investors also had confidence in the successful handling of capital outflows by the Malaysian Government. Second, along with the implementation of financial controls to obtain monetary policy independence, the Malaysian Government had also implemented financial and corporate restructuring to stimulate the economy. The government's policy focused on short-term capital flows, especially selling of domestic securities by nonresident holders, and tried to curb speculation by offshore hedge funds to prevent currency devaluation. Simultaneously, the government also made a long-term commitment to trade and investment liberalisation, and encouraged foreign direct investment, greatly increasing foreign investors' confidence in the economy.

Malaysia's capital flight in 1998 was largely due to scepticism about the country's political stability and pessimistic views of its macroeconomic future. The Malaysian Government adopted the policy toolkit of control over capital flows in the short term and support for foreign investment in the long term. Foreign investors' confidence was restored and their worries alleviated, hence problems were solved at the source.

Success case 2: The Icelandic experience of dealing with capital outflows in 2008

The 2008 GFC led to the bankruptcy of Iceland's three largest commercial banks. These three banks held an enormous amount of short-term foreign debt, a total of about six times the country's GDP.

The Icelandic Government took the following measures to deal with the subsequent capital outflows. First, the government prohibited all types of cross-border capital flows; second, it prohibited foreign exchange transactions in the offshore market; third, exporters were required to repatriate their income in foreign currencies; and fourth, limitations were placed on financial derivatives transactions in the domestic market.

With this intervention, capital outflow was curbed and the krona's exchange rate was stabilised quickly. These capital outflow measures achieved early results. Capital flow restrictions enabled the Icelandic Government to reduce interest rates and revitalise the domestic economy. Iceland exited from this seven-year restrictive policy with the imposition of a 'stability tax' in June 2015.

Failure case 1: Ukraine's approach to capital outflows in 2008

Before the 2008 GFC, Ukraine had experienced large-scale capital inflows, which triggered domestic credit and asset price booms. The loan-to-deposit ratio was at one time more than 150 per cent; signs of economic overheating were apparent. After the GFC, Ukraine suffered a serious banking and currency crisis under the impacts of both the current account deficit and capital outflows.

A banking crisis could easily lead to systemic financial crisis. At that time, domestic bank deposits had fallen by more than 20 per cent and the government had reduced the capital adequacy ratio of many banks to below minimum regulatory requirements. In the meantime, Ukraine's long-term pegged exchange rate system could not be maintained; even with the loss of 25 per cent of foreign exchange reserves, the currency was still forced to depreciate by about 35 per cent.

In response to the currency crisis, the Ukrainian central bank adopted the following measures. First, the central bank revised the method for banks to move bad foreign currency loans from the balance sheet and foreign exchange positions. This led to many banks (especially foreign banks) selling a significant amount of foreign exchange in the market. Second, more stringent banking practices were applied, including limiting early withdrawal of time deposits and prohibiting early repayment of foreign currency loans and currency exchange by non-domestic banks. Third, the banks suspended the deposit reserve requirement on banks' short-term foreign borrowings. Fourth, the bank implemented controls on foreign investment, especially the five-day compulsory waiting period for nonresidents' exchange of domestic currency into foreign currency. Fifth, other measures were implemented including prohibiting foreign currency loans to unhedged borrowers and a monthly quota on foreign exchange allowed for natural persons.

These measures gave only temporary relief. The hryvnia depreciated by 50 per cent in two months and foreign exchange reserves decreased by 30 per cent in six months, while nominal interest rates soared four times. The main reason for the policy's failure is that the effectiveness of the control measures was weakened by inherent contradictions between the policies. The inconsistency between the aforementioned first, second, fourth and fifth measures undermined confidence in the financial system. The third measure, which was intended to inject liquidity into banking institutions, instead boosted capital flight.

Failure case 2: Thailand's efforts to stop capital outflows in 1997

Thailand pegged its currency to the USD in 1984. From 1984–1994, as the USD continued to depreciate against other major currencies, the baht also depreciated, which increased Thailand's export competitiveness. Simultaneously, Thailand opened its capital account relatively early; by 1996, its capital account convertibility had largely been realised. This brought a large amount of active capital into Thailand, among which was a large amount of short-term capital in the form of loans that flowed into the real estate and stock market. This created significant asset bubbles, foreshadowing the future currency crisis.

By 1995, the USD had started to appreciate continuously. The baht also strengthened, greatly weakening Thailand's export competitiveness. The decline in exports led to the rapid expansion of Thailand's trade deficit. Simultaneously, due to appreciation of the USD, a large amount of short-term capital was withdrawn from the capital market and Thailand's asset prices began to fall. In 1996, the real estate market bubble burst, causing severe problems for commercial banks and financial companies. The banking system accumulated a large number of non-performing loans related to the real estate sector. In the following year, Thailand's stock index fell more than 60 per cent. Financial market turmoil and a deteriorating real economy exacerbated market expectations that the baht would depreciate.

Moreover, Thailand was hit not only by domestic financial turmoil, but also by international 'hot' money from Soros and others, and a significant amount of foreign capital began to flee from the country. The Thai Government needed to fight these capital outflows. However, it was also concerned that an interest rate rise would hurt the economy. As a result, Thailand took a series of capital flow management measures in early 1997, including restrictions on forward transactions, restrictions on the surrender of bills of landing in exports and a requirement that proceeds from securities sales be converted at the onshore rate.

Although the Thai Government addressed capital outflows actively, these measures did not bring about the desired results. Instead, the baht depreciated by 50 per cent, foreign exchange reserves declined by 20 per cent in six months, domestic interest rates continued to rise, and large spreads between onshore and offshore exchange rates resulted in evasion of regulations.

Thailand's capital flow management failed for three reasons. First, the Thai central bank raised interest rates to keep the pegged exchange rate with the USD. Higher interest rates further curbed investment and consumption demand, accelerating the economic recession. Due to high interest rates, enterprises had to seek low-cost capital in international financial markets, further expanding the scale of external debt and initiating a vicious cycle. The Thai Government was finally forced to abandon the fixed exchange rate system in July 1997. Second, Thailand's external debt reached US$90 billion in 1997, equivalent to 50 per cent of GDP, of which 60 per cent was short-term external debt. This undoubtedly exacerbated external risks to the Thai economy, particularly as the Thai Government lacked effective tools to prevent capital outflows. Third, Thailand had foreign exchange reserves of US$32 billion in June 1997, but US$30 billion were from foreign exchange swap transactions, and US$25 billion had to be paid off within a year. With interest expenses and external debt, Thailand's foreign exchange reserve was unable to meet these financial commitments. Even if the Thai Government had suspended foreign exchange forward transactions promptly, the existing swap transactions would still have been difficult to address.

Main conclusions

Maintaining the independence of monetary policy requires strengthening cross-border capital flow management. After the 2008 GFC, major developed economies implemented quantitative easing policy and injected significant liquidity into the international market. Sun and Li (2017) argued that not all this liquidity entered the real economy; some entered global financial markets through cross-border capital flows. These funds were significant, highly mobile and very unstable, leading to an increased importance of capital flows versus the other elements of the impossible trinity (i.e. 'capital flow–fixed exchange rate–independent monetary policy'). In the past, it was possible to abandon the fixed exchange rate system and realise the free flow of capital and monetary policy independence. However, even if governments abandon the fixed exchange rate system, this may not be sufficient to guarantee monetary policy independence under increased volumes of capital flows. To ensure the independence of a country's monetary policy, governments should not only make certain concessions on the fixed exchange rate system, but also actively realise the effective management of cross-border capital flows to reduce their impact on the economy. Transnational capital flows are becoming more frequent and rapid, and the scale is increasingly large. Because of this, the IMF and other international organisations, as well as various economies, are becoming aware of the rationality and necessity of cross-border capital flow management. It is likely that capital flow management will be a topic of discussion in the future.

Implementing cross-border capital flow management reduces the negative impact of short-term exchange rate fluctuations on the domestic economy. Capital flow management and macroprudential policy adhere to the same idea; both focus on reducing volatility and preventing risks to alleviate the impact of capital flows on an economy. Especially for developing countries, the prevalence of underdeveloped financial markets and currency mismatches constitute the 'original sin': a high probability exists that liberalising capital flows without careful planning will result in both currency and financial crisis. This is undoubtedly relevant to China's situation. If a country seeks rapid opening up to the outside world, while also attempting to maintain macroeconomic and financial stability, it must use capital flow management tools comprehensively and rationally.

Cross-border capital flow (especially capital outflow) management must follow several principles (Viñals & Moghadam, 2011):

1. Once a country opens its capital account, a certain degree of capital outflows and fluctuations are normal; these do not require the use of specific capital flow management measures.

2. Macroeconomic and financial policies should be the main tools for dealing with capital outflows.

3. To smooth fluctuations in capital flows, capital inflow management measures can be adopted in advance, following the IMF policy framework.

4. Faced with large capital outflows, currency depreciation and depletion of foreign exchange reserves during a crisis or imminent crisis, temporary capital outflow management measures must be undertaken to allow time for fiscal policy adjustment and financial sector stabilisation.

5. Priority should be given to control measures with no discrimination based on residence, such as those tailored to different types of currencies.

6. When formulating management measures, consideration should be given to specific national circumstances, such as administrative and regulatory capacity, as well as the degree of openness to capital flows.

7. Capital flow management measures should only be used to complement policies in response to a crisis. When the macroeconomic situation stabilises, market confidence is restored and foreign exchange reserves begin to rise, these controls should be abolished.

Additionally, regarding the use of specific policy instruments, governments must ensure the measures are non-discriminatory, transparent and temporary (Brockmeijer, Marston & Ostry, 2012). This is to avoid capital controls in the name of capital flow management. Simultaneously, it must be realised that capital flow management is not the fundamental solution to address the shocks of cross-border capital flows; it can only provide time for domestic structural reform and macroeconomic recovery.

Finally, the effective management of cross-border capital outflows requires certain conditions. The IMF proposes three key conditions: strong macroeconomic fundamentals, effective institutions and existing comprehensive restrictions (Saborowski, Sanya, Weisfeld & Yepez, 2014). Capital outflow restriction will be effective if at least one of these three conditions is met. When none of these are met, restrictions on capital outflows will be ineffective.

Part 3: The wave-like development of China's financial opening in recent years

Review and summary of China's capital account opening and RMB internationalisation in the new century

Capital account liberalisation

In the first stage, before 2003, reform was relatively cautious. Direct investment was the main area of opening during this time. Also, management of foreign currency loans was reformed and QFII investors were allowed to invest in domestic securities markets.

In the second stage, from 2003–2009, the pace of reform gradually accelerated. In 2003, for the first time, the Third Plenary Session of the 16th Central Committee of the Communist Party of China (2015) clearly stated the goal of the 'gradual realization of capital account convertibility'. Since then, China's capital account opening has accelerated. First, liberalisation was promoted in all areas; that is, areas of opening were expanded from direct investment to external credit and liability, securities investment and other cross-border capital and financial account transactions. Second, liberalisation was more balanced; that is, against the background of large-scale inflows, the idea of 'loose regulation on inflows and strict regulation on outflows' was gradually substituted with more balanced regulation on inflows and outflows. Third, the opening speed was adjusted based on domestic and international economic and financial conditions. During this period, China introduced about 40 capital account reform measures, including improvement of external debt management, the introduction of the QDII scheme, and the relaxation of regulations on QFII investment and overseas investment of insurance funds.

In the third stage, after 2009, reforms were further deepened. This period is characterised by 'reducing existing restrictions' and 'establishing new rules'. The former refers to the reduction of exchange restrictions on cross-border capital and financial transactions—convertibility for direct investment was basically realised—while convertibility for portfolio investment was steadily promoted through various channels, including QFII, RQFII, QDII, RMB Qualified Domestic Institutional Investor, the Shanghai–Hong Kong Stock Connect and the Shenzhen–Hong Kong Stock Connect (Pan, 2017). Simultaneously, new means of capital account regulation were explored, and cross-border capital flow was included in the framework of macroprudential management (see below).

RMB internationalisation

The pilot stage of RMB internationalisation was from 2003–2009. At the end of 2003, China's central bank issued a circular to provide clearing arrangements for banks with personal RMB deposits, currency exchange, bank cards and remittance services in Hong Kong. This was done to meet the needs of the market and standardise business development. This began a new stage of RMB internationalisation. In 2004, the central bank officially began to provide clearing arrangements to banks with personal RMB businesses in Macao. However, in this period, RMB businesses in Hong Kong and Macao were mainly for use by individuals, and only involved a small number of sporadic capital account transactions; trade and investment transactions were not yet covered (Tian, 2003).

The rapid development stage of RMB internationalisation was from 2009 to August 2015. In 2009, approved by the State Council, the central bank raised the curtain on RMB internationalisation with RMB cross-border trade settlement. First, the use of RMB in cross-border trade settlement was expanded to the whole country; the transactions covered were expanded from trade in goods to trade in services and other current account items. Second, the use of RMB in cross-border capital account transactions was liberalised significantly. A number of reform measures were introduced in relation to direct investment, portfolio investment and other investment. Third, offshore RMB centres represented by Hong Kong grew rapidly. Fourth, a breakthrough was made on the RMB's function as an international currency. Substantial progress was achieved not only in terms of bilateral currency swaps, but also the role and weight of RMB as the 'anchor currency', as a number of countries now included RMB assets in their reserves (PBC, 2016).

The period from August 2015 to the present is a new starting point for RMB internationalisation. In November 2015, the IMF announced the inclusion of the RMB in the special drawing right (SDR) currency basket at a weight of 10.92 per cent. On 1 October 2016, the IMF officially announced that the RMB had become the fifth currency in the SDR basket (in addition to the USD, euro, British pound and JPY). However, the RMB is facing new challenges after joining the SDR basket, especially regarding how to turn this into a policy dividend for real economic development (Wen, 2016).

Several important principles of financial opening

Several principles of financial opening exist. First is the principle of steady opening up. Under the premise of properly controlling risks—and following the general guidelines of step-by-step progress, overall planning, addressing easier issues before difficult ones and keeping options open—regulation of the capital account was relaxed gradually and selectively. RMB internationalisation was promoted steadily, ensuring the compatibility of the opening-up process with economic development, financial market conditions and financial stability.

Second is the principle of facilitation. Following market demand, the government streamlined administration, delegated government powers, clarified regulatory boundaries and abolished unnecessary administrative approvals to facilitate trade and investment.

Third is the principle of national treatment. The government gradually abolished the long-existing super-national treatment of foreign investment and unreasonable barriers to foreign investment. It also explored a pre-establishment national treatment and negative list approach, and created a fair business environment for enterprises with all types of ownership.

Fourth is the principle of balanced management. The government made an effort to facilitate the entry of foreign companies into China, as well as Chinese companies' expansions abroad. It also implemented regulatory policies to encourage two-way capital flows.

Significant progress in financial opening

As of the end of 2016, China had achieved partial convertibility[8] for 37 items under the capital account, three more items compared to the end 2012. The proportion of the total increased from 85 per cent to 92.5 per cent during the same period, leaving only three items nonconvertible (see Table 5-4). Moreover, as opening increased, China not only improved trade and investment facilitation, but also revamped the management of cross-border capital flows from a previous focus on pre-approval to an emphasis on operational and post-operational oversight. It also constantly improved macroprudential management tools, so that the market could play a more important role. After years of development, RMB use has expanded from the traditional regional use (that is, mainly in cross-border trade) to the financing and investment field. The circulation area has expanded to include the whole world and circulation volumes have continued to grow (see Figure 5-8). The RMB was admitted to the SDR currency basket at the end of 2015, an acknowledgement of its freely usable level and international currency status. According to the IMF, the global holdings of RMB reserve assets were US$84.5 billion by the end of 2016, accounting for 1 per cent of the total reserves. The yuan has become the seventh international reserve currency.

---

8   The IMF's Annual Report on Exchange Arrangements and Exchange Restrictions classifies the 40 items under seven types of capital account transactions into four degrees of convertibility: nonconvertible, partially convertible, basically convertible and fully convertible.

Table 5-4: Convertibility of China's capital account transactions (based on IMF classifications)

Item				2012	2016
1. Capital and money market tools	Capital market securities	Purchase of stocks or other equity securities	1. Purchase locally by nonresidents	Partially convertible	Partially convertible
			2. Sale or issue locally by nonresidents	Nonconvertible	Nonconvertible
			3. Purchase abroad by residents	Partially convertible	Partially convertible
			4. Sale or issue abroad by residents	Basically convertible	Basically convertible
		Bonds or other debt securities	5. Purchase locally by nonresidents	Partially convertible	Partially convertible
			6. Sale or issue locally by nonresidents	Partially convertible	Partially convertible
			7. Purchase abroad by residents	Partially convertible	Partially convertible
			8. Sale or issue abroad by residents	Partially convertible	Partially convertible
	Money market instruments		9. Purchase locally by nonresidents	Partially convertible	Partially convertible
			10. Sale or issue locally by nonresidents	Nonconvertible	Nonconvertible
			11. Purchase abroad by residents	Partially convertible	Partially convertible
			12. Sale or issue abroad by residents	Partially convertible	Partially convertible
	On collective investment securities		13. Purchase locally by nonresidents	Partially convertible	Partially convertible
			14. Sale or issue locally by nonresidents	Nonconvertible	Partially convertible
			15. Purchase abroad by residents	Partially convertible	Partially convertible
			16. Sale or issue abroad by residents	Nonconvertible	Partially convertible

Item			2012	2016
2. Derivatives and other instruments		17. Purchase locally by nonresidents	Partially convertible	Partially convertible
		18. Sale or issue locally by nonresidents	Nonconvertible	Nonconvertible
		19. Purchase abroad by residents	Partially convertible	Partially convertible
		20. Sale or issue abroad by residents	Partially convertible	Partially convertible
3. Credit business	Commercial credit	21. By residents to nonresidents	Basically convertible	Basically convertible
		22. To residents from nonresidents	Basically convertible	Basically convertible
	Financial credit	23. By residents to nonresidents	Fully convertible	Fully convertible
		24. To residents from nonresidents	Partially convertible	Partially convertible
	Guarantees, sureties and standby loan facility	25. By residents to nonresidents	Partially convertible	Basically convertible
		26. To residents from nonresidents	Partially convertible	Basically convertible
4. Direct investment		27. Outward direct investment	Fully convertible	Fully convertible
		28. Inward direct investment	Basically convertible	Fully convertible
5. Liquidation of direct investment		29. liquidation of direct investment	Fully convertible	Fully convertible
6. Real estate transactions		30. Purchase abroad by residents	Partially convertible	Partially convertible
		31. Purchase locally by nonresidents	Basically convertible	Basically convertible
		32. Sale locally by nonresidents	Fully convertible	Fully convertible

Item			2012	2016
7. Personal capital transaction	Loans	33. By residents to nonresidents	Partially convertible	Partially convertible
		34. To residents from nonresidents	Nonconvertible	Partially convertible
	Gifts, endowments, inheritances and estate	35. By residents to nonresidents	Basically convertible	Basically convertible
		36. To residents from nonresidents	Fully convertible	Fully convertible
	Settlement of debts abroad by immigrants	37. Settlement of debts abroad by immigrants	Fully convertible	Fully convertible
	Transfer of assets	38. Transfer abroad by emigrants	Basically convertible	Basically convertible
		39. Transfer into the country by immigrants	Fully convertible	Fully convertible
	Transfer of gambling and prize earnings	40. Transfer of gambling and prize earnings	Basically convertible	Basically convertible
Sum		Nonconvertible	6	3
		Partially convertible	19	20
		Basically convertible	8	9
		Fully convertible	7	8

Source: Collaborative Innovation Center of Financial Security (2016) and CF40 (2017).

($100 million)

%

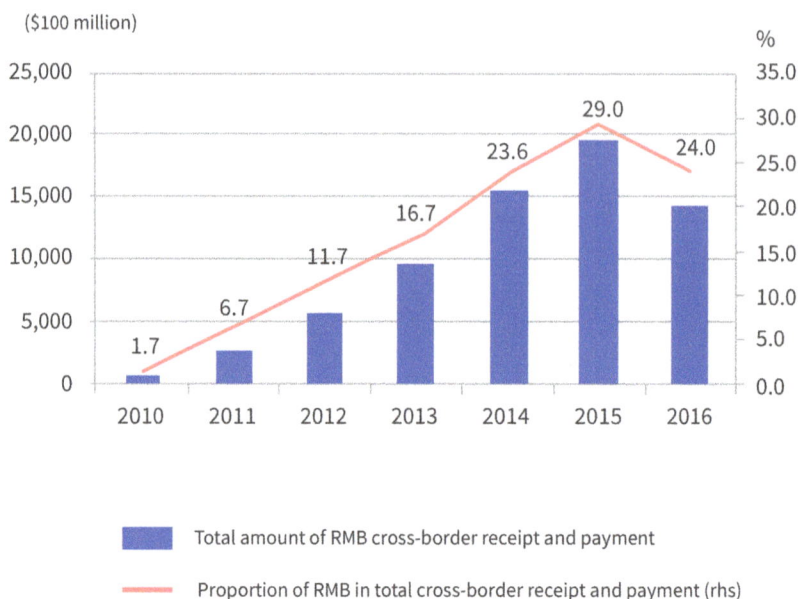

Figure 5-8: Cross-border RMB payments and receipts (2010–2016).
Source: SAFE (2016) and CF40 (2017).

Controversies and reversals of opening in recent years

Controversy exists over the timing and speed of China's capital account liberalisation and RMB internationalisation. Some scholars argue that China is facing a rare opportunity to promote the convertibility of its capital account. Several reasons are given for this: China's overall national strength is increasing, the fiscal situation and the financial system are basically stable, the market-oriented reforms of exchange rate and interest rate regimes are steadily advancing, the ability of international discharging is adequate, macro-control ability is significantly enhanced, and profound changes occurred in the global economy after the 2008 GFC. Therefore, China should accelerate capital account liberalisation and propel RMB internationalisation. In 2012, the PBC (2012) issued a report that deemed 'the conditions for China to speed up capital account opening are basically mature'. However, scholars such as Lin (2013) and Yu (2016) contend that the conditions for China to further promote financial liberalisation are not yet mature, as China's financial markets must evolve further to reach parity with developed countries. Further, implicit government debt is large, macro-control and financial regulation need to be improved, both the internal and external environments remain uncertain, and the risk of cross-border capital outflow has increased. In this context, rapid capital account opening and RMB internationalisation is similar to drinking poison to quench one's thirst—it may increase the vulnerability of China's financial system and induce cross-market arbitrage activities.

Recently, China's financial opening has shown certain signs of reversal. Especially after the 'August 11th' exchange rate reform in 2015, China's financial market experienced turbulence. RMB internationalisation indicators also fluctuated. SWIFT data show that the RMB's ranking in international payments fell from fifth in 2015 to sixth by the end of 2016, and its proportion in total payments declined from 2.31 per cent in December 2015 to 1.67 per cent in December 2016. At present, cross-border capital flow management has again shifted towards encouraging inflows and regulating outflows. One lesson here is that the earlier financial opening did not propel market-oriented exchange rate reform, but the absence of this hindered further financial opening. To promote further opening of the capital account, the following should be considered: the influence of internal and external factors; identifying the key points, rhythm and steps at different stages; promoting orderly reform; strengthening policy support; and ensuring that risk is basically controllable. The National Financial Work Conference held in July 2017 laid out plans for expanding financial opening and reaffirmed the stance of making progress with capital account liberalisation and RMB internationalisation while ensuring stability, with a particular emphasis on proper sequencing of opening policies.

Current policy measures on strengthening cross-border capital flow management

In an open economy, the 'impossible trinity' exists, which states that the use of either price tools (floating exchange rate) or quantitative tools (market intervention and capital flow management) is required in dealing with the shocks of excessive capital inflows or outflows. It is impossible to use neither (Guan, 2016). From 1998–2000, during the Asian financial crisis, China kept exchange rate and foreign exchange reserves stable by strengthening foreign exchange management. At present, when once again facing capital outflows, China has adopted a policy mix of floating the exchange rate, market intervention and capital flow management. Regarding specific policy instruments, China has further opened up its domestic financial market to encourage capital inflows and relaxed settlement restrictions, while also placing capital flows under macroprudential management. China has also strengthened authenticity and compliance checks on capital outflows.

Continue to promote the opening of domestic financial markets and relax restrictions on foreign exchange settlement

China further opened the domestic bond market, allowed foreign financial institutions including mid- and long-term institutional investors such as pension funds to invest in the interbank bond market through the registration system and determine their own size of investment. Simultaneously, China implemented macroprudential regulation in relation to foreign institutional investors. China also relaxed restrictions on foreign exchange settlement for capital account transactions, allowed the voluntary settlement of corporate external debt, unified the policy for domestic entities on the voluntary settlement of foreign exchange income from capital account transactions, and adopted a negative list management approach on the use of income from capital account items. It also simplified foreign exchange regulation for QFII, cancelled the investment limit for each investor, allowed investors to obtain their basic investment quota by registration, abolished the requirement for the investment principal to be received within a certain period, and reduced the lock period from one year to three months. It substantially relaxed entry barriers to the service sector, manufacturing and mining industries, and promoted fair competition between domestic and foreign entities. It launched the Shenzhen–Hong Kong Stock Connect, improved the Shanghai–Hong Kong Stock Connect mechanism, abolished the quota on total investment and retained only the daily limit. Additionally, a bond connect mechanism is being launched.

Introduce and improve the macroprudential management of cross-border capital flows

China implemented macroprudential management of cross-border financing, linked market entities' borrowing limit with their capital strength and debt repayment ability, and managed leverage ratios and currency mismatch risks through adjusting macroprudential parameters. It also improved the reserve requirement for nonresidents' RMB deposits, established a long-term mechanism for counter-cyclical adjustment of cross-border RMB flows, and guided foreign financial institutions to strengthen RMB liquidity management. Additionally, it established self-discipline mechanisms for the foreign exchange market, standardised quotation behaviour for the central parity rate, developed and implemented a code of conduct for the interbank market and over-the-counter foreign exchange sale and purchase and cross-border RMB businesses. It also dealt with transaction disputes between members and improved standardisation of the foreign exchange market by use of both self-discipline and outside discipline (Chen, 2016). China also implemented risk reserve requirements on foreign exchange transactions, requiring financial institutions to fulfil a 20 per cent reserve requirement on their forward purchase contracts (including options and swaps) to curb short-term arbitrage activities.[9]

Strengthen authenticity checks and compliance review on cross-border capital outflows

China has urged banks and enterprises to implement strict authenticity checks and compliance reviews for current account transactions, required enterprises to collect their export proceeds in a timely manner, continued to implement management on the repatriation of direct investment profits, further clarified the procedures for domestic institutions to register ODI and remit out funds, and strengthened the information reporting requirements for domestic institutions to retain overseas their foreign exchange proceeds from export or trade in services. China has also strengthened regulations of ODI. Four government departments have stressed the need to prevent risks with ODI, especially irrational investments in real estate, hotels, entertainment and other areas. The same approach was taken to the hidden risks associated with large non-core business investments, investment by limited partnership companies, 'small parent, large subsidiary' and 'fast out fast in' investment activities. China also improved the information reporting requirements for individuals' foreign exchange purchases, detailed the reporting content and reiterated that individuals could only use foreign exchange purchases for current account transactions and not for capital account purposes, while maintaining the annual purchase limit. It also strengthened the management of cross-border RMB outflows, and required enterprises to register overseas lending activity with the foreign exchange authority.

---

9   The ratio has been lowered to 0 per cent since 11 September 2017.

Achievements and problems of the cross-border capital flow management

The direction of financial opening has not changed but the focus and content have been adjusted

China will continue to move in the direction of making the RMB into a convertible and freely usable currency. However, in recent years, with the change in the foreign exchange market, the focus of financial opening has changed from a balanced management of inflows and outflows to encouraging inflows. Opening of the domestic financial market has been accelerated and restrictions on external financing have been loosened. The Shanghai–Hong Kong Stock Connect and Shenzhen–Hong Kong Stock Connect mechanisms have promoted two-way opening of the stock market and supported the marketisation and internationalisation of the A-share market. In June 2017, MSCI included China's A-shares in its key Emerging Markets Index. Moreover, China increased the speed of infrastructure building, including launching the RMB cross-border interbank payment system, introducing more RMB clearing banks, expanding RMB currency swaps, and further facilitating the holding and use of RMB abroad.

Regulations on cross-border capital outflows have been tightened, but have not moved beyond the existing policy framework

Overall, the measures introduced in recent years have mainly required market entities to comply with existing requirements and exercise self-discipline. They are not new controls on exchange or cross-border payment and receipt activities. For example, in improving the information disclosure requirements for individuals' purchases of foreign exchange, the annual quota remains unchanged. Additionally, policies on using foreign exchange for personal reasons, such as studying abroad or travel, also remain unchanged. In the case of domestic residents' purchase of insurance products abroad, no restrictions apply to current account transactions (such as purchase of travel insurance), but the purchase of investment and participating policy under the capital account is not allowed. In the past two years, some overseas insurance companies tried to sell large investment insurance products with 'capital flight' features to mainland residents through various means. This not only seriously interfered with the domestic foreign exchange market order, but also led to bubbles in the overseas insurance market and active underground bank activities. The SAFE has reiterated the bank card regulation policy that was first implemented in 2003. It has also strengthened category and quota management on using bank cards to purchase insurance products, ensuring the effective enforcement of regulatory policies and business rules.

Measures have been effective in balancing capital flows in the short term

China's further opening of the domestic interbank bond market, the implementation of full-calibre macroprudential management of cross-border financing and a few other measures have all helped expand capital inflows. In 2016, foreign investors' holdings of RMB bonds increased by RMB151.3 billion. From the second to fourth quarter of 2016, China's total external debt increased by US$89.2 billion, reversing the overall decline in external debt since 2015. With regard to risk prevention, several measures curbed the excessive (or even illegal) foreign exchange demand. These included stricter authenticity checks and compliance rules, strengthened monitoring and early warning of cross-border capital flows, and improved the self-discipline mechanisms of banks. In the first half of 2017, net inflows of direct investment were US$11.4 billion, compared with net outflows of US$17.7 billion for the same period in the previous year. During the same period, pressure on capital outflows gradually eased. Foreign exchange reserves rebounded by US$46.3 billion, compared with a decrease of US$125.2 billion a year earlier. Foreign exchange assets net of valuation effect increased by US$29.4 billion, compared to a decrease of US$163.6 billion a year earlier. This has stabilised market expectations and created the conditions for relaxation of capital flow management.

Capital flow management needs to be more effective

First, capital flow management still mostly resorts to administrative means; as such, it is prone to a one-size-fits-all solution. At times, it may restrict normal investment and reduce market efficiency. Window guidance and other administrative measures are not transparent and difficult to supervise. Additionally, excessive reliance on administrative means will likely result in policy reversal. For example, the policy on ODI has changed from encouraging enterprises to 'go out' to a tightening of controls. Second, the policy may fail. For example, the government wants to attract more capital inflows through financial opening, and the key would be for market participants to collect and settle more foreign exchange. However, this is difficult, because the enterprises decide for themselves how much to collect and settle. As another example, the marginal effect of authenticity checks and compliance review tends to diminish over time. Third, encouraging capital inflows has side effects. Capital outflows all start from earlier capital inflows—encouraging overseas financing, opening the bond markets and facilitating foreign investment in securities may all increase financial market volatility and vulnerability.

Part 4: Establishing a dual-pillar capital flow management framework

The trend of China's cross-border capital flow management

The '13th Five-Year Plan' clearly proposed promoting the marketisation of exchange and interest rates, realising RMB capital account convertibility in an orderly way, making the RMB a more convertible and freely usable currency, and steadily facilitating international use of the RMB. By 2020, with market-based exchange and interest rates and the gradual implementation of financial opening, China's international influence should extend from traditional trade and investment areas to the monetary and financial fields. The following sections describe possible trends in China's capital flow management framework.

Trend 1: The macroeconomic adjustment function of capital flow management will be less important

At present, the most important function of China's capital flow management is to serve macro-control goals, and the focus is on maintaining the balance of international payments. From the perspective of policy choices, capital flow management is a function of monetary policy independence and exchange rate marketisation. Monetary policy independence is China's priority, so it can be viewed as an exogenous variable. As a result, the higher the degree of exchange rate marketisation, the less the government's demand for capital flow management. China's dependence on capital flow management is largely decided by the progress of the market-oriented reform of the RMB exchange rate regime. Implementing capital flow management is only to buy time for the RMB exchange rate to realise a clean float. In the future, temporary use of cross-border capital flow management (balance of payments safeguard measures) will be required only in extreme cases (Rey, 2015). These may include situations in which global risk aversion is beyond a critical state, so that the flexible exchange rate system is insufficient to adjust external imbalances, or if exchange rate volatility is too high. Otherwise, the government should surrender the macro-control function to the market.

Trend 2: The micro-regulation function of cross-border capital flow management will be separated from the macro-control function

At this stage, the macro-control function of China's capital flow management is achieved through micro-regulation. This is not just a violation of 'Tinbergen's Rule' (that is, it is difficult for cross-border capital flow management tools to meet the policy objectives of currency convertibility and maintaining a balance of payments). Also, repeated changes in micro-regulation policy has distorted resource allocation, increased the cost of market entities, affected policy credibility and undermined China's national image. In the future, with a market-based exchange rate in place, capital flow management will focus on its original mandate. That is, it will promote RMB capital account convertibility, vigorously develop the foreign exchange market and promote RMB exchange rate marketisation. Simultaneously, it will strengthen micro-regulation; establish a new mechanism of anti-money laundering, anti-terrorism financing and anti-tax avoidance (based on international practice); and establish a new system of national security review and prudential and behaviour supervision (based on authenticity and compliance review).

Trend 3: Diversification and decentralisation will be a future reform direction of capital flow management

First, a single objective should be substituted by multiple objectives. Instead of one objective (i.e. maintaining balance of payments), multiple objectives should be developed to include preventing systemic financial risks and external shocks from international financial crises. At the micro level, objectives include not only review of the authenticity and compliance of capital flows, but also that of anti-money laundering, anti-tax avoidance and anti-terrorism financing, along with national economic security reviews on foreign mergers and acquisitions.

Second, the focus will shift from regulation of currency exchange to regulation of transactions. Capital flow management covers both exchange and transaction activities. As the balance of payments is closely related to cross-border capital flows, the management focuses on exchange and payment activities. In the future, with diversified objectives, regulation will cover the entire process of currency exchange and transactions, based on specific objectives, objects and characteristics, and, more importantly, on supervision of transactions.

Third, centralised regulation should be replaced by decentralised regulation. Currently, the monetary authorities (including the PBC and SAFE) are responsible for centralised cross-border capital flow management. In the future, with the diversification of management functions, regulatory agencies will become more diversified and decentralised. Monetary authorities will focus on anti-money laundering, tax departments will focus on anti-tax avoidance, national security departments will focus on anti-terrorism and the Ministry of Commerce and National Commission of Development and Reform will focus on national security reviews of foreign investment. Additionally, the monetary authority, China Banking and Insurance Regulatory Commission and China Securities Regulatory Commission will work on prudential supervision. This will help build supervisory synergy with division of labour and cooperation.

Establish a dual-pillar framework of cross-border capital flow management

The future framework of capital flow management will properly separate macro functions from micro-supervision. The macro-management tools will aim at a balance of payment and prevention of systemic financial risks. Micro-management tools will help promote capital account convertibility, exchange rate marketisation and diverse regulatory objectives. The two are relatively independent but closely linked, constituting a dual-pillar system for cross-border capital flow management.

Pillar 1: A two-dimensional macro-management framework for cross-border capital flows

The future of macro-management of cross-border capital flows is two-dimensional. The first is the policy transmission mechanism that serves the balance of payments objective (capital control). The second is the policy transmission mechanism that serves the risk prevention objective (macroprudential management).

To design a two-dimensional framework, the monetary policy transmission mechanism offers a lesson. The basic logic is that the regulators use certain tools to implement counter-cyclical adjustment or set up risk reserve, and assess the policy effects on the final goals (economic growth, full employment and price stability) through observing changes in intermediate objectives (e.g. balance of payments and systemic financial risks). Identifying the final goal, intermediate objective, operational objective and operational tools is at the core of this two-dimensional framework.

Under the two dimensions of capital control and macroprudential management, the goals are consistent: to promote economic growth, maintain price stability and achieve full employment. In other words, internal balance is the final goal. Balance of payments is not regarded as a final goal for several reasons. First, the balance of payments is important under a fixed exchange rate system, where it determines whether the foreign exchange market is cleared. In the context of free float exchange rates and free capital flows, international payments can reach an automatic balance, except during crisis periods. This is why Samuelson and other mainstream scholars in the West do not mention the four goals of macro-control. Second, China is a large open economy; internal objectives always have priority over external objectives, and, thus, monetary policy independence (sovereignty) is the highest policy objective. Too much emphasis on the importance of balance of payments is not consistent with China's status as a large economy.

Balance of payments could serve as an intermediate objective for the capital control dimension. In an open economy, balance of payments conditions could directly affect supply and demand in the foreign exchange market, changing the amount of funds outstanding for foreign exchange and base money, thus having a significant impact on money supply. Therefore, balance of payments is closely and directly linked to the final goals such as economic growth and price stability.

The structural indicators that reflect cross-border financial risks can serve as the intermediate objectives of the macroprudential dimension. Macroprudential management mainly aims to prevent systemic financial risks related to cross-border capital flows. From a policy perspective, risk in the financial system is central, whereas risks associated with specific businesses and individuals are not the focus of attention. China has just started to implement macroprudential management, and many indicators have been incorporated into the framework. Which indicators are more suitable as the intermediate objectives requires further study.

The tools for cross-border capital flow management can be organised as an inverted tree-like structure (see Figure 5-9). Of these, those that serve the macro-management function include macroprudential regulation in Area 1 (see Table 5-5) and capital control measures in Areas 2 and 3 (see Table 5-6).

Table 5-5: Macroprudential capital flow management tools

Asset-side tools	Liability-side tools	Capital-related tools	Market tools
Loan-to-value cap for foreign exchange loans	Levy on non-deposit foreign debts	Capital requirement on foreign currency loans	Levy on short-term capital flows
Foreign currency liquidity ratio	Foreign debt to income cap	Foreign currency counter-cyclical capital buffer	Financial transaction tax on foreign currency transactions
Foreign currency net stable funding ratio	Unremunerated reserve requirement	Excess reserves for foreign currency loans	Income tax on profits
Foreign currency liquidity ratio	Core foreign debt dependency ratio	Foreign currency leverage ratio	Margin requirement for financial transactions
Foreign currency loan provision ratio	Macroprudential management of cross-border capital flows		Interbank foreign exchange market transaction fee
Foreign currency provision coverage ratio			
Foreign currency loan concentration	Reserve requirement on nonresidents' RMB deposits		Limit on bank's net open foreign exchange position for foreign exchange sale and purchase business
Foreign currency liquidity gap			Risk provision for foreign currency derivatives
Foreign currency loan loss provision			Foreign currency risk exposure management
Foreign currency non-performing loan ratio			
Foreign currency asset profit ratio			

Note: Grey shading indicates areas in which China has implemented the measures.

Source: Bruno, Shim and Shin (2015).

Table 5-6: Characteristics of cross-border capital flow management tools

Measures	Capital control	Foreign exchange market intervention	Macroprudential management	Antidumping, countervailing duties and safeguard measures	Foreign investment review
Objectives	Balance of payments	Balance of payments	Prevention of financial risks	Prevention of financial crimes	Safeguard national security
Targets	Nonresidents	Nonresidents	Foreign currency	No restriction	Nonresidents
Entities	All entities	All entities	Financial institutions	All entities	Foreign enterprises
Characteristics	Discretional	Discretional	Mainly rule-based regulation	Rule-based regulation	Rule-based regulation
Frequency	Tentative measures	Tentative measures	Long term	Long term	Long term

Source: CF40 (2017).

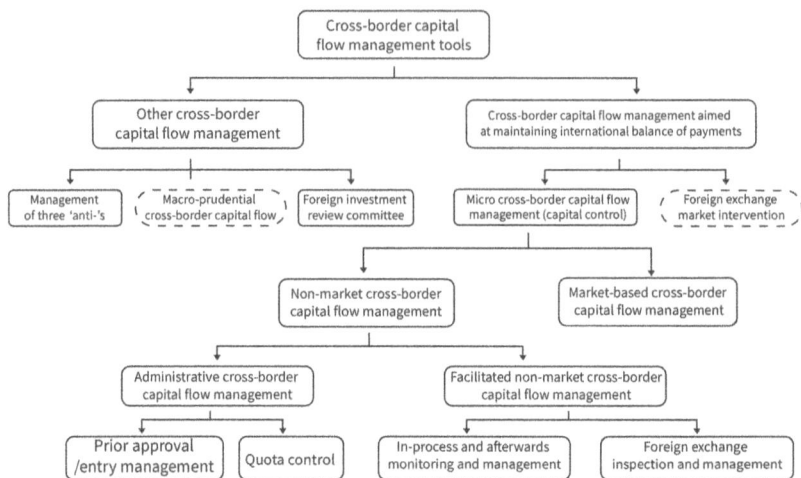

Figure 5-9: Cross-border capital flow management toolkit.
Source: Authors' original.

Pillar 2: Micro-management framework for cross-border capital flows

Based on the separation of macro- and micro-functions, the future micro-management of cross-border capital flows will no longer include the macro-control function of maintaining balance of payments. Instead, it will focus on capital account convertibility reform. This can help avoid policy reversals, provide a stable policy environment for the market, and improve policy transparency and credibility.

Gradually realise RMB capital account convertibility. The authorities should continue to push forward liberalisation of the capital account. In view of the potential risks, opening should be promoted steadily based on domestic and international situations. The liberalisation of capital inflows should be prioritised. Learning from the Organisation for Economic Co-operation and Development's approach, capital account convertibility can be achieved while the authorities retain prudential supervision or capital control over some high-risk transactions.

Increase the depth and breadth of the foreign exchange market. To better satisfy market needs for management of foreign exchange assets and liabilities, foreign exchange derivatives such as forwards, swaps and options should be improved. Increasing the variety of foreign exchange options and introducing foreign exchange futures in due course will meet market needs for more trading instruments. Introducing foreign currency exchange traded funds, margin trading and other transactions will increase the depth of the foreign exchange market. Other measures could also be implemented. These may include supporting domestic individuals' orderly participation in the foreign exchange market to meet investors' needs to diversify investments and manage exchange rate risks, relaxing restrictions on non-bank financial institutions (including securities firms and funds) so they may trade in the interbank foreign exchange market, and allowing qualified foreign entities to enter the domestic foreign exchange market.

Construct a new micro-management system based on the negative list approach. Current administration of foreign exchange should be streamlined. Based on the pre-established national treatment and negative list approach, most administrative procedures, such as approval requirements, should be abolished. Exchange restrictions on cross-border investment and financing should be cancelled gradually and the negative list reduced. On the other hand, operational and post-operational supervision should be strengthened, registration requirements for cross-border capital flow and financial transactions should be retained, the registration of contract information should be bolstered, and micro-agent solvency information should be collected periodically. In the future, negative list management will mainly apply to the following:

1. Foreign exchange business of financial institutions. Based on the risk levels of different businesses, no prior approval is required for low-risk businesses, while necessary thresholds should be set for higher-risk innovative businesses.
2. High-risk cross-border transactions. External debt, derivatives trading and other high-risk, high-leverage transactions should remain part of the negative list.
3. Improving the classified management of market entities, facilitating foreign exchange use by enterprises with good compliance records and implementing stricter prudential regulations over enterprises with poor compliance records, or those suspected of illegal activities.

Strengthen capacity building. This will be achieved through improving the operational and post-operational regulatory framework, strengthening the monitoring and early warning of abnormal and suspicious cross-border capital flows, implementing strict supervision and punishment measures, and increasing the cost of violating authenticity and compliance rules. To this end, future micro-supervision should focus on improving the four aspects of capacity building: 1) basic capacity (statistical reporting, process management, assessment and evaluation); 2) data analysis capacity (build irregular transaction screening capacity based on unified cross-border data platform and big data analysis tools, and detect the entities, items and territory of irregular transactions in a timely manner); 3) compliance regulation (self-discipline of banking institutions, regulators' meetings with financial institutions and window guidance); 4) capacity to gather information on the operation of systemically important financial institutions (regulators implement the principle of 'know the customers, know the business, and due diligence' and conduct on-site supervision of systemically important financial institutions and large multinational corporations to ensure comprehensive understanding of their operations).

Main conclusions and recommendations

First, the liberalisation and management of cross-border capital flows are connected. The '13th Five-Year Plan' gives a comprehensive summary on this topic. From an opening perspective, its intention is to 'facilitate two-way opening of the financial sector, realise RMB capital account convertibility in an orderly way, improve the convertibility and free usability of RMB'. From a management perspective, its intention is to 'strengthen the balance of payments monitoring' and 'improve the prudential management framework for external debt and capital flows'.

Second, with the implementation of market-oriented reform of the exchange rate regime, the importance of the macro-control function of cross-border capital flow management will be much reduced. Reform must focus on separating macro-management and micro-regulation functions and build a dual-pillar framework for cross-border capital flow management. During this process, both the policy transmission mechanism and the toolbox should see increased improvement.

Third, at the macro level, a macro-management framework for cross-border capital flows (see Figure 5-10) must be constructed. This should include the two dimensions of capital control and macroprudential management, while also accelerating improvements in the policy toolbox that serves macro objectives (see Table 5-7). These could include assessing the feasibility of adopting the Tobin tax (or similar measures) and other cross-border capital flow management systems. The Tobin tax has fewer distortions of resource allocation. This tax and similar approaches can not only enrich the policy toolbox, but also transform the foreign exchange management system and improve policy transparency. Additionally, a balance between macroprudential management and capital control should be maintained. Macroprudential management does not directly deal with imbalance of international payments, but has a significant role in addressing domestic and external economic balance. The monitoring, evaluation and stress testing for macroprudential management must be improved, and measures such as the Tobin tax and capital controls maintained as counter-cyclical adjustment and ex-post management tools.

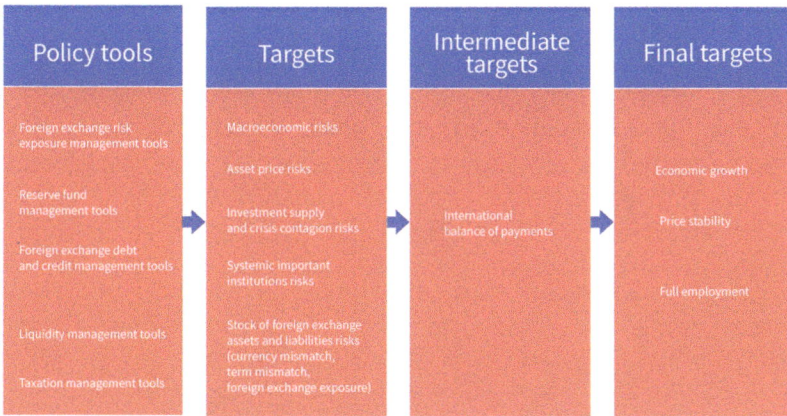

Figure 5-10: Transmission mechanism of the macro-management framework for cross-border capital flows.

Source: Authors' original.

Table 5-7: Policy tools for macro objectives

Policy tools	Operational targets	Intermediate objectives	Ultimate goals
Foreign currency risk exposure management tools	Macroeconomic risks	Balance of payments	Economic growth
Reserve management tools	Asset price risks		Price stability
Foreign currency loan management tools	Speculative supply or crisis contagion risks		Full employment
Liquidity management tools	Systemically important financial institutions risks		
Tax management tools	Foreign currency asset and liability risks (currency mismatch, maturity mismatch, foreign currency exposures)		

Fourth, the micro-management of cross-border capital flows should differentiate between regulation from macro control. Regulation should not include 'macro-control functions' and the regulatory system should be kept relatively stable. Future micro-management should focus on 'facilitation' and 'improvement'. Facilitation will promote capital account convertibility, facilitate trade and investment, and ensure the decisive role of the market in resource allocation. On the other hand, the approach of foreign exchange management should be improved to emphasise 'strict' regulation, change the focus from prior approval to operational and post-operational supervision, and strengthen authenticity and compliance rules. Other measures could include efforts to balance principle-based and rule-based supervision; improve banks' self-discipline and external supervision; enhance monitoring, analysis and early warning capacities; strengthen foreign exchange inspection; crack down on illegal activities; and build cross-departmental supervision and cooperation mechanisms.

Fifth, the micro-management of cross-border capital flows should differentiate between regulation and capital control. Capital controls should be temporary measures. Any such measure will lead to market distortion and increase transaction costs. Cross-border capital flow management should be used to buy time for other reforms. These may include reforms to improve monetary policy independence and achieve stable and rapid economic growth, curb capital outflows and dispose of financial risks, and help the private sector better adjust their assets and liabilities to adapt to more flexible exchange rates.

References

Brockmeijer, J., Marston, D. & Ostry, J. D. (2012). *Liberalizing capital flows and managing outflows.* International Monetary Fund. Retrieved from www.imf.org/external/np/pp/eng/2012/031612.pdf

Bruno, V., Shim, I. & Shin, H. S. (2015, June). *Comparative assessment of macro prudential policies* (Working Paper No. 502). Bank for International Settlements. Retrieved from www.bis.org/publ/work502.htm

Central Committee of the Communist Party of China. (2015, November). *Recommendations for the 13th Five-Year Plan for Economic and Social Development.* Beijing: People's Publishing House.

China Finance 40 Forum (CF40). (2017). *China financial reform report 2016 - cost and return analysis of RMB internationalization*. Beijing: China Financial Publishing House.

Coats, W. (2009). *Time for a new global currency. New Global Studies, 3*(1). doi.org/ 10.2202/1940-0004.1070

Collaborative Innovation Center of Financial Security (Southwestern University of Finance and Economics). (2016, March). *China financial security report 2015*. Beijing: China Financial Publishing House.

Corker, R. & Tseng, W. (1991). *Financial liberalization, money demand, and monetary policy in Asian countries* (Occasional Paper No. 84). International Monetary Fund.

Gilpin, R. (2003). *A postscript to the Asian financial crisis: The fragile international economic order. Cambridge Review of International Affairs, 16*(1), 79–88.

Guan, T. (2016). Policy options to deal with the shock of capital flows: Two 'impossible trinities'. *China Money, 6*.

International Monetary Fund (IMF). (2001). *Agreement of the International Monetary Fund*.

International Monetary Fund (IMF). (2009). *IMF annual report*. Retrieved from www.imf.org/-/media/Websites/IMF/imported-flagship-issues/external/ pubs/ft/ar/2009/eng/pdf/_ar09engpdf.ashx

International Monetary Fund (IMF). (2011). *Financial stability issues in emerging market and developing economies*. Retrieved from www.imf.org/external/np/ g20/pdf/110211.pdf

International Monetary Fund (IMF). (2016a). *Capital flows—review of experience with the institutional view*. Retrieved from www.imf.org/-/media/Files/ Publications/PP/PP5081-Capital-Flows-Review-of-Experience-with-the-Institutional-View.ashx

International Monetary Fund. (2016b). *Annual Report on Exchange Arrangements and Exchange Restrictions 2016*. Retrieved from www.imf. org/en/Publications/Annual-Report-on-Exchange-Arrangements-and-Exchange-Restrictions/Issues/2017/01/25/Annual-Report-on-Exchange-Arrangements-and-Exchange-Restrictions-2016-43741

Korinek, A. & Sandri, D. (2015). *Capital controls or macroprudential regulation?* (Working Paper No. 15/218). International Monetary Fund.

Kose, M. A., Prasad, E., Rogoff, K. & Wei, S. (2010). *Financial globalization and economic policies* (Working Paper No. 06/189). International Monetary Fund.

Krugman, P. (1995). *Increasing returns, imperfect competition and the positive theory of international trade.* Cambridge, MA: MIT Press.

Krugman, P. (1999). Balance sheets, the transfer problem, and financial crises. *International Tax and Public Finance, 6,* 459–472.

Li, L., Wang, B., Liu, X. & Hao, D. (2016). Short-term capital flows, monetary policy and financial stability. *Journal of Financial Research, 9,* 18–32. Retrieved from www.jryj.org.cn/CN/abstract/abstract173.shtml

Lin, Y. (2013, 21 July). *Why I do not support complete capital account liberalization.* Keynote speech at the CF40's 'Bi-week Roundtable' internal discussion. Retrieved from www.cf40.org.cn/plus/view.php?aid=7798

Masciandaro, D., Nieto, M. & Quintyn, M. (2009). Financial supervision in the EU: Is there convergence in the national architectures? *Journal of Financial Regulation and Compliance.* Retrieved from www.emeraldinsight.com/doi/abs/10.1108/13581980910952540

National Bureau of Statistics. (2016). *National GDP data.* Retrieved from data.stats.gov.cn/search.htm?s=GDP

Obstfeld, M. (1994). The logic of currency crises. *Cahiers Économiques et Monétaires, 43,* 189–213.

Obstfeld, M. (1996). Models of currency crises with self-fulfilling features. *European Economic Review, 40*(3–5), 1035–1047.

Pan, G. (2017). Policy framework and management approach of China's foreign exchange market. *Modern Bankers, 5.* Retrieved from www.cnki.com.cn/Journal/J-J6-DJRJ-2017-05.htm

People's Bank of China (PBC). (2012, 23 February). *Conditions are ripe for China to speed up opening of the capital account.* Retrieved from www.pbc.gov.cn/diaochatongjisi/116219/116221/116241/2860754/index.html

People's Bank of China (PBC). (2016, December). *2016 report on RMB internationalization.* Retrieved from www.pbc.gov.cn/goutongjiaoliu/113456/113469/3117603/index.html

Rey, H. (2015, May). *Dilemma not trilemma: The global financial cycle and monetary policy independence* (Working Paper No. 21162). National Bureau of Economic Research.

Ruggie, J. G. (1981). The politics of money. *Foreign Policy, 43.*

Saborowski, C., Sanya, S., Weisfeld, H. & Yepez, J. (2014). *Effectiveness of capital outflow restrictions* (Working Paper No. 14/8). International Monetary Fund.

State Administration of Foreign Exchange (SAFE). *Chinese balance of payments data.* Retrieved from www.safe.gov.cn/safe/tjsjkbcx/index.html

Sun, G. & Li, W. (2017). *Monetary policy, exchange rate and capital flow: From 'equilateral triangle' to 'non-equilateral triangle'* (Working Paper No. 2017/3). People's Bank of China.

Tian, J. (2003, 20 November). Providing settlement arrangements for individual RMB business of Hong Kong banks. Press conference of the People's Bank of China. *People's Daily*, p. 2. Retrieved from finance.sina.com.cn/g/20031120/0722526552.shtml

Tobin, J. (1998). Comments by Professor James Tobin. *Journal of Applied Econometrics, 12*(5), 647–650.

Viñals, J. & Moghadam, R. (2011). *The multilateral aspects of policies affecting capital flows.* International Monetary Fund. Retrieved from www.imf.org/external/np/pp/eng/2011/101311.pdf

Wen, Y. (2016). *RMB officials becomes the fifth currency included in SDR basket.* Retrieved from www.xinhuanet.com/politics/2016-10/01/c_129308907.htm

Yu, Y. (2016). *The last barrier – capital account liberalization and RMB internationalization.* Beijing: Orient Publishing Center.

6

Promoting China's Financial Market Reform and Innovation with Opening Policies

Xu Zhong,[1] Zhang Xuechun,[2] Cao Yuanyuan,[3]
Tang Yingwei[4] and Wan Tailei[5]

Reform and opening are mutually reinforcing. Reform inevitably requires opening and vice versa. Opening consists of two levels. The first is to attract foreign institutions and encourage domestic institutions to go overseas. The second is to develop domestic financial markets based on the development pattern of mature financial markets and adapt to international market rules and practices. This will ensure ultimate integration with the international financial market. The second level is actually a higher level of openness. China's financial market was established and developed after reform and opening was launched in 1978. Adhering to a market-oriented development philosophy and international patterns are the drivers for China's financial market prosperity. The first level of opening will not be successful without the second. And promoting the first level will propel the second level.

---

1   Director-General of Research Bureau, People's Bank of China (PBC).
2   Deputy Director-General of Monetary Policy Department II, PBC.
3   Staff at Financial Market Department, PBC.
4   Head of Strategic Planning Department, Shanghai Commercial Paper Exchange.
5   Head of International Department, National Association of Financial Market Institutional Investors.

As China's four decades of practice shows, the development of financial markets is faster when the development patterns of advanced financial markets and international rules are followed. Without these, development will be problematic and may reverse. Over the past four decades, China's financial market has grown from humble beginnings to achieve remarkable growth. This shows that China can only integrate with the international market through an understanding of the country's practical needs. With the continuous expansion and deepening of China's markets, the importance of opening is increasing—opening has become an indispensable part of reform.

Currently, it is particularly important to institute reform and open China's financial market. Only an open financial market can possess real breadth and depth. Such a financial system can form effective price signals, attract more capital and investors, and support development of the real economy. China has almost completely integrated into the global economy. The country also requires a stable and open financial market at every stage of development in order to fully integrate into the international financial market.

China is committed to becoming an advanced economy. This requires China to resolve structural problems in its financial market and establish an advanced financial system that matches its global status and supports sustainable development of the real economy. This financial system must be all-encompassing, well structured, efficient, stable, inclusive and competitive. To this end, China should promote reform and development through opening, respect and abide by the rules and norms of the international market, emphasise top-level design and policy coordination, and strengthen macroprudential regulation. On this basis, China should aim to open further and establish a healthy development pattern that pushes forward both domestic reform and liberalisation.

Part 1: Key drivers of China's financial market development

To construct a socialist market economy, China's financial market began from nothing after the reform and opening launched in 1978. China has since achieved remarkable success. It has formed a comprehensive multilevel financial system that covers the money, bond, stock, insurance, gold, foreign exchange and derivatives markets. As of the end of March 2017, bonds in custody amounted to CN¥65.9 trillion, ranking third globally and second in Asia. The amount of outstanding corporate bonds is the second largest globally and the largest in Asia. The interbank bond market has a complete series of products and diversified trading tools. It has become the main element of China's bond market, and perhaps its entire financial market. As of the end of 2016, the Shanghai and Shenzhen stock exchanges listed a combined total of 3,052 companies. Of these companies, A-share stocks numbered 3,034, with a total market value of CN¥55.68 trillion. According to statistics from the World Federation of Exchanges, the total market capitalisation of China's stock market in 2015 was second only to that of the United States (US).

China's financial market takes a different development path from developed countries

The development of China's financial market has been a successful process of promoting reform and development through opening. This opening process largely followed international financial market development patterns. Initially, China made some ineffective decisions and did not follow international patterns. The country encountered some problems and had to begin again. To analyse the current situation more effectively and determine the future prospects of China's financial market development, it is necessary to understand the history of China's financial market. Lessons can then be drawn from its experiences and mistakes.

Over hundreds of years, the financial markets of developed countries have encountered various problems and experienced both crises and improvements. In the US, the *Glass–Steagall Act* (introduced after the Great Depression in 1930) separated investment banking business from commercial banking in a strict sense. In the 1980s, the US passed the *Financial Institutions Reform, Recovery, and Enforcement Act* in response to the savings and loan crisis. The *Sarbanes–Oxley Act* was passed in the 1990s after the Enron scandal to strengthen corporate governance and audit standards and improve accounting guidelines. At the turn of this century, the rollout of the *Gramm–Leach–Bliley Act* marked the US financial industry's entry into an era of mixed operation. The *Dodd–Frank Wall Street Reform and Consumer Protection Act* was introduced after the 2008 global financial crisis to control systematic risks. History shows that US financial market legislation always follows crises or problems. The regulatory authorities analysed the causes of problems and then improved regulation at the legislative and institutional level.

China's financial market has taken a different development path from that of more mature countries and, therefore, it has its own characteristics. First, China started its development late. Only four decades have passed since the launch of economic reform in 1978. Second, the development is government led. China did not follow the steps of financial market evolution in other countries, instead following the requirements of its own economic and financial development. Third, the financial market is focused on serving the government's economic agenda. The Chinese Government was short of capital at the beginning of the reform and opening. When the government tried to issue bonds, this could only be done through compulsive apportionment. In the early 1990s, when the government attempted to reform state-owned enterprises, the Shanghai and Shenzhen stock exchanges were established to support the reform. Fourth, the development of China's financial market differs from its economic reform. Economic reform began outside the system. It was driven by the market and then expanded to other areas. However, China's financial market has taken a few wrong turns while serving the government's economic needs.

China's financial market was established in the absence of a sound credit system. According to economist Richard Hicks, the commercial prosperity of Western countries relies on three factors—currency, law and credit. In the early days of China's reform and opening, only collective credit, rather than individual credit, existed. Departments with more power had more creditworthiness. However, the development of financial markets must be built on individual credit, or significant problems will result. Notably, collective credit also played a vital role in the transition from a planned to a market economy. During this process, the individual credit system had not yet been fully established. With the continued development of accounting, credit reporting, credit rating and other systems in recent years, the individual credit system is gradually progressing, creating beneficial conditions for financial market development. Many problems arising in today's financial market are connected to deficiencies in individual credit and related supporting systems, such as accounting, auditing and rating.

Respecting market law is the key to financial market development

A review of some cases in China's financial market development history clearly shows that this development would have been more rapid if common patterns and international rules had been followed. Without these elements, the development process can encounter severe problems or even fail. When China's bond market was first established, the original intention of issuing bonds was to support the reform of state-owned enterprises. Some mistakes were made that led to major risk events in the 1980s and 1990s. In the 1980s, government bonds were administratively apportioned, and a unified national bond market had not yet been established. At that time, market prices and transaction prices of government bonds varied in different places. The Wuhan exchange and repurchase transactions in Tianjin both witnessed major risks. In terms of corporate bonds, the earliest issuers were enterprises affected by ineffective management and a lack of capital and needed guarantee by banks. This kind of bond issuance is not based on enterprises' creditworthiness, and the pricing was not market-oriented but administrated pricing, which clearly contrasts with the bond markets of developed countries. The earliest issuances of corporate bonds were conducted over bank counters. If a company defaulted, bondholders would ask banks for repayment even though such requests were unreasonable.

A typical case was the 'March 27 government bond futures incident' in 1996 before the 1997 Asian financial crisis. Wanguo Securities's investment in futures led to the company's collapse. It was the largest bond company at that time. The incident showed that the rollout of financial products did not fully consider market conditions or take a gradual approach. Rather, it was based on the arbitrary decisions of regulatory authorities. Several reasons lie behind the incident. First, China's interest rate was not market based. Second, the discount rates stipulated by the Ministry of Finance were not transparent. Third, the securities exchanges lacked an understanding of the risks related to bond futures. In short, the market was not ready for bond futures.

Such incidents drove the Chinese Government to develop a more unified, healthy and transparent market. In 1997, the State Council approved the establishment of the interbank bond market. The government paid more attention to experiences from the international market and followed the rules of market development. China's domestic bond market was dominated by natural persons and characterised by collective deal-making. Per the government's aim, the interbank bond market consisted mainly of institutional investors and that engage in over-the-counter transactions, and the market emphasised financial reporting, information disclosure, credit rating and other disciplinary mechanisms. In the past two decades, the market has developed rapidly and is now the world's third largest.

China's bond market achieves development through deepening reforms

The development of China's bond market is generally driven by social needs, not administrative authorities or ideologues. Progress was made through deepening reforms, not administrative intervention. The experience over the past two decades shows that a time of great challenges is usually the best time for reform. Only in difficult times can people reach consensus on reform more easily. The real solution is to deepen reform, rather than to step back—this is an important lesson drawn from the practice of China's bond market development.

First, if the bond market is to evolve to a higher level, it must adhere to a market-oriented direction. Administrative approval or other types of restrictions should not be imposed. Reducing administrative approval procedures does not mean relaxing market regulation. Instead, issuing corporate bonds strengthens, rather than relaxes, discipline on enterprises. In the past, companies only obtained loans from banks, but now they can have multiple investors. Historically, companies could default on debt, but now they cannot operate without good credit. If a company defaults on its debt, it will be difficult for the company to issue new bonds. If an issuer releases false information, investors may sell their bonds immediately and the issuer may not find new investors. While reducing administrative approvals, the government should also strengthen market regulation—these can be achieved simultaneously. An important lesson for the development of the bond market is to reduce implicit guarantee of repayment by the government. In the past, whoever approved bond issuance had to bear the risks. Later, the regulators began to exercise control and essentially stopped approving new issuance. No approval means no risk. However, other problems arose. Companies could not raise capital from the financial market. To address the underdevelopment of direct financing in China, the PBC established the National Association of Financial Market Institutional Investors (NAFMII) in 2007. The aim was to promote the development of corporate credit bonds using market forces. The direction of development was to strengthen market discipline while reducing administrative approvals. Such market constraints include information disclosure, auditing of financial statements and various arrangements for bond custody and clearing.

Second, a significant breakthrough in the past 10 years is the development of institutional investors. Individual investors can invest in bonds through funds, asset management products offered by banks and other institutional investors. Institutional investors can manage their risks more effectively and obtain higher returns. Institutional investors can identify the risks of financial products and bond products in a more professional manner than can most retail investors. The easiest way for retail investors to invest is to purchase government bonds at banks, but these rarely achieve high returns. With the help of institutional investors, consumer savings can be channelled to the interbank bond market through a wide range of products. The bond market can achieve faster development and retail investors who lack knowledge about the bond market can avoid being cheated. As bond investors are mostly institutional investors, the bond market differs from the stock market in the custody, trading, clearing and settlement approaches.

Third, bond market development should comply with and serve the diversified needs for investment and financing of the real economy. Although China's bond market has a great number of products, it still falls short of the needs of the real economy. To meet these needs, new types of corporate credit bonds have been rolled out, including capital supplement bonds for the banks along with credit and asset-backed bonds. These products are not innovation for innovation's sake; they have been introduced to meet the needs of the real economy and to improve the financial market's ability to serve the real economy. This is also a major difference between China's bond market and some Western bond markets.

Additionally, in the interbank bond market the government has minimal influence. More intermediaries and self-regulatory organisations have been empowered to take on more important roles. For example, NAFMII was established in the banking industry and bond market in 2007. NAFMII currently has more than 3,000 members. Some important financial products are not developed by the PBC or other regulators, but by market participants. All market participants meet with lawyers and accountants to discuss proposals of new products. After balancing all interests and conflicts and assessing the risks, the design and rules of the product will be developed and registered with the regulators. Regulators mainly review the procedures of product development and the new product's compliance with risk control regulations. Regulators will also check whether the product proposal reflects a consensus among all market players. Market forces play an increasingly important role in innovation. There is no administrative approval during the registration process, only issuers and investors are involved. Issuers require more convenient financing, investors require more secure protection, and a balance between the various interests will be reached in the end. Such a products design process is more sophisticated and mature than one led by government officials. This is also an important factor that led to the success of the Chinese bond market. China should continue in this direction and aim for greater innovation in bond products.

Overall, China's bond market has basically followed the development patterns of the world's major bond markets over the past 30 years. This is why China has achieved substantial progress. Despite these achievements, China's financial market has prominent structural problems compared to the markets in developed economies. To develop its financial market further, China must promote reform and development continuously through opening, while also adhering to the market-oriented philosophy and development patterns of international financial markets.

Part 2: Assessing the opening of the major financial submarkets

China's financial market does not have a long history and neither does the opening process. The bond and foreign exchange markets were opened up relatively late (in 2005 and 2004 respectively). Although the stock market opened up first (in the early 1990s), the degree of its openness was quite limited and the primary market remains closed. Although the bond market has had a higher degree of openness, it is still well below the level of openness of the bond markets in developed countries. This part summarises the openness of the bond, stock and foreign exchange markets and analyses problems in the opening process of each market.

The bond market

China's bond market began to open in 2005, when international development institutions such as the International Finance Corporation and the Asian Development Bank were approved to issue RMB bonds in the interbank bond market. The Pan Asia Fund and Asian Debt Fund were also allowed to invest in the interbank bond market.

After the 2008 global financial crisis, the USD and other major currencies experienced drastic fluctuations. To reduce exchange rate risks, there was an increasing demand from domestic and foreign enterprises to use the RMB for cross-border trade settlement. In this context, cross-border RMB business began to thrive. The rapid development of cross-border RMB settlement created a need to invest offshore RMB back into China. In 2010, the PBC allowed foreign central banks and monetary authorities, RMB clearing banks in Hong Kong and Macao, and foreign participating banks to invest in China's interbank bond market. When these institutions were approved to invest, they were able to engage in interbank market bond business, but within a certain limit. With the development of cross-border RMB business, the scope of overseas institutions that are allowed to invest gradually expanded to include sovereign wealth funds; international financial institutions; RMB clearing banks in regions other than Hong Kong and Macao; and insurance companies in Hong Kong, Taiwan and Singapore.

Since 2013, as the scope of RMB cross-border business and international use gradually expanded, the RMB's international status rose significantly. The bond market opened at a quicker rate and adopted a more market-oriented approach.

In terms of bond issuance, international development institutions, overseas non-financial enterprises, financial institutions, foreign governments and issuers have issued RMB bonds in the interbank bond market. In 2013, Daimler issued CN¥5-billion worth of RMB bonds in China, demonstrating that foreign non-financial institutions could raise money with RMB bonds. In 2015, the Hong Kong and Shanghai Banking Corporation Limited and the Bank of China (Hong Kong) Limited were allowed to issue RMB bonds in the interbank bond market, a first-time issuance by international commercial banks following international development institutions and foreign non-financial enterprises. In 2015, Canada's British Columbia and South Korea completed registration for

CN¥9 billion of RMB bonds. In 2016, the World Bank issued special drawing right (SDR)–denominated bonds of CN¥500 million. This is strategically significant for expanding SDR use, promoting RMB internationalisation, and opening China's financial market. At the end of April 2017, foreign issuers of all types had issued a total of CN¥7.81 billion of RMB bonds. Domestic institutions issuing bonds overseas are also making progress.

Regarding investment, the scope of foreign institutions and variety of products in the domestic bond market are expanding constantly, and management is becoming more market oriented. The Qualified Foreign Institutional Investor (QFII) and RMB Qualified Foreign Institutional Investor (RQFII) schemes allowed foreign investors to conduct spot transactions in the interbank bond market in 2013. In 2015, policies were introduced to facilitate overseas banking institutions' entry into the interbank market. The entry process was simplified to a filing system; the investment cap was lifted; and the investment scope was extended to include spot transaction, bond repurchase, bond lending and bond forwards, interest rate swaps, forward rate agreements and other business approved by the PBC. In 2016, the PBC issued Notice No. 3, allowing all types of financial institutions registered legally overseas and long-term institutional investors such as pension funds to invest in the interbank bond market through the filing system. The notice also allowed issuers to decide on the size of their investment independently. Currently, the secondary interbank bond market has been opened completely to qualified foreign investors. And the same standards are applied to domestic and foreign institutions. As long as they have the proper licences and their products fulfil all requirements, they can enter the interbank bond market through the filing system without approval from administrative departments. Moreover, there are no quotas on a single foreign institution or on the total investment of all foreign institutions. The size of investment is decided entirely by foreign institutions themselves, and the PBC implements only macroprudential management. Additionally, no restriction exists regarding the source of RMB funds for foreign institutions to invest in the interbank bond market. They can be derived from RMB cross-border business, or the onshore or offshore foreign exchange markets. However, if foreign institutions want to obtain RMB from the onshore foreign exchange market, they must follow foreign exchange regulations regarding remittance, repatriation, purchase and settlement procedures. Currently, there are about 480 foreign investors in the market, with a total investment of over CN¥800 billion.

As China's bond market continues to open, major bond indices across the world have begun to consider including the Chinese market in their coverage. In March 2017, Bloomberg launched two new hybrid, fixed income indices that include RMB-denominated China bonds and global indices: the Global Aggregate + China Index, which combines the Global Aggregate Index with the treasury and policy bank bond component of the China Aggregate Index; and the EM (Emerging Market) Local Currency Government + China Index, which combines the EM Local Currency Government Index and the treasury bond component of the China Aggregate Index. Earlier, in 2004, Bloomberg had introduced the China Aggregate Index, which included China's onshore bonds, but the aforementioned hybrid indices were the first time that onshore RMB bonds were included in Bloomberg's global indices offering. Citigroup later announced that China's onshore bonds were qualified to enter its emerging markets and regional government bond indices, including the Emerging Markets Government Bond Index (EMGBI), Asian Government Bond Index (AGBI) and the Asia Pacific Government Bond Index. Citigroup also announced that if Chinese bonds continued to meet the necessary criteria over the next three months, Citigroup would eventually include China in the three indices (i.e. by February 2018) and introduce EMGBI-Capped and AGBI-Capped due to the large size of the Chinese market, with Chinese bonds weighing up to 10 per cent and 20 per cent respectively. According to Goldman Sachs, if Chinese bonds were included in all three major global bond indices (Citigroup, JP Morgan Chase and Barclays), the ratio of foreign holdings would increase from about 4 per cent at present to about 15 per cent, and US$250 billion would be expected to flow into the Chinese market.

In May 2017, the PBC and Hong Kong Monetary Authority jointly announced plans to connect the Hong Kong and mainland bond markets in the 'Bond Connect'. Bond Connect signifies that China's interbank bond market is opening further, but is still subject to existing capital account management, qualification requirements for medium- and long-term institutional investors, requirements on the collection of investment and trading information, and other regulations. Bond Connect provides a new channel for foreign institutions to enter the market more efficiently. It can do so with the help of increased connectivity between domestic and foreign infrastructures in a mode that is well accepted in the international bond market. The experience of other countries shows that foreign investors can either enter the market by opening accounts in the domestic market, or by investing in the country's bond market through the connectivity of infrastructure. The first model places higher requirements on foreign investors who need to possess a comprehensive and in-depth understanding of a country's bond market regulatory system and market environment. The second model has become common practice globally. It enables foreign investors to access the global bond market conveniently via infrastructure connectivity and multilevel custody. Bond Connect operates according to the second model. By connecting the infrastructure of two bond markets, international investors can participate easily in the mainland bond market without changing their business practices, provided they comply with the regulations of the mainland market. Bond Connect will be implemented step by step with the overall planning and deployment of China's financial market liberalisation. To meet the current needs of international investors to invest in the mainland bond market, the current priority is 'Northbound' trading, which will be expanded to 'Southbound' trading in the future.

Compared with international practice, China's bond market still has a long way to go. At the end of 2016, overseas holdings of US Treasury bonds accounted for about 38.1 per cent of the total investment, and Japanese Government bonds for around 10.5 per cent. Foreign holdings in China's bond market accounted for less than 2 per cent and the lack of diversity in product structures is reflected in the high proportion of treasury and policy bank bonds. China's bond market has yet to be included in major international bond indices.

The stock market

China's stock market started to open in the early 1990s when the country's capital account was not yet open. To develop a channel for domestic companies to raise funds from overseas and facilitate foreign investors to invest in the domestic market, the State Council approved the Shanghai and Shenzhen stock exchanges to test issuing B-shares. In 1992, the B-share market was officially established. B-shares, also known as special RMB shares, are denominated in RMB and subscribed and traded in foreign currencies at the Shanghai and Shenzhen stock exchanges. Companies listed in the B-share market are all registered in China. Before February 2001, the B-share market was only open to foreign investors. It was then opened to domestic investors.

To further expand the channel for overseas financing and enhance the status of Chinese enterprises abroad, the Joint Working Group on Mainland–Hong Kong Securities Affairs was established in July 1992 with the approval of the State Council. Its main task was to provide consultations on state-owned enterprises going public in Hong Kong. After concluding the negotiations and completing the corresponding institutional arrangements, Tsingtao Brewery successfully issued H-shares and was listed on the Hong Kong Stock Exchange in July 1993, becoming China's first state-owned enterprise to list overseas. Since then, China has experienced a wave of mainland enterprises going public in the overseas market. In December 2012, the China Securities Regulatory Commission (CSRC) issued the 'Regulatory Guidelines in Relation to the Document Submission and Review Procedure for Overseas Stocks Issuance and Listing by Joint Stock Companies', which further strengthened supervision on domestic companies applying to issue shares and publicly list overseas.

With the gradual opening of the capital account, China introduced the QFII and Qualified Domestic Institutional Investor (QDII) schemes. As transitional arrangements, QFII and QDII are special ways to open the securities market orderly and prudently in countries and regions where the capital account is not yet fully opened. In December 2002, the CSRC and the PBC jointly issued the 'Interim Provisions on the Administration of the Domestic Securities Investments by Qualified Foreign Institutional Investors', and the first trade by QFII was made in July 2003. To open the capital account further, achieve a more balanced RMB exchange rate and give domestic investors the opportunity to participate in the global market, the QDII scheme was officially put into practice in July 2006, when the State Administration of Foreign Exchange (SAFE) approved a US$500 million quota to the Bank of Communications. In recent years, regulatory authorities have gradually eased qualification requirements and foreign exchange management and have raised investment quotas continuously. By the end of March 2017, SAFE had approved 280 QFIIs with an investment quota of US$90.3 billion and 132 QDIIs with an investment quota of US$90 billion.

In recent years, with the accelerated internationalisation of the RMB and liberalisation of the capital account, the depth and breadth of China's stock market opening has increased rapidly. In December 2011, the CSRC, PBC and SAFE jointly issued the 'Measures for Pilot Domestic Securities Investment Made by RQFII of Fund Management Companies and Securities Companies'. This allowed the Hong Kong subsidiaries of qualified fund and securities companies to conduct RQFII business. The early pilot quota was set at about CN¥20 billion. By the end of 2016, RQFII global pilot zones had been increased to 18, with a quota cap of CN¥1.5 trillion. By the end of March 2017, 182 RQFIIs had been approved and their investment quota reached CN¥541.4 billion. In November 2014, the PBC issued the 'Notice of the People's Bank of China on Matters Concerning the Overseas Securities Investment by RMB QDIIs', allowing qualified investors to invest in RMB-denominated products in overseas financial markets with their own or RMB funds raised onshore. Different from the approval system for QDII's quota, RMB Qualified Domestic Institutional Investor's (RQDII) quota is based on the amount of funds they actually raise.

To promote two-way opening and the sustainable development of the mainland and Hong Kong capital markets and increase the overall level of openness while integrating with the international market, the State Council approved the 'Shanghai–Hong Kong Stock Connect' in April 2014. After six months of preparation, the CSRC and Securities and Futures Commission of Hong Kong (SFC) issued a notice to officially launch the Shanghai–Hong Kong Stock Connect in November 2014. Further, to strengthen financial cooperation between the mainland and Hong Kong markets and to capture the regional advantages of the Shenzhen and Hong Kong stock exchanges, the State Council officially passed the 'Implementation Plan for Shenzhen-Hong Kong Stock Connect' in August 2016. In December 2016, the CSRC and SFC issued a notice to officially launch the Shenzhen–Hong Kong Stock Connect. Since then, qualified domestic individuals and institutional investors can trade stocks directly in the Hong Kong market, and foreign investors can trade stocks directly in the Shanghai and Shenzhen stock exchanges. Currently, both the Shanghai–Hong Kong Stock Connect and Shenzhen–Hong Kong Stock Connect are operating in a smooth and orderly manner, and cross-border capital inflows and outflows are approximately equal. China has achieved a cross-border trading system with proper regulation.

As the mainland and Hong Kong markets continue to deepen cooperation in financial products and services, in May 2015, the CSRC and the SFC announced plans for the joint development of the fund market. They signed a Memorandum of Understanding on Mutual Recognition of Funds (MRF) between the mainland and Hong Kong, and the CSRC simultaneously issued the corresponding 'Interim Provisions on the Administration of Recognized Hong Kong Funds'. In December 2015, the first seven mainland–Hong Kong MRFs were registered with the CSRC and SFC. In January 2017, the mainland–Hong Kong MRF service platform was launched. As new initiatives to open the capital market, the MRF, Shanghai–Hong Kong Stock Connect and Shenzhen–Hong Kong Stock Connect could complement each other, attract long-term capital and deepen capital market opening. By the end of February 2017, Hong Kong funds issued and sold on the mainland had generated a net outward remittance of CN¥7.3 billion, and mainland funds issued and sold in Hong Kong had a net inward remittance of CN¥97.45 million.

With increasing capital account convertibility, China's stock market is becoming more open, and its structure and mechanisms are becoming more diversified. In terms of the primary market, B-shares and H-shares have provided channels for domestic enterprises to raise capital overseas and for foreign investors to invest in domestic companies. Regarding the secondary market, schemes like QFII and RQFII have facilitated capital inflows, while QDII and RQDII schemes have facilitated capital outflows. Mechanisms like the MRF, Shanghai–Hong Kong Stock Connect and Shenzhen–Hong Kong Stock Connect have facilitated the two-way flow of capital, catering to the needs of various types of investors.

However, China's stock market is not as open as its international counterparts. At the end of 2014, the total market capitalisation of companies listed in London was £1.7 trillion, of which 54 per cent was held by overseas investors, a significant increase from 30.7 per cent in 1998. Foreign holdings reached 16 per cent in the US stock market, the world's largest stock market. Shares held by foreign investors in the South Korean stock market have remained at a constant level of over 30 per cent. Although foreign capital can now enter China's A-share market, the combined shares held by foreign investors through schemes such as QFII, RQFII, the Shanghai–Hong Kong Stock Connect and Shenzhen–Hong Stock Connect totalled less than 5 per cent in 2017.

The foreign exchange market

China's interbank foreign exchange market began to open in 2004, with the Bank of China (Hong Kong) and the Macau branch of the Bank of China entering the market first. With the introduction of cross-border RMB settlement business in 2009, the interbank foreign exchange market opened to foreign clearing banks with offshore RMB business. In 2015, the PBC allowed foreign central banks (monetary authorities), other official reserve management institutions, international financial organisations and sovereign wealth funds to participate in China's interbank foreign exchange market through agents, direct market access and other channels. They were allowed to conduct various types of foreign exchange trading, including spot, forwards, swaps and options, without quota restrictions. In January 2016, the PBC allowed internationally influential and regionally representative foreign banks involved in large-scale RMB selling and buying business to enter the interbank foreign exchange market. These banks could now participate in various types of foreign exchange trading, including spot, forwards, swaps and options. In February 2017, to help foreign investors participating in China's interbank bond market better manage their foreign exchange risk, qualified settlement agents were allowed to conduct foreign exchange derivatives business for foreign investors. They had to follow the principle of conducting trading based on real needs; however, foreign investors were only allowed to hedge foreign exchange risk exposure caused by investing in the interbank bond market with inward remittances. So far, China's interbank foreign exchange market has achieved varying degrees of openness for different types of investors. It now covers a full range of trading products and is more internationalised than ever. The entry of foreign investors has not only helped trading entities in the interbank foreign exchange market become more diverse, but is also an important force that enhances market liquidity and integration. By the end of May 2017, 66 foreign institutions were participating in China's interbank foreign exchange market, including 18 overseas RMB clearing banks, 19 foreign participating banks and 29 foreign central banks.

Apart from the introduction of different types of investors, China has also focused on developing direct and regional trading to further open the interbank foreign exchange market. To support RMB cross-border trade settlement, direct trading between the RMB, Malaysian ringgit and Russian ruble was launched in 2010, bypassing the USD cross rates. In 2014, RMB–Kazakhstani tenge interbank trading was launched. This bilateral direct exchange rate formation mechanism reduced trading costs and improved market transparency. To facilitate RMB internationalisation and implementation of the Belt and Road Initiative, in 2016, the interbank foreign exchange market launched direct trading mechanisms between the RMB and 11 currencies, including the United Arab Emirates dirham, South African rand and Saudi Arabian riyal. At present, 25 currency pairs exist in the interbank RMB foreign exchange market. This covers not only major international reserve currencies like the British pound and Japanese yen, but also the currencies of countries involved in the Belt and Road Initiative. In 2016, the trading value of these currencies amounted to nearly CN¥50 billion, twice the size of the previous year.

The interbank foreign exchange market is opening at a steady pace. It is cooperating with international mainstream institutions to construct a community of common interests and achieve gradual deployment in the global financial market. In 2015, following the Sino–US Economic and Strategic Dialogue and discussions between Chinese and German leaders, the China Foreign Exchange Trade System (CFETS) signed agreements with the Chicago Mercantile Exchange Group and the Deutsche Bank. These agreements clarified the shared objectives of achieving interconnectivity in financial infrastructure and financial products (such as exchange rate products) and of developing RMB-denominated offshore spot and derivative exchange rate products.

The interbank foreign exchange market is also actively promoting the internationalisation strategy, aiming at building a global service network, improving international financial service infrastructure and establishing a market with a higher degree of openness. Since January 2016, trading time in the market was extended to 23:30 Beijing time, covering European trading hours and part of US trading hours. This has facilitated the involvement of foreign investors. The service support time for all types of markets was also extended accordingly, enhancing the ability to serve global participants. Since 2015, the CFETS has released RMB exchange rate data based on the International Monetary Fund's (IMF) Special Data Dissemination Standard and RMB reference rates, providing pricing references to the IMF and other international organisations. In particular, since December 2015, the CFETS has compiled and issued the CFETS index, which has gained a widespread influence in the domestic and international markets.

The openness of China's foreign exchange market is much lower than that of advanced economies. For example, about 70 per cent of the trading volume in London's foreign exchange market—the world's largest—comes from foreign institutions. Seven out of the top 10 traders are non-British institutions, and the participants are very diversified and include multinational corporations, investment banks, mutual funds, hedge funds, foreign exchange funds and insurance companies. As for China, foreign investors participating in the interbank foreign exchange market only account for around 10 per cent of total investors, and their trading volume is less than 1 per cent. Further, the variety of foreign participants in the Chinese market is very limited, with banks being the only type of commercial institution participating.

Assessing the openness of China's financial market

Overall assessment

Although China's financial market is less open compared to other developed markets, its pace of opening has attracted worldwide attention.

In terms of the onshore market, China's stock, bond and foreign exchange markets have all opened up, but the degree of openness varies. The bond market has the highest degree of openness, followed by the stock market and then the foreign exchange market. In the primary market, although nonresidents cannot issue shares in the domestic stock market, various types of nonresidents (such as international development institutions, foreign non-financial enterprises, financial institutions and foreign governments) can issue bonds in the interbank market to raise funds. In the secondary market, the stock market introduced the QFII scheme in 2002, and then the RQFII scheme, Shanghai–Hong Kong Stock Connect and Shenzhen–Hong Kong Stock Connect. The interbank bond market has been fully opened to qualified foreign investors. The same entry standards are applied to both overseas and domestic institutions. Investors are not subject to any quota, but are subject to macroprudential management implemented by the PBC. Foreign investors participating in the interbank bond market can also participate in foreign exchange derivatives trading based on real demand.

The scale and geographic scope of the offshore market is expanding, and the products and participants in the offshore market are becoming increasingly diversified. Since 2010, the overseas offshore RMB market has developed steadily and rapidly with Hong Kong as the centre. A variety of RMB products have emerged, including credit, foreign exchange, bonds, funds and forwards. Trading activities are also very dynamic. The balance of RMB deposits in major offshore markets totalled about CN¥1.12 trillion at the end of 2016 (People's Bank of China, 2017). Fourteen locations, including New Zealand, London, Frankfurt, Seoul, Paris, Luxembourg, Doha, Toronto and Sydney, now have RMB clearing banks, covering Asia, Africa, America, Europe and Oceania. However, there is a spread between onshore and offshore RMB products and RMB exchange rates, which shows that capital control still exists and that financial market openness is still limited.

Regarding capital account convertibility, an increasing number of items under the capital account are gradually becoming convertible, and investment in the primary market is being liberalised at a steady pace. According to the classification of capital account transactions by the IMF's 'Annual Report on Exchange Arrangements and Exchange Restrictions' (seven major categories and 40 items), 37 items in China are fully convertible, basically convertible or partially convertible, accounting for 92.5 per cent of all items (see Chapter 5). Inconvertible items concentrate in the domestic primary financial market, which is still off-limits to nonresidents. Partially convertible items with more restrictions mostly relate to trading in the secondary market, which is not yet fully opened to the outside world.

Problems of the major financial submarkets in the process of reform and opening

Overall, the financial submarkets have different levels of openness, and China's financial market still has plenty of room to open to foreign investors. Market access for foreign investors and capital flows are still subject to many restrictions. Moreover, China's market system, market rules and regulations still need to gear up to international standards, which directly affects the participation of foreign investors in China's domestic market.

The bond market. Although the bond market is the most open market in China's financial system, the breadth and depth of its openness is still far from desirable. In particular, the rules and institutions of China's financial market differ significantly from those in the international market, and foreign issuers and investors often find it inconvenient to participate in the Chinese market. Some deep-rooted problems are hidden beneath the surface, damping the spirit of issuers and investors both at home and abroad.

First, China's accounting and auditing standards have caused much inconvenience for foreign issuers and have raised the cost of issuing bonds in the domestic market. According to existing regulations, the financial statements disclosed by overseas institutions should follow China's accounting standards, or equivalent standards as approved by the

Ministry of Finance. They should also be audited by accounting firms with securities and futures business qualifications in China, unless their country or region of origin has signed an agreement on the equivalence of public oversight over CPAs and auditing with China's Ministry of Finance. As Hong Kong is the only place that meets the aforementioned accounting and auditing requirements, foreign issuers from other countries or regions have to re-prepare their financial statements if they want to issue bonds in China. This has greatly constrained market development.

Second, China's rating industry lacks credibility. Therefore, it cannot meet the needs of international investors. China's rating services began late and are plagued by problems such as insufficient inspection on default rates, unrealistically high credit ratings and lack of ability to differentiate between bonds of varying quality. It is common practice for rating agencies to 'assign the rating based on the price' and to 'set the price based on the rating'. In China, enterprises with high ratings make up a significantly high proportion of the total. For example, enterprises with AA– or above constitute 97.13 per cent of all enterprises, much higher than the levels in the US, Japan and other countries. Conversely, enterprises with low ratings comprise a very small proportion of the total. As more enterprises end up with high ratings, enterprises with the same credit rating can have different risk levels, and it is difficult to distinguish the credit risks of enterprises with the same credit rating. When international investors allocate their assets globally, they develop their risk control system based on global rating standards. These are not shared by Chinese rating agencies. Concerns over China's rating quality prevent investment in China's bond market. In regard to bond issuers, as foreign issuers are usually experienced issuing entities, requiring them to hire unfamiliar Chinese rating agencies to undertake another rating would increase the cost of issuing bonds in China.

Third, market participants are subject to entry filing, one-level custody and centralised trading in China's bond market, which differs significantly from the international practice of investor suitability system, multilevel custody and decentralised trading. This situation has led to many technical obstacles for foreign investors investing in China. When the bond market opened up in 2005, foreign investors were required to comply with domestic regulations regarding market entry, trading, custody and settlement. Due to differences in the legal system, as well as in trading and settlement habits, foreign investors have encountered many technical problems, resulting in a slow pace of opening. In terms of filing for entry, foreign investors can only open an account after they submit a filing notice with the PBC's Shanghai headquarters via a settlement agent. In terms of transactions, the natural evolution of overseas markets has led to the formation of a hierarchal structure of dealer-to-dealer and dealer-to-customer trading. Within this structure, ordinary investors trade mainly through dealers. However, the Chinese market is flat and market makers have not developed enough, meaning that the ratio of one-on-one transactions among investors is especially high. In terms of settlement, the international market has adopted a multilevel custodian system, in line with the structure of trading. Investors need to open a nominal account in a custodian bank, and the custodian bank opens a custodial account in a central depository. With this model, the custodian bank can provide investors with a series of post-trade services, such as custody, clearing and settlement, and accounting reconciliation. In the one-level custodian system in China, investors must open an account directly at a central securities depository, and the settlement agents will provide trading and settlement services, but not all post-trade services. As the central depository deals directly with all investors, it is unable to cater to every investor's need. In terms of the settlement cycle, the overseas market is generally around T + 3, due to layered trading and multilevel custody, while the domestic market is generally T + 0, as the flattened structure enables higher settlement efficiency. This also creates unease among foreign investors.

Fourth, there is a limited variety of foreign exchange and derivative products related to bonds, which has slowed the opening process. Foreign institutions lack hedging instruments against exchange rate and interest rate risks when they invest in RMB bonds. Meanwhile, China's derivatives market is still at an early stage of development, with a small market size, homogenous participants and many technical obstacles for foreign investors. When foreign institutions invest in fixed income products, they usually develop a systematic trading strategy (called FICC) that integrates fixed income products, commodities and currency products. However, in China, different products have different levels of openness to foreign investors. The bond market opened up ahead of the derivatives market and the foreign exchange market. In this case, foreign investors cannot use derivatives and foreign exchange instruments effectively to develop their investment strategies.

Fifth, international cooperation on financial market infrastructure can be improved further. Foreign institutions involved in the domestic market have to deal with very complex technical details due to the lack of unified and transparent rules and institutions. The adoption of a case-by-case model can destabilise foreign investor expectations. Further, China's financial market infrastructure cannot fully meet the needs of foreign institutions. International electronic trading platforms are very developed after years of market competition, through which foreign investors can monitor market movements, place orders and conduct transactions. However, China's trading terminals lag behind in terms of language service and convenience. The major international bond markets have formed a multidimensional network with multilevel custody arrangements, enabling investors to access the global market easily, while providing them with services such as margin trading, data and research. In the process of opening, China must integrate further with international infrastructure.

The stock market. Securities investment has adopted a channelled approach to opening and is yet to open up completely. Although A-shares have been included in MSCI's EMs review list since 2014, it was not until June 2017 that MSCI announced that it would incorporate A-shares into the MSCI EM Index starting in June 2018 (MSCI, 2017). The A-shares will only account for 0.7 per cent of the index, far below China's proportion of economic size, trade volume and stock capitalisation globally (14 per cent, 14 per cent and 15 per cent respectively).

In terms of investment, although the stock market introduced QFII as early as 2002 and gradually extended to RQFII, the Shanghai–Hong Kong Stock Connect, the Shenzhen–Hong Kong Stock Connect and other mechanisms, foreign investors entering China's stock market are still subject to many restrictions. The QFII scheme imposes a quota for monthly capital redemption, and pre-approval by exchanges is required for financial products related to A-shares. Moreover, the QFII and RQFII schemes do not share unified standards for market access. The requirements for entry are high, and the scope of investors qualified to apply is limited. Long-term foreign capital that entered the domestic market through the QFII or RQFII schemes is restricted in areas such as quotas and liquidity. Such restrictions may reduce the enthusiasm of long-term investors and affect the abilities of such schemes to improve investor structure, promote long-term investment and enhance the governance of listed companies.

Individual investors abroad can only invest in underlying stocks listed in the Shanghai and Shenzhen exchanges via the Shanghai–Hong Kong Stock Connect and Shenzhen–Hong Kong Stock Connect.

In terms of financing, the development of bi-directional cross-border financing is not balanced. Foreign enterprises are not yet allowed to engage in equity financing in the A-share market. Although domestic enterprises can now raise money overseas through the H-share market without much obstruction, the approval system for overseas refinancing is not capable of seamless convergence with fast tracks such as lightning placement. The B-share market has basically lost its financing capability for now.

The foreign exchange market. The principle of 'trading on real needs' has somewhat limited further opening of the foreign exchange market. At present, the domestic foreign exchange market is a regulated market based on the principle of servicing real demand, while the international market has no such principle. Data analysis shows that less than 10 per cent of trading volume in the international market is driven by real trade. Based on the principle of real needs, the interbank foreign exchange market has been prudent when engaging foreign investors. Although foreign central banks and clearing banks can now enter the market, investment banks, commercial banks, insurance institutions, pension funds, hedge funds and large enterprises are still not allowed. This problem is also reflected in the structure of domestic investors, which is dominated by commercial banks, with non-bank financial institutions and non-financial enterprises accounting for a relatively small proportion. The limited type and number of market participants leads to similar trading behaviour. It also homogenises market demands and lowers the demand for foreign exchange derivatives. Further, the volume of trading in the domestic market lags far behind the international level.

To facilitate initiatives such as the Belt and Road Initiative launched in recent years, the CFETS introduced dozens of new currency pairs in a short period. However, the participants have not been very active, leading to a low trading volume and liquidity shortage. The trading between the RMB and non-US currencies accounted for a market share of less than 5 per cent. Small currencies that saw active trading was concentrated in China's neighbouring countries or developed economies, while the remaining small currencies remained quiet. Regional currencies, such as the Kazakhstani tenge, were basically not traded at all.

Financial infrastructure. The organisation of China's financial infrastructure is markedly different from that of the international market. The international market usually uses a multiple-level custodian system and a more developed market maker system. China's financial infrastructure is replete with Chinese characteristics and tailored to China's national condition, such as the fact that China's market is still at an early developmental stage and the governance of companies remains imperfect. Because of this, China's financial infrastructure is relatively centralised. To address the imperfections of companies' governance structures and the risk of clients' securities being misappropriated, as well as enhance information monitoring, improve transparency and provide a normalised trading platform, the interbank bond market has constructed a unified electronic trading platform for bond custody and settlement, implemented real-name centralised custody and one-on-one bidding. Therefore, China's centralised infrastructure is well adapted to the country's economic and financial environment. Additionally, this system showed its merits during the 2008 global financial crisis. Even the regulatory reforms introduced after the crisis were directed towards infrastructure centralisation.

However, in the process of opening, these Chinese characteristics have not been very compatible with international conventions and technical operation, especially in areas such as opening accounts, custody, transactions and settlements. This inconsistency has negatively affected investment from foreign institutions in the domestic market. Since China's bond market started to open up in 2005, only 480 foreign investors have invested in the market and their holdings amount to CN¥800 billion, only 1.2 per cent of the total. This is not only far lower than the proportion of 30–40 per cent in developed European countries and the US, but is also lower than the 10 per cent in Russia, Malaysia and other emerging economies.

Part 3: Promoting a higher level of openness of the financial market

At present and in the near future, further development of the financial market through opening is necessary for China to enhance its international competitiveness. Only an open financial market can possess real scope and depth. Such a financial system can form price signals that are truly representative and effective, attract more capital and investors, and support development of the real economy. China has now consolidated its position as the world's second-largest economy after the US and its economy has entered a 'new normal' phase. For now, China's market reforms on interest rates and exchange rates have entered the final stage, capital account liberalisation has basically been achieved, and the international status of the RMB has been further improved with its inclusion in the SDR basket. However, it should also be noted that China does not have the ability to completely reshape the rules of the global financial system and still needs to conform to international standards. In the process of opening, China should seek inclusion and cooperation, rather than putting its own needs first. By actively adapting to international rules and gradually integrating into the international financial order, China can establish a healthy pattern that combines domestic reform with opening-up to the outside world.

Solve the structural problems of China's financial market in the process of reform and opening and uncover market potential

Since its reform and opening up, China has established a financial market and institutional system that aligns with the socialist market economy and that has made important contributions to the sustained and healthy development of the Chinese economy. However, China's financial market has only played a limited role in promoting capital formation, optimising resource allocation and enabling economic transition and structural adjustment. Compared to advanced market economies, China's financial market has prominent structural problems. First, the proportion of direct financing is too small. Second, shadow banking is putting pressure on the bond market, a situation similar to 'bad' money driving out 'good' money. Third, the structure of the bond market needs to be improved. Fourth, equity financing is underdeveloped, and retail investors are its main participants. Fifth, the financial derivatives market remains underdeveloped. In the future, China should persist in respecting and adapting to international market rules and practices. The reforms of the domestic financial market should be deepened on the basis of opening. Further, the financial regulatory framework should be improved to achieve coordinated development between direct financing and indirect financing, between equity financing and debt financing, and between basic products and derivatives products. Only in this way can China establish an advanced financial market system that matches its economic status and supports sustainable development of the real economy. This financial market system needs to be all encompassing, properly structured, efficient, stable, inclusive and competitive.

Open the financial market through overall coordination and improve the framework of macroprudential management

China should open its financial market in a methodical way, following a suitable roadmap and sensible timetable. First, there must be an overall plan and the process can be adjusted as required. Factors that should be considered include domestic and international economic and financial situations, China's foreign debt serving capacity and balance of payments position, the real economy's demands on financial services, and the impact of two-way financial opening. Cross-border regulatory capacity should be strengthened. A roadmap and a timetable for two-way opening should be prepared. Second, domestic financial development and opening policy should be better coordinated. For now, China should aim for a higher level of openness based on respecting international market rules and practices. It should simultaneously open the foreign exchange derivatives markets in a coordinated manner. In the process of opening, authorities should focus on integrating domestic rules with international standards and avoid overemphasising Chinese characteristics.

China should improve the macroprudential management framework and control the risk of cross-border capital flows. The macroprudential policy framework for foreign debt and cross-border capital flows should be improved to strengthen the risk management capacity under enhanced convertibility. The match of currency types and maturity of assets and liabilities should be considered, the size of foreign debt should be subject to adjustment and the structure of foreign debt should be optimised. It is important to monitor foreign debt and keep risks under control. It is also necessary to curb short-term speculative capital shocks through market-based measures and strengthen regular monitoring and risk warnings about foreign investor behaviour and large amounts of abnormal cross-border flows. Alongside these measures, China should also urge participants to perform obligations such as monitoring and information reporting to prevent illegal transactions and control the risk of abnormal cross-border capital flows.

Open the credit rating market in an orderly manner

First, China should allow the entry of international rating agencies into the domestic bond market for credit rating business. Detailed requirements should be clarified in respect of international rating agencies. Unified administrative rules for rating agencies should be established and improved, and a unified registration and supervision system should be established. As long as ratings are released 'for regulatory purposes', an agency should be subject to regulation, regardless of whether it is domestic or foreign. Meanwhile, an investor- and market-oriented evaluation mechanism should be established, and a mandatory exit mechanism introduced. Additionally, as rating agencies have entered the market in different ways, they should also be regulated differently. International rating agencies that have engaged in rating business by building a commercial presence in China should be treated in the same way as domestic agencies. International rating agencies that provide cross-border rating business services must learn from international experience and coordinate with regulators in their country of origin. It is necessary to refrain from overregulation and avoid regulatory conflicts, as rating agencies may feel uneasy and confused and their business may decline. It is also important to avoid oversights and loopholes so that rating agencies will have no opportunity to conduct arbitrage activities. In the early stage of opening the rating industry, it is viable to only consider supervising the business of international rating agencies conducted in China. Possible regulatory measures could be inquiries and access to their working papers. Ultimately, it is necessary to strengthen cooperation with international regulators and achieve coordinated supervision by signing cooperation agreements.

Second, China should take advantage of international rating agencies and gradually liberalise the domestic bond rating business. The bond market should reduce its reliance on credit rating and stop treating ratings as a prerequisite for issuing bonds. Historically, China has been overprotective of the rating industry and required all bonds be rated before being issued. This was an administrative intervention that helped rating agencies gain dominance. As China's bond default rate is very low, it is almost impossible to effectively verify the accuracy of ratings. This has prompted rating agencies to prioritise market share over their own credibility. Once mandatory rating requirements for bond issuance are lifted, rating agencies will focus more on their credibility to gain recognition from investors, and international rating agencies will play a bigger role in improving the quality of domestic ratings. It is also vital to coordinate the global rating system with the local rating system and to open the domestic rating industry methodically. International rating agencies use global rating standards. These specify that the ratings of Chinese enterprises cannot surpass China's sovereign rating (A+ or AA–). However, the highest rating given by domestic rating agencies to domestic enterprises is AAA. In this context, the same issuer may have very different ratings at home and abroad. In the early stages of opening, attention should be paid to the coordination between the two systems to avoid pricing confusion. In this sense, it is necessary to gradually liberalise the rating business. At an early stage of the process, foreign institutions planning to issue Panda bonds or domestic institutions that have raised funds overseas can be rated by international rating agencies.

Implement multilevel management to offer foreign issuers greater flexibility in terms of auditing and accounting

First, China should allow foreign issuers to choose their own accounting standards to prepare financial reports. Most participants in China's bond market, especially in the interbank bond market, are qualified institutional investors with the capacity to identify risks and make judgements about the financial statements of foreign institutions. Foreign institutions that issue bonds to qualified institutional investors can be allowed to prepare their financial statements based on accounting standards that align with China's accounting standards for business enterprises or are recognised by China's Ministry of Finance. However, they should note the differences between their own and China's accounting standards. Regarding the statement of important differences, foreign government agencies (including sovereign governments and local governments), international development institutions and other foreign institutions with high credit worthiness and international influence only need to disclose the major differences. Financial institutions, non-financial enterprises and other foreign commercial institutions must make adjustments on the differences between their accounting and China's standards while disclosing reconciliation statements. Moreover, in the case of foreign institutions issuing bonds to certain qualified institutional investors, considering the limited number of investors involved and their familiarity with the issuers, the two sides may be allowed to negotiate the type of accounting standards between themselves.

Second, China should allow qualified foreign accounting firms to provide auditing services to foreign institutions issuing bonds to qualified institutional investors in China. International practice shows that when Chinese institutions issue bonds to qualified investors in the US market, they often refer to the audit opinions issued by Chinese accounting firms. US regulators had never asked to sign a cooperative agreement on audit regulation with China. At present, the legal framework for the capital market's opening is still under development. Signing cooperative agreements on audit regulation with countries where the overseas accounting firms are based can help China improve its regulation and facilitate cross-border recourse efforts in relation to bond default. For now, the Hong Kong Special Administrative Region is the only jurisdiction that has signed such a cooperative agreement with China. This lack of agreements has increased the cost and dampened the spirits of foreign institutions issuing bonds in China. It is proposed that China accelerates the process of reaching agreements with other countries and regions on audit regulation, while simultaneously allowing accounting firms to proceed with their audit service after filing with the Ministry of Finance. No filing procedure is required for accounting firms based in Hong Kong; they only need to follow the guidance of the signed cooperation agreement.

Finally, China should issue a set of unified administrative rules for foreign institutions participating in China's bond market as soon as possible. It is important to clarify the requirements, including accounting and auditing policies, for foreign government agencies, international development institutions and foreign business institutions that plan to issue bonds in China. Such requirements should be more transparent and standardised.

Clarify tax codes for foreign investors planning to enter China's bond market

First, China's finance and taxation departments should immediately clarify the tax details for foreign investment in China's bond market so that more foreign institutions will be willing to invest in China. On issues such as whether and how to levy corporate income tax and value-added tax, China could learn from international practice and develop highly operable, clear and specified tax policies. The requirements concerning withholding tax should be made clear for registration and custody agencies in the interbank market.

Second, China should clarify regulations concerning preferential tax policies in international agreements and tax treaties. For example, the suitable objects, application methods and procedures should be specified clearly.

Third, regarding foreign investors' interest income and the spread income from investing in Panda bonds in China's interbank bond market, it is necessary to exempt these types of income from corporate income tax and value-added tax to avoid double taxation and enhance transparency.

Additionally, the tax department should promote the publicity of tax policy, creating a fairer and more transparent policy environment for foreign institutions investing in China's interbank market.

Construction of financial infrastructure should consider China's actual conditions and international practice

A practical approach for adapting to the different habits and characteristics of investors would be to adopt a centralised custody system for domestic investors and a multilevel custody system for foreign investors. The former suits China's actual conditions, while the latter aligns with international practice.

The Bond Connect launched in July 2017 is characterised by multilevel custody, nominal holdings, centralised trading and 'penetration supervision'. Such institutional arrangements are a reasonable and effective way to further open the bond market and attract international investors. From a macro perspective, the Bond Connect essentially helps foreign investors to conveniently and effectively allocate RMB bond assets through internationally accepted arrangements that they can understand and accept. Bond Connect can lead to smoother capital inflows and debt outflows. It can also help with China's balance of international payments, support economic and financial deleveraging, reduce financing costs and consolidate financial security. From a micro perspective, Bond Connect, which introduced multilevel custody into Chinese banks, offers a historic opportunity for Chinese financial institutions to participate in international custody business. This can enhance their global competitiveness and ability to safeguard financial security.

References

MSCI. (2017). *MSCI announces results of the 2018 annual market classification review*. Retrieved from www.msci.com/market-classification-2017

People's Bank of China. (2017). *2017 report of RMB internationalization*. Retrieved from www.nbd.com.cn/articles/2017-10-19/1155154.html

7

Building China's Overseas Investment and Financing Cooperation

Zhu Jun,[1] Guo Kai,[2] Ai Ming,[3] Bai Xuefei[4]
and Zhao Yue[5]

Introduction

The 2008 global financial crisis reshaped the global economic and investment landscape. Outbound investment of developed economies decreased, and China's proportion steadily rose (United Nations Conference on Trade and Development [UNCTAD], 2016). In 2015, China ended the surplus in foreign direct investment (FDI) inflow that had lasted for more than 30 years, and its outward foreign direct investment (ODI) exceeded FDI inflow for two consecutive years (Ministry of Commerce [MOFCOM], National Bureau of Statistics [NBS] & State Administration of Foreign Exchange [SAFE], 2017).

According to statistics from the MOFCOM, NBS and SAFE, in 2016, China's utilisation of foreign capital reached CN¥813.2 billion (US$126 billion). The country's ODI flows amounted to CN¥1.1299 trillion

1   Director-General of the International Department, People's Bank of China (PBC).
2   Deputy Director-General of the International Department, PBC.
3   Staff researcher at the International Department, PBC.
4   Staff researcher at the International Department, PBC.
5   Staff researcher at the International Department, PBC.

(or US$170.1 billion), ranking second globally, only after the United States (US). China's Belt and Road Initiative, which has drawn global attention, is linked strongly to the previously launched 'go global' strategy and international cooperation on industrial capacity. Both of these strategies regard overseas investment as vital. The scale of China's overseas investment and construction projects is likely to expand further at a rapid pace. With continued promotion of the 'go global' policy, international industrial capacity cooperation and the Belt and Road Initiative, the room for growth is tremendous.

Enterprises cannot 'go global' without appropriate financial support, and the rapid development of overseas investment and project construction poses greater demands on China's overseas investment and financing system and corresponding cooperation.

Meanwhile, many host countries of China's overseas construction projects and investments are developing and emerging economies with tremendous capital demand. However, financial systems in some of these countries and regions remain underdeveloped and unable to provide adequate financing to meet investment needs. Given the huge demand for investment and financing in related projects, any single country is unable to provide sufficient funding purely from its own sources and China is no exception (Zhou, 2017). To meet such investment needs and ensure the sustainability of China's overseas interests, China should establish an investment and financing cooperation framework to facilitate enterprises' 'going global', encourage international industrial capacity cooperation and promote financial integration.

To address the aforementioned concerns, China should follow the basic principles of market-oriented operation and have enterprises play the primary role in overseas investment and financing. It should also clarify the roles of market, government and international institutions in the process. Although on an international scale there is no lack of capital in the private sector overall, enthusiasm remains relatively low for projects with long cycles, slow payback and uncertain profitability. This requires the government to play a guiding role and help eliminate institutional constraints and information asymmetry faced by the supplier and demander of funds. If necessary, the government should use public funds to leverage funds from the private sector and international institutions.

Specifically, the role of government and the market should vary in relation to different investment and financing projects. In general, three project categories exist. First, projects that can be operated entirely on a profit-oriented basis should be undertaken by the private sector. Second, in terms of projects that are profitable but face certain information asymmetries and defects in the regulatory environment, the government should facilitate private investment by improving the investment climate, instead of intervening directly. It should eradicate institutional obstacles and reduce information asymmetries. Third, with projects that are extremely capital intensive, highly susceptible to political situations and impossible for the private sector to take on alone, but that also possess some strategic benefits—such as those with high risk and slow payback elements and those in definite need of public and concessional funds—the government should play a leading role. It should deliver support through credit enhancement, guarantees and other services, and leverage capital fully from international development institutions, private sector and financial institutions at home and abroad. Regarding highly strategic and policy-based projects that are still operating in the red despite public backing, as they can no longer be viewed as commercial investments they will not be discussed in this chapter.

Additionally, the role played by public funds in investment and financing cooperation should vary in different host regions. When investing overseas in Europe, the US and other developed economies where the market is completely competitive and the legal, institutional, investment and financing systems relatively sound, Chinese-funded enterprises should be allowed to compete freely with their international counterparts and gain project funding from the market. Conversely, overseas projects in developing and emerging economies may find it difficult to use local funds. It is highly possible that investment and financing services formerly covered by the private sector are now in short supply, and government engagement is needed. Public funds can be used to attract and obtain the required capital.

Starting with the characteristics and problems of overseas investment and financing cooperation, this chapter studies how the government could facilitate investment and financing cooperation, especially for large-scale and long-term projects in underdeveloped regions that lack private sector support, while adhering to market-oriented operations.

Part 1: An assessment of China's overseas investment and financing cooperation

Chinese enterprises 'going global' and investing abroad are experiencing a period of fast development, with the level of investment flow and stock at record-high levels. Alongside this, problems have developed in relation to China's overseas investment and financing cooperation framework. Taking the Belt and Road Initiative as an example, most countries in the relevant regions are emerging and developing economies with a shortage of capital and an excess of historical burdens associated with infrastructure and interconnection projects. These countries rely heavily on external funding and are in urgent need of international support. They also have certain expectations about concessional rates of funding. Meanwhile, although China's overseas investment is expanding rapidly, it had a late start. The investment and financing framework still requires improvement. Investment and financing cooperation is also facing various challenges. This part briefly introduces the basic features of China's overseas investment and financing, evaluates the opportunities and risks of overseas investment and financing cooperation, and conducts an in-depth analysis of existing problems.

Basic features of Chinese enterprises' overseas investment

First, despite its late start, China's overseas investment is expanding rapidly, and the growth outlook is highly optimistic. China's ODI has soared in the past decade. The NBS estimates that the average annual growth rate of China's newly added non-financial ODI from 2000–2016 reached 33.9 per cent. The ODI stock of Chinese mainland reached US$1.0979 trillion, exceeding the trillion-USD mark for the first time in 2015. China's ODI grew to US$1.281 trillion in 2016, ranking China sixth globally after the US, Hong Kong, the United Kingdom (UK), Germany and Japan (see Table 7-1). The flow of China's ODI in 2016 (see Figure 7-1) stood at US$170.1 billion, second only to the US. Although China has the highest growth rate and largest stock of overseas investment among emerging economies, the gap between China and the major advanced economies remains large. At the end of 2016, China's ODI stock was equivalent to 11 per cent of its gross domestic product (GDP), significantly lower than the US's 34 per cent, Japan's 28 per cent,

Germany's 39 per cent, France's 51 per cent and the UK's 55 per cent. When compared to other countries, China's potential for ODI growth is great. This is due to the advancement of China's reforms and opening, as well as continuous integration with its neighbouring countries.

($100 million)

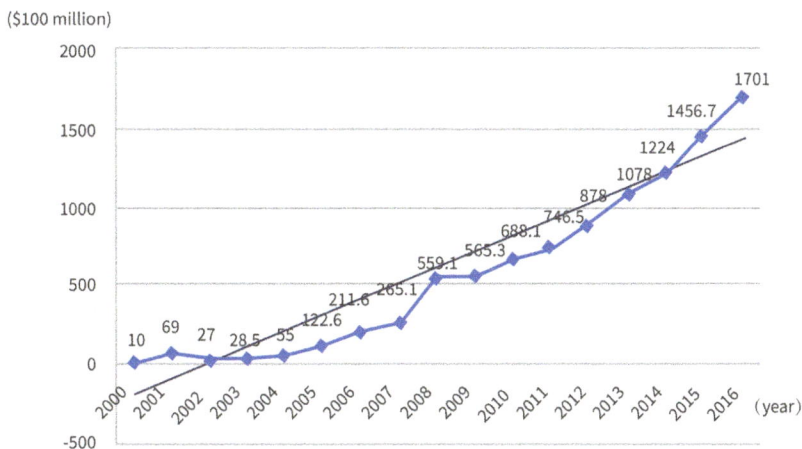

Figure 7-1: China's ODI flow since 2000 (US$100 million).
Source: MOFCOM, NBS & SAFE (2017).

Table 7-1: Comparison of ODI between China and major countries/regions

Countries/regions	ODI stock (US$100 million)		
	2000	2010	2016
US	26,940	48,096	63,838
Hong Kong China	3,793	9,439	15,279
UK	9,402	16,863	14,439
Japan	2,784	8,311	14,007
Germany	4,839	13,646	13,654
China	278	3,172	12,810
France	3,659	11,730	12,594
Netherlands	3,055	9,681	12,560
Canada	4,426	9,985	12,200
Switzerland	2,322	10,413	11,309
US	26,940	48,096	63,838

Source: UNCTAD (2017).

Second, the focus of investment and financing cooperation has gradually expanded from Asian economies to developed countries in Europe and the US. In the past decade, advanced economies have remained a major destination for global FDI, and they received 59 per cent of total global FDI in 2016 (UNCTAD, 2017). However, as international experience indicates, in the initial stage of overseas investment, a country prefers to invest in surrounding regions and in economies at a similar developmental stage. As a country's economy grows, the destination of its overseas investment gradually extends to developed economies. This experience reflects the trajectory of China's outbound investment. The stock of China's foreign investment in Asia reached US$768.9 billion at the end of 2015, 70 per cent of China's total foreign investment. Most of this flowed into developing economies. In the same period, only 10 per cent of China's total overseas investment went to Europe and the US. Notably, although the share of investment outflow to developed countries is still relatively small, it shows an upward trend. This is occurring because Chinese-funded enterprises are becoming increasingly competitive internationally and their appetite for advanced technologies and entry into the markets of developed countries continues to grow. Advanced economies in Europe and the US are gradually becoming popular destinations for Chinese investment and acquisitions. China's investment in Europe and the US accounted for 25 per cent of its total outbound investment flow in 2015. As the Boston Consulting Group (2015) highlighted in its report on China's overseas mergers and acquisitions (M&As) over the past decade, the focus and target of China's overseas M&As has shifted and is increasingly aimed at acquiring technology, brands and market share.

Third, a noticeable shift has occurred in the distribution of target industries. Mining has traditionally been a major recipient of China's overseas investment, accounting for 48.4 per cent of the total outflow in 2003. However, Chinese outbound investment has been gradually diversifying as Chinese enterprises accelerated their pace of 'going global' and participation in international industrial capacity cooperation. Some countries reduced FDI restrictions to attract foreign capital after the 2008 global financial crisis. Sectors such as business services, financial services and manufacturing have also witnessed substantial growth. In terms of ODI flows, the three industries that received the highest proportion of China's ODI in 2015 were leasing and business services, financial companies and manufacturing companies, accounting for 24.9 per cent, 16.6 per cent and 13.7 per cent respectively. ODI in the manufacturing sector has grown rapidly, while ODI in the mining sector has dropped out of the top three. In terms of ODI stock, the leasing and business sector came first with US$409.57 billion at the end of 2015, 37.3 per cent of the total stock. This was followed by the financial sector with US$159.66 billion, 14.5 per cent of the total stock. The mining sector came third with US$142.38 billion, or 13 per cent of the total stock (see Figure 7-2). These statistics reveal that China's overseas investment is experiencing an obvious structural transformation. Apart from traditional industries, such as infrastructure and energy and resources, business services, financial services and manufacturing sectors are all developing fast. Increasing diversification in target industries is evident.

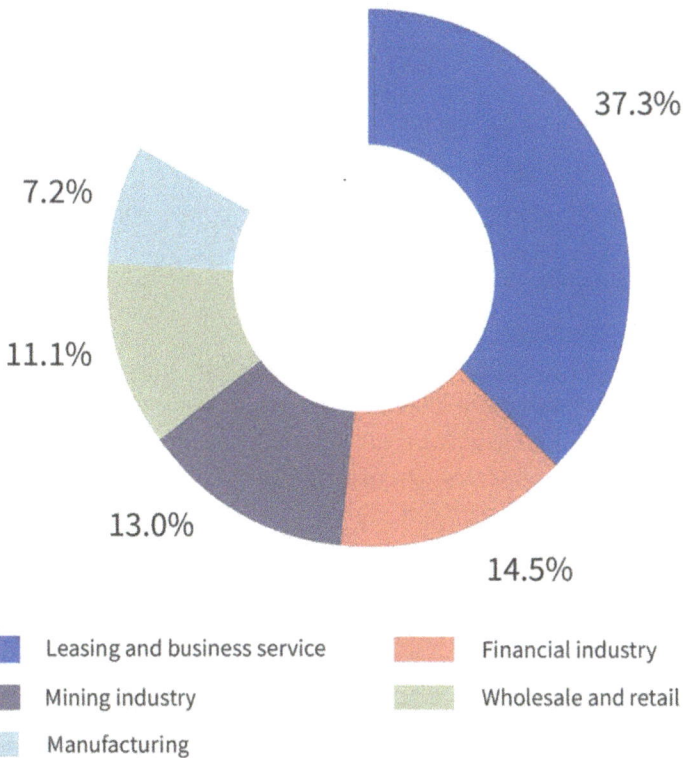

Figure 7-2: Distribution of China's overseas investment stock by industry in 2015.

Source: MOFCOM, NBS & SAFE (2017).

(year)

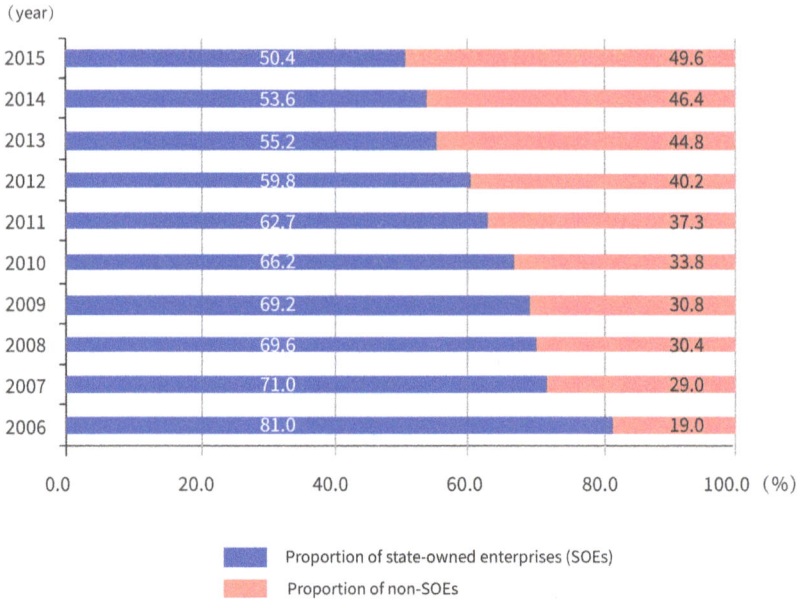

Figure 7-3: Distribution of China's overseas investment stock by ownership in 2015.
Source: MOFCOM, NBS & SAFE (2017).

Fourth, non-state-owned enterprises (non-SOEs) have become the dominant driving force for China's outward foreign investment. At the end of 2006, the share of ODI stock by state-owned enterprises (SOEs) was 81 per cent, whereas that held by non-SOEs (including limited liability companies, companies limited by shares, and private enterprises) was 19 per cent (see Figure 7-3).

At the end of 2015, the share of SOE investment in ODI stock dropped to 50.4 per cent, whereas that of non-SOE investment increased to 49.6 per cent. In terms of flow and the number of investment entities, non-SOEs (especially companies with limited liabilities) have already become the main driving force in China's ODI. Clearly, China's overseas investment is becoming diversified and multi-layered.

China's foreign investment is characterised by its long cycle, large scale and high risks, and opportunities and challenges coexist in investment and financing cooperation

In general, many Chinese ODI projects have long cycles, are large scale and face relatively high risks. First, in terms of regional distribution, although China's investment in developed countries has grown rapidly in recent years, developing countries in the vicinity have still absorbed most of China's ODI. In fact, 80 per cent of China's ODI stock goes to projects in developing economies, including many major cooperation projects along the Belt and Road regions (MOFCOM, NBS & SAFE 2017). In most of these countries and regions, financial markets are still underdeveloped and the level of marketisation requires further improvement.

Second, in terms of industry distribution, although business and financial services take up a relatively large share of China's ODI, infrastructure construction, energy and resources, and equipment manufacturing are still important target sectors (Wang & Li, 2017). Investments in these areas are typically large, long term and have slow payback. Such projects have relatively high demands for long-term equity funds. However, the financial market can only offer a limited amount of medium- and long-term equity funding.

Third, in terms of industry sensitivity, energy and resources, one of the major target sectors of China's outbound investment, is highly sensitive and protected. Host countries increasingly prefer to reserve the benefits of exploitation and subsequent increments to local firms and, therefore, impose strict regulatory and supervisory requirements on the entry, shareholding ratio, export and taxes of foreign investors (Li, 2015).

The aforementioned characteristics of China's overseas investment not only pose challenges, but also create opportunities for China to conduct investment and financing cooperation with other countries. Enterprises that 'go global' often face many difficulties and constraints in overseas financing. For example, many Chinese enterprises lack sufficient credit records in host countries, making it difficult for them to obtain funds from local financial institutions. Additionally, the credit records of newly established subsidiaries of Chinese enterprises are often relatively brief and, thus, they cannot access funds at low costs. Meanwhile, it takes time for enterprises to adapt to overseas financing procedures and legal environments.

Conversely, as developing and emerging economies are the major destinations for China's overseas investment, where capital shortage is a common issue, private sector investment and financing services are often absent. Chinese-funded enterprises can also face bottlenecks and constraints when seeking funds through domestic financial institutions or their overseas branches. For example, these branches are distributed mostly in developed economies instead of emerging or developing countries where most Chinese outward investment is destined. Taking the Bank of China (BOC) and Industrial and Commercial Bank of China (ICBC) as examples, these two Chinese banks have the largest overseas branch networks, but cover only 40 countries or regions, overlapping minimally with the distribution of China's overseas investment. Conventional commercial financial institutions can only provide short-term loans, which are typically due in less than five years. They seldom offer medium- and long-term financing. Domestic banks in general do not accept foreign property as collateral. They tend to 'favour the rich and disdain the poor' and are more likely to refuse lending requests from non-SOEs for overseas investment projects out of risk management considerations.

In terms of opportunities, transnational corporations from advanced economies have already begun to seek market opportunities and resources across the globe, occupying relatively mature markets and sectors. Because of the aforementioned features of China's target regions and industries, Chinese-funded enterprises have the opportunity to break into regions and industries where developed countries have traditionally found entry difficult. As such, with good planning and a reasonable cooperative framework for overseas investment and financing, China has a real chance to achieve 'corner overtaking' in its ODI.

In practice, rather than performing well, some Chinese-funded enterprises have suffered setbacks and frustrations in the overseas investment process. For example, of the 106 Chinese-funded companies that hold shares abroad, only three made a profit at the end of 2014 (Wang, 2015). The China Mining Association notes that 80 per cent of Chinese enterprises incurred losses for overseas mine purchases (China Mining Association, 2014). Additionally, statistics from the All-China Federation of Industry and Commerce show that 67 per cent of private enterprises venturing abroad experienced disappointments and only 10 per cent made a profit. Such poor performances can be partially attributed to risk factors such as political, legal and cultural differences, along with management, project selection and economic cycle issues. However, in some cases, the failure of an enterprise is linked directly to unreasonable and inflexible financing arrangements. For example, some Chinese-funded enterprises use cash instead of stock as consideration in overseas M&A transactions, and a lot of capital is raised through external debts. Additionally, the underdeveloped direct financing systems in China and the dominant role of bank credit in financing such investments have each partially contributed to this phenomenon. More notably, there is a tendency among Chinese enterprises to overpay because most of their transnational M&A deals are pro-cyclical and conducted across industries. The long running-in period after M&As and comparatively high debt leverage could also lead to potential risks. To address the problems and risks faced by enterprises, the government should provide guidance and develop innovative institutional arrangements. The ultimate goal is to improve the sustainability of overseas investment and create a favourable financial environment for Chinese enterprises to 'go global' and engage in international industrial capacity cooperation.

The capital demand of developing and emerging economies for construction projects is massive and can hardly be satisfied by China alone, thus, a sound investment and financing cooperation framework is needed.

Developing and emerging economies are the primary host countries of China's overseas projects and investment. Their demand for capital for economic and social development is tremendous. The Asian Development Bank (ADB) estimates that the demand for infrastructure investment in Asia will amount to US$26 trillion between now and 2030, equivalent to US$2.5 trillion per year. According to the Hong Kong Monetary Authority, the annual capital requirement for construction-related infrastructure along the Belt and Road regions is between US$0.8 and US$1 trillion. In a report published in 1994, the World Bank proposed a policy objective that set the share of infrastructure investment at no less than 5 per cent of GDP (Yuan, 2016). Based on this target, the authors have conducted a simple linear prediction of the annual investment demand for infrastructure construction in major Belt and Road regions (see Table 7-2).

Table 7-2: Forecast of the infrastructure investment demand along the Belt and Road regions (US$100 million)

Share	Countries/regions	2017	2018	2019	2020	2021	Total	Annual average
Low (3%)	Emerging economies and developing countries in Asia	5,125	5,569	6,053	6,593	7,177	30,519	6,104
	Commonwealth of Independent States	619	646	671	702	737	3,376	675
	Middle East and North Africa	979	1,039	1,101	1,173	1,254	5,546	1,109
	Total	6,724	7,255	7,826	8,468	9,168	39,441	7,888
Medium (5%)	Emerging economies and developing countries in Asia	8,542	9,282	10,089	10,989	11,961	50,864	10,173
	Commonwealth of Independent States	1,032	1,077	1,119	1,170	1,228	5,626	1,125
	Middle East and North Africa	1,632	1,731	1,836	1,954	2,090	9,244	1,849
	Total	11,207	12,091	13,044	14,114	15,279	65,735	13,147
High (6%)	Emerging economies and developing countries in Asia	10,251	11,139	12,107	13,187	14,354	61,037	12,207
	Commonwealth of Independent States	1,239	1,292	1,343	1,405	1,474	6,752	1,350
	Middle East and North Africa	1,958	2,078	2,203	2,345	2,508	11,092	2,218
	Total	13,448	14,509	15,652	16,937	18,335	78,882	15,776

Source: Authors' original calculation based on statistics from the IMF's World Economic Outlook database.

We divide the infrastructure investment to GDP ratios into three categories—low, medium and high—and set their values at 3 per cent, 5 per cent and 6 per cent respectively. The size of investment demand is then obtained by multiplying the GDP forecasted by the International Monetary Fund (IMF) by the infrastructure investment to GDP ratio. As shown in Table 7-2, the annual demand for infrastructure investment in Belt and Road regions is likely to reach US$0.8 to US$1.6 trillion between 2017 and 2021.

In sharp contrast, according to MOFCOM data, China's total 2016 investment in the Belt and Road regions was US$14.53 billion, lagging far behind the demand for investment and financing indicated above. Most of China's investment goes to developing and emerging economies, where the financial systems are underdeveloped and neither public nor private financing can satisfy local capital needs. Conversely, as the world's second-largest economy, second-largest foreign investor and largest holder of foreign exchange reserve, China is widely considered to hold large amounts of capital. Concessional funds from China are also expected. Therefore, to conduct overseas investment and financing cooperation more effectively, including infrastructure construction projects along the Belt and Road regions, and to meet the huge demand for investment and capital, China must fully mobilise resources from all stakeholders. This will not only promote economic growth in host countries, but will also facilitate the 'going global' of Chinese enterprises, equipment and technologies. In doing this, Chinese investors can also achieve better returns.

Nevertheless, it is important to note that developing funding platforms and facilitating financial integration to help enterprises 'go global' and attain international industrial capacity cooperation does not mean one-way financial support or unilateral interest concessions (Zhou, 2017). In a reasonable investment and financing cooperation framework, funds must be operated in accordance with market and commercial principles, with risks and losses borne by the institutions themselves. Behaviour must also reflect self-discipline; that is, all parties' resources must be fully mobilised, with each party both undertaking responsibilities and enjoying the benefits. In this way, a positive incentive mechanism can be formed and sustainable development secured. Additionally, due to limited government resources, overseas investment and financing cooperation cannot rely mainly on public funds. Instead, it needs to reinforce the division of responsibilities and cooperation between the government and market, only using public funds to free up and leverage other funds. China should follow the leading principles of market-oriented operation and primary role of enterprises to secure sustainable investment and financing.

Existing problems in China's overseas investment and financing cooperation

With the continuous integration of China into the world's economy, the potential for China's overseas investment and financing is enormous. However, in the process of 'going global', Chinese-funded enterprises face increasing conflicts and problems. Some of the most pressing challenges confronting Chinese financial institutions and enterprises are detailed below.

First, disorderly competition occurs when some financial institutions compete for projects. For example, many financial institutions have reported that it is common for domestic financial institutions to rush to fund the same high-quality overseas projects. Overheated competition and a lack of proper incentive mechanisms then cause lending conditions to be excessively relaxed. Chinese-funded financial institutions should base their overseas funding and expansion decisions on specific project requirements and their own specialties. To address hasty expansion and disorderly competition, financial regulatory authorities should provide a favourable environment, improve market access conditions and tighten the supervision of overseas operations. It is necessary to strengthen top-level design and create a mechanism for the unified coordination of major projects. The goal is to integrate the respective advantages of, and create solidarity among, Chinese enterprises and financial institutions for overseas investment.

Second, some enterprises have overlooked the risks and invested blindly. Poor understanding of local environments and social norms may lead to environmental pollution and violations of religious, labour and cultural customs, damaging the business and reputation of the financial institutions and corporations involved in an investment. For example, according to media reports, the State Power Investment Corporation initiated the Myitsone Dam project in December 2009 with the Myanmar Government's permission. However, in September 2011, the Myanmar Government halted the project, citing public concerns as the main reason. Many thought this project could destroy Myitsone's natural scenery and local culture, affect the harvest of local rubber plantations and crops, and lead to various climate and environmental problems. Although the Myanmar Government later established an inquiry committee to determine an appropriate solution, the project remains suspended at the time of writing and Chinese investment of more than US$2 billion is facing grave uncertainty. As it is uncertain when the project may resume, any possible return on investment appears distant (Bao & Li, 2015).

Third, monitoring and accountability mechanisms for public and concessional funds are inadequate. Only when capital provider values return will they focus on the effectiveness of capital utilisation instead of investing blindly and wilfully (Yin, 2017). Taking the light rail project in Mecca, Saudi Arabia, as an example, the Chinese listed company China Railway Construction Corporation (CRCC) won the bidding for this project in 2009. At that time, a Saudi Arabian corporation more familiar with the local engineering specifications submitted a quotation of US$2.7 billion, compared to the quotation of US$1.7 billion by CRCC. Although the project was delivered on time, was high quality and was well received after operation began, CRCC's misjudgement of the project's costs, along with mistakes made during the project management process and contract alterations, caused a total deficit of 4.15 billion RMB by the time of completion in 2010. To reduce shareholder losses, CRCC (the parent corporation) covered the shortfall. Although the Mecca light railway project won a good reputation for Chinese railway projects abroad and created favourable social effects, financially it brought about an unexpected and massive loss. Throughout the process, risk management and accountability mechanisms had clearly failed to fulfil their intended role (Bao & Li, 2015).

Fourth, enterprises also encounter some bottlenecks and constraints when they seek financing from domestic financial institutions or their overseas branches. To begin with, Chinese financial institutions have yet to extend their operations to cover a large number of developing and emerging economies. In terms of coverage, Chinese enterprises have already spread across 180 countries or regions. However, the overseas branches of Chinese commercial banks cover only 60 or so countries or regions and are concentrated in advanced economies. They are yet to form a global network and, as such, are unable to fully support Chinese enterprises' overseas financing needs. Regarding investment banks, their coverage is even smaller, and their overseas branches are similarly clustered in advanced economies. Overseas branches serve important purposes as they allow financial institutions to play a frontline role. Therefore, whether better coverage can be achieved will significantly influence the ability of Chinese financial institutions to support the enterprises' overseas investments.

Moreover, the capability and services of existing overseas branches of Chinese financial institutions must improve. In recent years, as the 'going global' efforts of Chinese enterprises have taken increasingly various forms, needs have developed for more diverse financial services. Besides traditional services, such as financing, payment and settlement, and bank guarantees, there is growing demand for M&As, equity investment, derivatives transaction, investment consulting and other investment bank services and insurance-related financial services. Although Chinese financial institutions have gained remarkable expertise in recent years, they are still relatively inexperienced in international operations compared with their long-established international counterparts. They have yet to develop the ability to navigate the international financial market and integrate domestic and foreign financial resources with ease. For example, with limited capital reserve, financial institutions' overseas branches enjoy little advantage in terms of financing size and interest rates. They are also less knowledgeable about the compliance risks in host countries than local financial institutions. Their ability and efficiency in helping enterprises circumvent supervision and avoid legal risks remains underdeveloped. Gaps also exist with foreign financial institutions in terms of providing innovative and comprehensive products and services. Increasing the competitiveness of overseas branches of Chinese financial institutions is an urgent task.

Fifth, the scale of Chinese enterprises' cross-border M&As is expanding rapidly, and a high proportion of these are backed by debt financing. ODI is divided into cross-border M&As and green field investment. The former has grown rapidly in recent years. In 2016, Chinese enterprises conducted 742 cross-border M&As with a total transaction value of US$107.2 billion, achieving a year-on-year growth of 167 per cent. With such explosive growth, debt financing has also become common, leading to an increase in corporate leverage and a subsequent rise in overseas operational risks. Statistics jointly released by the MOFCOM, NBS and SAFE show that, on average, 28.9 per cent of China's ODI capital from 2009 onwards came from loans and other types of debt financing from domestic banks (see Table 7-3). Given that some projects may secure debt financing overseas, and that the newly added capital stock of subsidiary corporations is likely secured partially through parent corporations' debt financing in China, the de facto share of debt financing may be even higher.

Table 7-3: Financing method of China's ODI (2009–2015)

Year	Newly added capital stock (%)	Reinvestment of current profit (%)	Loans, etc. from domestic banks (%)
2009	30.5	28.5	41.0
2010	30.0	34.9	35.1
2011	42.0	32.8	25.2
2012	35.5	25.6	38.9
2013	28.5	35.5	36.0
2014	45.3	36.1	18.6
2015	66.4	26	7.6
Average	39.7	31.3	28.9

Source: MOFCOM, NBS & SAFE (2016).

Additionally, according to statistics from Thomson Reuters, in international M&As the median debt to EBITDA ratio[6] is around 3.0 globally, whereas that of Chinese enterprises involved in overseas M&As in 2015 was 5.4. This is a telltale sign of high leverage. This can be partially explained by the dominant position of banks in China's financial system and the high threshold of equity financing. It is also closely related to the fact that China's financial system remains underdeveloped.

China's overseas investment is placed mainly in developing and emerging economies. These investments are characterised by long cycles, large scales and high risks. Government bodies and official funds should make targeted efforts to facilitate overseas investment. It is necessary to refine the cooperative framework of overseas investment and financing; leverage capital from various parties with governmental funds; and address the financing difficulties and financial risks instigated by the mismatch of risk, return and duration of projects. The Chinese Government should also provide a favourable macroeconomic and financial environment for Chinese enterprises to participate in international economic competition and collaboration and should actively integrate itself into global production and value chains. Moreover, the flow of capital should be

---

6   Debt to EBITDA ratio reflects the corporation's ability to sustain and support its debts with profits. The smaller the value, the greater the solvency of the corporation.

directed into overseas investment projects that are important for China's industrial upgrading and strategic positioning within the international production chain. Additionally, China should uphold a market-oriented approach and maintain the dominant role of enterprises, improve risk management and accountability mechanisms for concessional funds, optimise the financing structure of enterprises' overseas investment, and support qualified domestic enterprises to conduct authentic and legitimate investment abroad. This will ensure the sustainability of investment and financing.

Part 2: Guidelines for conducting overseas investment and financing cooperation

The key to overseas investment and financing cooperation is diversification of interests and decentralisation of risks. From a long-term perspective, one-way fund support from China to developing and emerging economies is hard to sustain. An effective mechanism must be established for all parties to share costs, risks and returns. This mechanism should use market force to mobilise all available resources, ensure the sustainability of funds and maximise the interests of overseas investment. Based on the aforementioned considerations, we argue that China should uphold the following principles in overseas investment and financing cooperation.

Mobilise various parties to participate in overseas investment and financing cooperation

As mentioned previously, it is impossible for a single country to meet the capital need for overseas projects and international industrial capacity cooperation. Therefore, collaboration is essential. China should engage a broad range of stakeholders and mobilise various resources to use global capital effectively, alleviate China's financing strains and diversifying investment risks.

Engaging more stakeholders helps mobilise capital from more sources. A number of overseas cooperation projects in which China has participated featured long construction periods and slow returns. Without the timely commitment of funds, project implementation may be delayed and economic benefits reduced. This may also cause negative political influence. Therefore, investment and financing should be sustainable, which requires collaboration between all parties and sharing of costs and interests. To this end, the government and market should work together to mobilise the resources of stakeholder countries to provide multi-channel, medium- to long-term, sustainable funding for projects and reduce the burden on China.

Engaging more stakeholders also helps with risk prevention. Capital users will only seriously consider how to place funds where they are needed most when they bear the cost of the capital (Yin, 2017). Therefore, introducing capital from host countries helps to reduce project risks. Apart from collaborating with host countries, China could also foster common interests with some competitors to promote the sustainability of overseas projects. For example, the Myanmar Government suspended the Myitsone Dam project (in which China invested) out of environmental concerns, but the China–Myanmar Oil Pipeline project was not affected because of the joint participation of Myanmar, South Korea, India and other countries. This pipeline started pumping successfully in June 2017 (China Economic Net, 2017). As such, China should establish a framework of overseas investment and financing, and encourage countries with the capital, experience or demand for projects to collaborate. In this situation, each party can exert its strength based on the principle of mutual benefits, to share both risks and benefits.

Building on international experience, China should adhere to the following principles. First, for major projects, Chinese enterprises may cooperate with entities from other countries, including financial institutions in advanced economies, to share costs, risks and profits. It could also relieve concerns and increase international pressure on borrowers in relation to debt default. Major projects generally require significant amounts of funds, meaning they cannot be bankrolled by a single financial institution. Instead, these projects could be raised through international syndicated loans, with the participation of financial institutions in developed economies. In this way, the integration of funds and distribution of risks can be achieved, and long-term, large-scale, stable funding support and matching financial services for major projects secured. China can also simultaneously learn from the experiences of financial institutions in advanced countries.

Moreover, China may enhance cooperation with commercial banks in host countries to share benefits and risks. By encouraging the contribution of capital stock from local investors, financial institutions and investors in host countries will attach more importance to the operation and profitability of projects, thus ensuring the safety of Chinese investment.

Finally, multilateral development institutions—which have been working extensively in host countries for many years—often bring obvious advantages and are more experienced with risk control. Thus, cooperation with multilateral development institutions in investment and financing should be reinforced. This may include establishing joint investment funds and conducting co-investment business.

Optimise industry layout and conduct overseas investment and financing based on regional comparative advantages

In recent years, Chinese enterprises have sped up their 'going global' efforts. They have established various industrial parks abroad, transferred production capacities where needed and expanded their overseas markets. As each region is unique, with its own distinctive comparative advantages, China should pay attention to the choice of industry and location for overseas investments to optimise the spread of China's industries.

Since the reform and opening, China has successfully developed labour-intensive industries by making use of its comparative advantage of cheap labour. This has made a significant contribution to China's economic growth and employment. Nonetheless, after decades of rapid development, the situation has changed. In terms of demographic structure, China's working-age population has begun to shrink. In terms of wage levels, China's annual per capita GDP has increased from US$300 in the early stages of reform and opening to the current level of US$8,000. GDP per capita in coastal regions, where export industries are concentrated, has approached or reached the level of high-income economies. There has been a clear increase in labour costs. These data suggest that China's comparative advantage of cheap labour, which once propped up its labour-intensive industries, is disappearing. Conversely, after years of investment China's capital stock has increased substantially, with progress in education and research. Technology and labour quality have also advanced remarkably.

Compared with the early stages of reform and opening, or when China joined the World Trade Organization (WTO), there has been substantial change in the quantity and price of labour, capital and technology in China. The shift in comparative advantage and industrial upgrading is not only a natural outcome of China's economic development, but is also necessary for sustaining relatively high growth. With this change, some industries could move overseas to countries and regions with complementary conditions to China. Against this backdrop, to maximise returns on overseas investment, Chinese enterprises should pursue a differentiation strategy and choose target industries and locations based on local characteristics and complementary comparative advantages.

Clarify the positions of the market and government in overseas investment and financing cooperation

In the process of overseas investment and financing cooperation, the market should play a decisive role in resource allocation. Only through allocating capital under market-oriented and commercial principles will investors and projects be self-disciplined, take responsibility for risks and losses, and pursue a balance between benefit and risk. In this way, the efficiency of financial resource allocation will be improved and sustainable development realised. Additionally, given the huge scale of the capital required by China for outward investment, it is essential that the market should play a decisive role in capital allocation. It should provide well-tailored financial services on a case-by-case basis to improve the effective integration of resources.

As previously mentioned, some host countries require much improvement in terms of marketisation and financial systems. From an industry perspective, infrastructure, energy and resources, and equipment manufacturing industries all have long investment cycles and slow payback schedules. As a result, market failures sometimes occur. For example, a lack of investment and financing services in the private sector may hinder some public welfare projects that have slow cost-recovery periods, long investment cycles and great risks. Despite the positive externalities of such projects, they are hindered by uncertain profit outcomes or the long period required to reach profitability. Therefore, the government should play a supportive role and also be a sweeper—using public funds to leverage other types of funds, reducing or eliminating obstacles that impede private funds, and promoting the incubation and launching of projects.

However, special attention should be paid to efficiency when public funds play a supplementary role. It is only when the fund provider pays due attention to benefits, instead of providing financial resources wilfully, that such funds can be invested where they are most needed. If funds are used inefficiently, problems such as moral hazards in the host country and an over-reliance on preferential funds may arise. This will not boost the economic growth of developing countries and may restrain their development and hinder further cooperation (Zhou, 2017). Therefore, before using government resources for investment and financing, the following issues should be considered. First, is it possible for the project to be fully financed by the private sector through the market or commercial means? Second, if no private sector companies are willing or able to provide financing due to problems such as high levels of risk or market failure, is it possible for the government to introduce corresponding policies or conduct-related reforms to reduce investment risks and improve the market environment, thereby providing a more welcoming environment in which the private sector can participate? Third, if government funds must be used, this should primarily be to reduce risks and should leverage resources from all possible parties, including funds from the private sector.

Given the limited government resources, it is not appropriate to rely mainly on them for overseas investment and financing cooperation. Instead, it is necessary to strengthen the division of responsibilities and cooperation between the government and market. The market should play a decisive role in resource allocation, and official funds can be used to leverage resources from other sources if necessary. Meanwhile, adherence to the principles of market-oriented operation and having enterprises play the primary role will ensure the sustainability of investment and financing. Additionally, strategic projects should also be differentiated from commercial projects. In terms of strategic projects (that are necessary and possess significant positive externalities), emphasis should be placed on quality over quantity so that public funds are most effectively allocated and used.

With a well-designed mechanism in place, some medium- and long-term strategic projects will also gain economic benefits. First, it is necessary to identify project users effectively and impose reasonable charges to generate economic returns. Second, due to factors such as large scale, long cycles and various uncertainties, some projects may have unapparent or minimal economic benefits in their early stages. In these circumstances, it is advisable to reduce uncertainties in project investment, construction and operation through reasonable mechanism designs, appropriate risk diversification and well-tailored financial tools to improve the economic returns.

Utilise overseas investment and financing cooperation to facilitate RMB internationalisation

Currently, many enterprises that have 'gone global' reflect that most of their foreign investments are financed in USD or RMB. Meanwhile, proceeds are received in the local currency. Due to unstable political and economic conditions and imperfect foreign exchange mechanisms, local currencies can fluctuate violently, leading to high exchange risks. Many projects have comparatively long construction periods, sometimes even spanning one or two decades. Yet, in general, the longest term of hedging tools for managing exchange rate risk is five years. Moreover, a majority of the Belt and Road countries have underdeveloped financial markets. Risk hedging tools in these countries are severely inadequate, making it difficult for Chinese corporations to hedge exchange rate risks.

In 2016, the RMB was officially added to the IMF's basket of currencies that make up the special drawing right, thus gaining status as an internationally recognised reserve currency. Increasing the RMB's use in the investment and financing of overseas Chinese projects can not only mitigate currency exchange risks, but also promote RMB internationalisation. Promoting international use of a domestic currency through investment and financing cooperation is not a new concept. From 1986–1991, Japan launched a US$65-billion capital recycling program in three phases (Liu, 2012). The goal was to alleviate international pressure on the current account surplus and, in the meantime, promote internationalisation of the JPY. To a certain extent, this program was successful (see Box 7-1).

Box 7-1: Japan's capital recycling program

Since 1980, the sharp increase in Japan's current account surplus has placed it under substantial international pressure. At that time, Japan could not promote the outflow of the JPY through trade. To promote internationalisation of the JPY, ease trade friction and take advantage of the financing needs of developing countries in Asia, Latin America and other regions, Japan designed a program to return part of the surplus to developing countries. It did this by providing them with official development assistance (ODA) and commercial loans. As surplus is recorded on international balance sheets in black, this program was dubbed the 'capital recycling program'.

The capital recycling program was conducted from 1986–1991 in three phases, covering a total of US$65 billion. The first phase was initiated in September 1986, focusing on contributing capital to the IMF and establishing the Japan Special Fund in the World Bank and the ADB. The total amount introduced in this phase was US$10 billion. This was mainly used to encourage international development agencies to issue JPY-denominated bonds in Japan, promote the participation of Japanese banks in syndicated loans of international development agencies and provide developing countries with JPY loans as a form of bilateral aid. The second phase began in May 1987, with a total commitment of US$20 billion. The third phase was launched in July 1989, with the total contribution in this phase reaching US$35 billion. The goal was mainly to support the US in implementing the Brady Plan and help manage the Latin American debt crisis.

Funding for the program came mainly from ODA budgetary fund and private capital, with latter accounting for 71 per cent of the funding (i.e. US$46 billion). Loans provided through the capital recycling program include project and non-project loans. Project loans targeted firms in the infrastructure, energy and raw material export sectors in developing countries in the Asia-Pacific region. These loans had relatively high concessional rates, longer repayment terms and fewer auxiliary conditions. Non-project loans were granted through the IMF and other international financial institutions, primarily to assist borrowing countries improve their international payment position and adjust domestic industrial structure.

Japan achieved substantial financial, political and diplomatic gains through the capital recycling program. It not only reduced trade friction and improved foreign relations, but also accelerated internationalisation of the JPY, supported the globalisation of Japanese firms and financial institutions, and increased Japan's international influence.

At present, many developing countries are in great need of funds, and urgently need to develop their domestic manufacturing industry and infrastructure. Therefore, a huge demand exists for full sets of equipment, project construction and other products and services from China. Additionally, overseas projects constructed by Chinese companies will also increase the demand for equipment from China. These demands have laid a solid foundation for the RMB's use in overseas investment and financing cooperation. Foreign parties can use the RMB earned through China's ODI to import Chinese goods and services. In this way, RMB flow back will be facilitated. RMB investment in suitable industries can further release the growth potential of other developing countries, while promoting the purchase of Chinese goods and services, export of Chinese equipment and RMB internationalisation. Additionally, investing and financing in RMB could reduce dependence on the USD and other currencies, boost confidence in and increase the attractiveness of the RMB, promote the development of offshore RMB markets, reduce the risks created by exchange rate fluctuations, and maintain stability in the foreign exchange rate and financial market. An important future direction for China to pursue is to use the RMB more frequently in overseas investment and financing cooperation. China should always uphold a market-oriented approach and the dominant role of enterprises in this process.

To date, China has made several attempts to explore RMB use for overseas investing and financing. First, at the Belt and Road Forum for International Cooperation held in May 2017, China announced that it would inject another CN¥100 billion into the Silk Road Fund. China also encouraged financial institutions to conduct overseas RMB fund business, which is estimated to total CN¥300 billion. Second, China has founded a number of RMB investment and loan funds, such as Sailing Capital International, to provide commercial investment plans and financial support to Chinese enterprises in their overseas investment and M&A activities. The total scale of Sailing Capital International has reached CN¥50 billion, of which CN¥12 billion came from the first round of fund raising. The fund also mobilised capital from other sources through various methods such as fund of fund, combination of investment and loans, and issuance of bonds. Third, development and policy-based financial institutions, such as China Development Bank (CDB) and Export-Import Bank of China (EIBC), have already issued many cross-border loans in RMB. For instance, loans granted by EIBC in RMB account for more than 60 per cent of its total overseas loans. Moreover, the proportion of overseas financing in RMB undertaken by EIBC has increased continuously. Fourth, commercial financial institutions have also begun to make loans in RMB in accordance with market-oriented approaches.

Part 3: Seize current strategic opportunities and build China's framework for overseas investment and financing cooperation

The Belt and Road Initiative and international cooperation of industrial production capacity have initiated ample strategic opportunities for creating a framework for China's overseas investment and financing. With the guidelines proposed above, we argue that China should encourage innovation in the design of investment and financing mechanisms; reduce uncertainty in overseas investment; and improve economic benefits through introducing sound financing arrangements, risk-sharing mechanisms and appropriate financial instruments. More specifically, China should use development finance effectively, refine policy-based financial tools such as export credit and promote the formation of an overseas financial operation network. It should also fully mobilise government and market funds, financial resources from host countries and the international capital market, and capital from multilateral development institutions. China should also make better use of equity funds and develop a market-oriented, sustainable framework of overseas investment and financing.

Promote development finance

According to international practices, enterprises that 'go global' mainly receive three types of financial support. The difference between them lies in the different value orientation towards market profits and national strategies. Commercial finance pursues profits following market principles. Policy-based finance serves national interests instead of market profits. Development finance, while aspiring to fulfil national strategies, also seeks to achieve breakeven or narrow profits to ensure sustainability (Zhou, 2015). There is a corresponding cost gradient, with commercial finance incurring the highest cost of capital and policy-based finance the lowest.

Of the three types, policy-based finance may face problems of low capital efficiency and increased fiscal burden. Additionally, its effect is relatively limited while there is a vast demand for capital by overseas investment and financing. Commercial capital performs well in terms of providing medium- and short-term financial support. However, it does not offer much long-term financing. The effectiveness of market-driven resource allocation in this field is less than ideal. Meanwhile, the actions of commercial financial institutions are typically pro-cyclical and 'favour the rich and disdain the poor'.

In such circumstances, development finance has its own advantage. It can fill the gap between policy-based finance and commercial finance. Development finance is an extension of traditional policy-based finance. It serves national strategies and relies on the credit worthiness of projects, rather than government subsidies. Run autonomously, it operates under market principles, emphasises long-term commitment and seeks financial sustainability with zero or modest profits. It is a financial model between policy-based finance and commercial finance, but leans towards the commercial side (Zhou, 2017). Currently, China's overseas investment and financing programs, including those along the Belt and Road Initiative, are characterised by slow payback timelines and a large capital requirement. In these cases, development finance could make significant contributions by exerting its strength in market-oriented operations, financial sustainability and medium- to long-term commitment. Indeed, existing practices have shown that development finance is advantageous in many aspects. With the support of government credits, it can secure long-term, stable funds at a relatively low cost through the issuance of policy-based financial bonds. Accordingly, it can provide long-term financial support for programs of its choice. Thus, the needs of medium- and short-term overseas investment can be met through commercial finance (market capital). However, commercial finance may avoid long-term programs with a slow return on investment (even if they are profitable) or if the cost of capital is too high to accept. This opens investment and financing services for the involvement of development finance.

Over the last few years, as long-term public resources have fallen short, the world's major development institutions are in the process of transforming their business models and increasingly emphasise the commercial feasibility and financial sustainability of projects. They are also seeking to leverage investment from the private sector through capital raised at a low cost from the international bond market, fully mobilise resources and support the economic development of all concerned countries. China has already been leading the world in this field, with the CDB and EIBC playing vital roles in enterprises 'going global'. The CDB is the largest investment and financing cooperation bank in China and the largest development financial institution in the world. Taking advantage of its medium- to long-term investment and financing capability, the CDB had extended over US$160 billion worth of loans to countries in the Belt and Road regions by the end of 2016, with an outstanding investment balance of US$110 billion. It has over 500 projects in its investment portfolio. Most projects are concentrated in the areas of infrastructure, energy and resources, and industrial production capacity cooperation, all of which require long-term financing. Apart from supporting international trade, government concessional loans and preferential buyer's credit, the EIBC has also established a special investment fund to participate actively in the investment of overseas projects. Development capital from the two banks is mainly provided in the form of loans. Recent years have also witnessed the involvement of equity investment in some overseas investment projects with high capital demands, long construction periods and slow return schedules. These projects have both a demonstration effect and positive externality. Thus, they share some common features with public goods and development finance. According to the authors' estimation, China possesses a development capital pool of US$200–300 billion for supporting the 'going global' of enterprises, international cooperation of production capacity and projects in the Belt and Road regions.

Considering the characteristics and costs of various funds (see Table 7-4), we may conclude that development funds will become the main support for overseas investment in the priority projects of developing countries. Meanwhile, from the perspectives of market development and project life cycle, the functions of policy-based, development and commercial funds in relation to each other can be described as 'incubation—laying the groundwork—follow-up'. Together, these form a sustainable framework of investment and financing.

Table 7-4: Estimation of cost of external funding for 'go global' enterprises

Policy-based funds	
Financial subsidies, soft loans, etc.	The cost of capital is negligible since profit maximisation is not the goal.
Government concessional loans and preferential buyer's credit	The annual interest rate is around 2–3%.
Development funds	
CDB and EIBC loans	The annual interest rate of export credit is about 4–5%. The annual interest rate of an overseas loan is about 6–7%.
Various equity-based funds	In the case of equity investment, the cost of capital equals its return on equity.
Commercial funds	
Medium- and long-term export credit of commercial banks	The annual interest rate is usually above 7%.
Medium- and long-term loans of commercial banks	The annual interest rate is usually above 7%.

Source: Authors' original calculations based on data extracted in early 2017 from open sources.

For important overseas investment projects eligible for government policy support, different types of funds can be introduced and play a complementary role in providing financial support at different stages of a project's life cycle. Given their low capital cost and indifference to profit, policy-based funds could engage in unprofitable yet indispensable projects that have significant positive externalities and provide fiscal and interest subsidies. Nevertheless, excess fiscal burden should be avoided. Meanwhile, development funds can assist projects at low-profit stages. They can provide capital support at a low cost, help the project grow and subsequently partake in the growth dividends. Commercial funds can become involved when projects are mature and generating steady returns. At this stage, projects would already have been running for some time, accumulating a certain level of credibility. Therefore, should they seek market financing, the cost of capital will be much lower than it would have been at the beginning stage.

For instance, infrastructure projects require a large amount of capital. They are also characterised by long cycles and slow payback timelines. Development financial institutions can enter at the beginning stages, bringing investment from the private sector. Through their unique advantage in connecting government and markets, integrating various resources, providing long-term credit support to those with special needs, and playing a demonstration role for commercial finance, development finance institutions can achieve reasonable returns and sustainability.

Policy finance: Improve the export credit system and provide investment and financing support for Chinese enterprises 'going global'

The export credit system is an important facilitator in the 'going global' of China's products, services, technology and labour. It is also a vital component of China's overseas investment and financing cooperation. Strictly speaking, to date, there has been no widely accepted international rules for export credit. France, Italy, Spain and the UK founded the Berne Union in 1934, which marked the beginning of international export credit coordination.[7] In the 1970s, major developed countries began competing fiercely for export orders from developing countries as their demand for

---

7   The Berne Union, also known as the International Union of Credit and Investment Insurers, was named after the location of its headquarters in Bern, Switzerland.

capital goods grew. The chaotic situation and ever-increasing export credit subsidies led to the emergence of a so-called 'gentlemen's agreement'. To coordinate export credit policies among developed countries, the Organisation for Economic Co-operation and Development (OECD) developed the 'Arrangement on Officially Supported Export Credits' (the 'gentlemen's agreement') after rounds of negotiations. However, this is only an agreement among developed countries. It does not have the status of international covenants, nor is it legally binding as is international law.

The 'gentlemen's agreement' has undergone constant revision since its promulgation. The Wallen Package adopted in 1987 was an important step in the process of phasing out interest rate subsidies. The package stipulated that the lowest interest rate of export credit provided to high-income countries would not be set below the relevant commercial interest reference rate (CIRR). It also set a minimum quantitative requirement for the concessional level of aid credits. The Helsinki Package, introduced in 1991, was another important revision; it prohibited tied aid for wealthier developing countries and for projects that could be financed commercially. It also ended the bundling of export credit with the procurement of a country's goods and services, clarified that loans from donor governments and their financial institutions should not favour domestic firms and products, and stated that procurement should be conducted by means of open and competitive bidding (OECD, 2011).

In the past, developed countries were the main providers of export credit. However, in recent years, China's export credit has flourished and has taken over some of the market share previously occupied by the US and European countries. This has led to some controversy. The global proportion of China's officially supported export credit rose from 2 per cent in 2001 to 36 per cent in 2014, while that of the G7 declined from 91 per cent to 32 per cent. Instead of following the 'gentlemen's agreement', which distinguishes strictly between concessional and non-concessional loans, China has adopted a more flexible policy that allows for a mix and match between the two types of loans. Generally speaking, the terms and conditions of China's export credits are more favourable than those stipulated in the 'gentlemen's agreement', but less favourable than with aid loans. This has created considerable controversy. Since 2010, the US and European Union have frequently mentioned the international rules of export credit to China, accusing the latter of being too flexible with its export credit schemes and of not abiding by existing international standards. Under such circumstances, the clash between different export credit models has become increasingly acute.

Based on the commercial viability of projects, the 'gentlemen's agreement' divides export credits into two groups: general officially supported export credits and tied aid. For the former, the core principle is 'not too favourable'. In terms of interest rates, the CIRR (the benchmark interest rate of each country plus 100 basis points) has been adopted as the minimum interest rate of fixed rate loans. Specifically, for countries with low levels of interest rate liberalisation, the CIRRs are determined by external standards under the WTO framework.

Regarding repayment terms, the 'gentlemen's agreement' classifies countries into two categories according to their per capita income as estimated by the World Bank. For credit provided by high-income OECD countries, the term is five years, and this can be prolonged to 8.5 years after prior notification. For credit provided by all other countries, the maximum repayment term is 10 years.

Tied aid aims to provide support for countries or projects with little or no access to market financing. To minimise trade distortion, 'the gentlemen's agreement' sets strict rules about the eligibility of countries and projects and the minimum levels of concessionality. The underlying principle is 'favourable enough'. In terms of eligibility, only countries with lower-middle incomes or low-income levels qualify for tied aid. Meanwhile, commercially viable projects, whether public or private, are ineligible. In terms of concessionality levels, the minimum level for tied aid is set at no less than 35 per cent, and no less than 50 per cent for the 'least developed countries' (OECD, 2015).

In general, instead of classifying export credits according to a project's commercial viability, China applies export credit schemes based on the project's specific needs, often using a blend of concessional and non-concessional loans. Subsequently, China's non-concessional export credits are more favourable and its concessional export credits less favourable than those established in the 'gentlemen's agreement'. If China conforms to the agreement's rules, the rapid development of export credit will be affected.

The 'gentlemen's agreement' is not an international custom and it certainly does not reflect the new international pattern of export credit. First, the basic goal of the agreement was to coordinate competition among developed countries in ex-colonial regions and break free of the constraints imposed by the notion of colonial territories. This goal lacks universality. Second, the agreement mainly targets the regulation of export credits from developed to developing countries; hence, the derivation of the phrase 'aid loan'. However, investment and financing cooperation between China and developing countries falls within the scope of 'South-South Cooperation', which stresses the mutually beneficial nature of the relationship. This is completely different from the original goal of the 'gentlemen's agreement'. Finally, the division of export credits based on a project's commercial viability is oversimplified. It fails to capture the diverse financing needs of developing countries. Therefore, China should propel reforms and improve international rules around export credit to provide investment and financing support for the export of its equipment, products and services.

China should also make full use of the communication platforms at various levels to create synergy for the establishment of new international rules on export credit. Specifically, China should make more emerging economies aware of the drawbacks of the 'gentlemen's agreement' and build a consensus through multilevel communication channels. This will improve coherence and coordination in the country's dialogue with developed countries. Internally, China should also promote domestic reform of its export credit system, adjust the procedures of government concessional loans and preferential export buyer's credit, and establish and improve the relevant management systems. In the meantime, to ease controversy, China could raise the concessionality level of its concessional loans by lowering the interest rate and extending the credit period. Further, measures should be taken to clarify the risk profile of commercial export credit vis-à-vis policy-based export credit to ensure capital recovery.

Commercial finance: Improve the overseas network of Chinese financial institutions and services

In recent years, the overseas activities of Chinese enterprises have taken diverse forms, such as cross-border M&As and equity swaps and establishment of overseas factories, research and development centres and industrial parks. This calls for more varied services from financial institutions. Apart from the traditional financial services, including financing, payment, settlement and bank guarantee, an increasing need exists for investment banking services such as M&A, equity investment, derivative transactions, investment consulting, account management, export credit and overseas investment insurance.

Financial institutions should establish a network to share risks and benefits through alignment of financial services, connection of capital markets and financial infrastructures, and communication and collaboration of financial supervisory authorities. (Zhou, 2017). First, Chinese financial institutions should actively develop overseas operation networks. Financial institutions, with their overseas branches at the forefront, play a major role in facilitating financial interconnection. Currently, many developing and emerging economies rely heavily on financial institutions from developed countries for financial services. China's financial institutions must develop and optimise their overseas operation networks, improve professional competence, expand the range of services they provide and initiate financial innovations to serve the needs of Chinese enterprises more effectively. They should provide effective service in investment and financing, financial consulting, insurance and risk management to help enterprises 'go global'.

In the past decade, the global strategy of major international banks has undergone profound changes. Before the 2008 global financial crisis, these banks were in a race to open branches or gain market share through M&As outside their home countries, creating a highly globalised business network in the process. For example, the networks of HSBC, Citibank and Deutsche Bank are spread over 100 countries globally. More than half, perhaps even 70–80 per cent, of the revenue from a few major international banks came from foreign markets. However, in the wake of the 2008 global financial crisis, they made a major adjustment to their global strategy. To deal with the aftershock of the crisis, international banks scaled down foreign operations and shifted the focus—especially the focus of retail business—back to more familiar home markets. This contraction in the global business indicates a relative decline in the capital strength of these banks. This provides great opportunities for China's financial institutions to develop their overseas operation network and achieve internationalisation.

In terms of geographical distribution, the branch offices of Chinese banks are concentrated mainly in Southeast Asian and West Asian countries. Their presence in Central Asian and Commonwealth of Independent States countries is less visible and lags far behind their major international competitors such as HSBC, Citibank and Standard Chartered. According to the authors' survey, the 15 major Chinese banks (ICBC, Agricultural Bank of China, China Construction Bank, BOC, Bank of Communications, CDB, EIBC, China Minsheng Bank, Shanghai Pudong

Development Bank [SPDB], Guangdong Development Bank [now China Guangfa Bank], China Merchants Bank, China Everbright Bank, Ping An Bank, CITIC Bank and China Industrial Bank) have established 220 overseas branches in over 50 countries and regions. Of these, 180 branches belong to the top five banks (49 to the ICBC and 56 to the BOC). Most banks have plans for further expansion, which will lead to an additional 39 overseas branches in total (SPDB, the most ambitious, is preparing to open seven). These branches will be located mainly in Asia and Europe. Specifically, 16 will be in Asia (including Hong Kong Special Administrative Region, Macau Special Administrative Region and Taiwan), 13 in Europe, five in America, three in Africa and two in Oceania. Institutions like the CDB also plan to upgrade their country working groups into representative offices.

In addition to accelerating the overseas network expansion of Chinese financial institutions, emphasis should be placed on expanding the width and depth of their cross-border business and improving services. For instance, China should promote the exploration of cost-sharing mechanisms between banks and enterprises, encourage Chinese banks to provide preferential terms to major overseas projects and receive dividends when the projects begin to make profit. It should also improve hedging tools against currency exchange risk in long-term investments and lower the requirements for sovereign guarantees of project financing in host countries to an appropriate level. China can also relax the full collateral coverage requirement for financing guarantees to reduce the liquidity pressure on 'going global' enterprises.

Correspondent banking is an important component of the international payment system. Through correspondent banking services, the respondent bank can access overseas financial systems for products and services that may not be available in the bank's own jurisdictions. Unfortunately, recent years have witnessed a decline in global correspondent banking business. While increased compliance costs due to tightened supervision is one reason behind this, the downsizing of financial institutions of developed countries also appears to be behind the decision of major transnational banks to reduce or terminate correspondent relationships. Their withdrawals have raised international concerns over potential financial exclusion in developing countries (Bank for International Settlements & World Bank, 2015).

China should deal with the decline of correspondent banking from the aspect of both respondent and correspondent banks. Large correspondent banks are more likely to withdraw from countries with weak supervision, especially of anti-money laundering and counter-terrorist financing. Therefore, those countries should strengthen their supervision capacity building. More importantly, the following measures can be taken. First, differentiated requirements for anti-money laundering and counter-terrorism should be applied to prevent financial exclusion that could be caused by one-size-fits-all rules. Second, the regulators should adopt a pragmatic approach, consult fully with the private sector and key stakeholders in the process of policy design (especially guidelines and procedures) and observe the effects of policy through multiphase deployment. Third, information exchanges between financial institutions should be reinforced to reduce asymmetry and, thereby, improve supervisory effectiveness. Finally, information transparency in cross-border capital flow should be improved.

Additionally, syndicated loans could play a more substantial role in meeting the financing needs of large enterprises and projects and diversifying risks. Syndicated lending is one of the most important forms of financing on the international financial market. It enables the sharing of risk and benefits among financial institutions. In the case of contract breach, lenders can come together to exert pressure on the borrower or determine appropriate solutions. According to statistics from Thomson Reuters, many major international projects and M&As are financed by syndicated loans. In 2014, global syndicated loans totalled US$4.7 trillion. With the rapid globalisation of Chinese enterprises, Chinese banks are becoming increasingly active in international syndicated lending. The BOC and ICBC are among the top 10 lending banks in Asia and the Pacific region. Nevertheless, international syndicated loan business is still at a developing stage in China and Chinese banks do not have an adequate sense of risk diversification. Further, China has yet to establish a standardised secondary platform for syndicated loan transfers. Channels of distribution, buy-back and securitisation remain underdeveloped (Rong, 2017).

China could take the following steps to make full use of syndicated loans in overseas investment and financing cooperation. First, more financial institutions should be engaged. Banks from developed countries with mature mechanisms can help share the capital burden and diversify risks. Financial institutions in host countries could help mitigate commercial and political risks. Domestic financial institutions could partner with each other to avoid disorderly competition. Second, China should promote securitisation of syndicated loans to increase secondary market liquidity, free up more funds, increase the rate of return, and diversify and transfer credit risks in time. Finally, priority of claims in bankruptcy liquidations should be properly designed to reduce the risks.

It is worth mentioning that the financial supervisory authorities should seize the momentum of financial institutions' overseas expansion and encourage them to facilitate 'going global' enterprises. First, the authorities should support expansion of financial institutions based on their functional expertise to achieve differentiated competition and create synergy for supporting the 'going global' of enterprises and the Belt and Road Initiative. Second, the authorities should raise awareness among Chinese financial institutions about risk factors such as the host country's political and economic stability, degree of openness in the local financial market, legal and regulatory provisions, financial supervision, market size, client resources and credit environment. In this way, they will conduct proper due diligence and feasibility studies prior to making any commitment, avoid unnecessary risks, make wise decisions regarding the location of overseas units and ensure sustainable operation. Third, to fully mobilise resources through various channels, China should propel cooperation between Chinese financial institutions and their foreign peers, further open its domestic financial market and grant qualified foreign financial institutions permission to open branches in China. Fourth, China should strengthen communication and coordination between domestic and foreign financial supervisory bodies. A global tightening of supervisory standards in recent years, due to the implementation of various domestic and international programs, suggests that, for Chinese financial institutions, the likelihood to trigger regulatory action overseas is now higher than ever. Therefore, coordination between regulatory bodies is vital. It is also needed to clear regulatory obstacles hindering the overseas expansion of Chinese financial institutions.

Host countries, multilateral development banks, capital markets of developed economies and international financial centres should play their role in overseas investment and financing cooperation

Domestic funds available for overseas investment and financing cooperation are limited. A sizable amount of capital can be gained on the international market. Thus, China should make full use of various kinds of capital. The first of these is the host country's financial resources. According to the World Bank, up until 2014, the gross savings of countries participating in the Belt and Road Initiative amounted to US$9 trillion. Credit loans in 70 per cent of the countries accounted for more than 40 per cent of their GDP. The Sino-Central and Eastern European Financial Holdings Company Limited is a typical example of mobilising the host country's financial resources (see Box 7-2).

Box 7-2: Sino-Central and Eastern European Financial Holding Company

On 24 November 2015, during the Fourth Summit of China and Central and Eastern European Countries, China proposed the establishment of a Sino-Central and Eastern European Financial Holding Company to support production capacity cooperation among member states. The holding company, which comprised China and all Central and Eastern European member states, was officially inaugurated in Latvia on 15 November 2016.

The holding company is an addition to the existing group of international multilateral financial institutions. Established by an intergovernmental agreement between China and Central and Eastern European countries, and operated by member state–authorised financial institutions, the holding company aims to promote production capacity cooperation among the member states through commercialised multilateral financial cooperation. The company adopted a two-tier structure. At the upper tier is the policy-oriented holding company funded by government-authorised institutions. At the lower tier, multiple subplatforms of private equity, investment banking, leasing, insurance and other elements run on commercial principles.

The company enjoys the advantage of super-sovereign credits and the consequent reduced cost of financing. It can achieve an amplifying effect on government funds, using them as seed money to attract and channel social capital and capital from other sources through its commercial subplatforms. Meanwhile, the company will adopt corporate governance practices and commercial approaches. All member countries are shareholders. Together they participate in rulemaking and project selection based on commercial principles. The ICBC, CDB and EIBC were involved in the establishment of the holding company on behalf of China.

China should also draw support from the expertise and capital of multilateral development banks such as the World Bank, IDB Bank, ADB, European Bank for Reconstruction and Development (EBRD), Asian Infrastructure Investment Bank and New Development Bank to promote successful implementation of cross-border projects. To date, China has invested a total of US$7 billion in co-financing programs with multilateral development institutions such as the IDB Bank, ADB and IFC (a member of the World Bank Group), and a further €250 million in the equity participation fund established by the EBRD. Through these co-investment schemes, China can effectively mobilise resources from multilateral development banks and other investors. In addition, given the extensive experience of multilateral development banks in risk management and their influence over and familiarity with host countries, joint investment with these institutions can help mitigate risks.

China's financing model using public funds to leverage multisource capital has been emulated by some major international institutions. For instance, with the European Commission's Fund for Strategic Investments providing first-loss protection, the Investment Plan (the so-called 'Juncker Plan') intends to trigger €315-billion worth of public and private investment. Similarly, World Bank Group programs such as the Managed Co-Lending Portfolio Program and Green Cornerstone Bond Fund provide first-loss coverage with public funds, thereby improving project risk ratings and enticing capital injections from institutional investors such as insurance companies, pension funds and sovereign wealth funds. At the 2016 G20 Hangzhou Summit, multilateral development banks issued a joint declaration. They confirmed their commitment to support infrastructure investment; ensure the high quality and sustainability of projects; explore multipartite cooperation financing models; catalyse private financing; and address the risk elements facing private investors through risk guarantees, credit enhancements and increasing local currency financing.

China should make full use of international capital such as sovereign wealth funds and the capital market of developed economies. According to the World Bank, globally, US$8.55 trillion are placed in negative-yielding bonds, US$24.5 trillion in low-yielding government bonds with a rate of return below 1 per cent, and a further US$8 trillion lies in cash. In other words, for the aforementioned three kinds of funds, over US$40 trillion is unused—this is a potential source of capital for higher yield investments in developing and emerging countries, if investment-grade assets are available. This measure could also provide China with risk management professionals and tools on the international financial market for its overseas investment and financing cooperation.

Finally, international financial centres such as Hong Kong and London should play to their advantages. Some regional and international financial centres (London, New York, Frankfurt and Singapore) are important platforms for international investment and financing. They have mature capital markets and a large number of institutional investors. Further, their connections to institutional investors worldwide would allow China to attract international capital and investors. China can enter cooperation agreements with financial centres with clearly defined capital contribution obligations. In this way, they can use Chinese funds to mobilise international capital, playing to the natural advantages of these financial hubs. In addition, China could turn overseas projects, including infrastructure projects, into financial products and investment opportunities and access global institutional investors through international financial centres to raise funds for these projects.

Taking Hong Kong as an example, in response to the urgent capital needs for infrastructure development in the Belt and Road countries, the Hong Kong Monetary Authority established the Infrastructure Financing Facilitation Office (IFFO) in July 2016 as a one-stop platform for facilitating infrastructure investments and financing. IFFO is running smoothly at present. Over 60 institutions, including financial institutions, banks, pension funds, sovereign wealth funds and insurance companies, have joined as partners. Among these are the IFC, MIGA, ADB, EIBC, China-Africa Development Fund and Blackstone. Taking London as another example, the city boasts an abundance of innovative financial instruments such as investment guarantee funds and underpinnings and could provide Chinese enterprises with services not available elsewhere. Indeed, London is host to China's first green asset–backed security, which went public in 2016.

Meanwhile, the clustering of major financial institutions and professional services firms in international financial centres creates extensive connections and world-leading expertise in areas such as trade finance, marine finance, insurance, financial operation and risk management. This can be used to China's benefit, to prevent various risks associated with finance, environment, regulation and markets. Major financial centres are also important RMB trading centres and offshore RMB markets, offering abundant RMB-related financial products. With the RMB's increased use in investment and financing, these centres can provide easily accessed RMB services to investors worldwide.

Use multiple investment and financing models and make full use of equity investment

China should use all types of investments and financing tools, especially equity investment. Overseas investments create financial needs for infrastructure financing, trade financing, risk management in cross-border transactions, cross-border trade settlements and financial infrastructure. Therefore, a diverse set of financial instruments is needed, each playing to its own advantage and together creating synergy.

Meanwhile, a high demand exists for equity investment among enterprises investing overseas. Equity investment can serve as high-powered funds in overseas investment and financing cooperation. Generally speaking, equity investment can enhance the capital strength of projects and investing firms and leverage debt financing, such as loans. Moreover, equity investment can also provide greater control over investment and project operations. To tackle problems faced by many host countries of Chinese investment, such as high leverage ratios and limited access to foreign credit, the proportion of equity investment should be increased and various models such as direct, entrusted and joint investment should be used to make full use of equity funds and private equity investment. In this way, risks can be diversified, and the sustainable development of investment and financing achieved.

Simultaneously, equity funds can help enterprises mobilise Chinese resources, by combining direct investment with policy agendas such as economic structural adjustment, the 'going global' of technical standards, cooperation in equipment manufacturing and RMB internationalisation, to reap long-term rewards and improve the overall efficacy of overseas investment and financing projects. However, it is worth mentioning that despite the advantages listed above, the risks and uncertainties associated with equity investment are higher compared to other types of financing, such as loans. Therefore, proper measures should be established to control relevant risks.

In conclusion, first, China should give full play to equity investment funds such as the Silk Road Fund, China-Africa Industrial Production Capacity Cooperation Fund, China-Latin America Industrial Production Capacity Cooperation Fund and overseas RMB funds. This will increase the proportion of equity investment; absorb capital, technology and experience from relevant countries; and enhance the overall benefit of projects. Second, allocation of resources should be made more efficient, and the interests of all parties should be maximised, rather than assuming that China is providing aid to economies in need. Third, the government should provide guidance and support for equity investments that produce public goods or have the feature of development finance projects. This will ensure their sustainability.

China should also pay special attention to the international coordination of rules regarding equity investment and actively participate in the making and improvement of these rules. For instance, at present, multilateral developmental institutions such as the World Bank have a co-investment policy that asserts co-investment is reserved only for the private sector, not for government-funded institutions. Such policies do not accord with the international community's principle of mobilising all types of resources for project construction, nor do they meet the actual needs of developing countries and emerging economies. Therefore, it is necessary to bring multilateral development institutions on board in terms of improving existing rules to foster win–win cooperation. Meanwhile, from the perspective of investment sustainability, China can play an active role in forming international rules in new and emerging areas such as environmental risk management and green finance. For instance, China has the largest green finance market. Many countries and international organisations have a strong intention to cooperate with China in establishing global green finance standards. A leadership role in the development of such standards could help promote China's image among people in host countries and ensure the smooth and sustainable operation of investment projects.

Equity investment institutions have made useful attempts to connect capital and industry, improve market openness and promote the complementarity of production factors. The Silk Road Fund is a medium- to long-term development investment institution established to support the Belt and Road Initiative. As of May 2017, the fund had signed 15 projects and pledged a total of US$6 billion in investment in Russia, Mongolia, Central Asia, South Asia, Southeast Asia, West Asia, North

Africa and Europe. The projects cover infrastructure development, resource exploitation, industrial production and financial cooperation. The fund has also committed another US$2 billion to set up a sub-fund for China–Kazakhstan industrial production capacity cooperation. So far, equity investment accounts for more than 70 per cent of the total investment of the Silk Road Fund. Apart from equity funds, the fund also combines several investment vehicles such as credits, loans and funds to meet differentiated financing demands. Meanwhile, the fund places much emphasis on serving China's benefits in investment decision-making. It plays an active role in promoting the engagement of Chinese enterprises in international production capacity cooperation, the 'going global' of China's equipment manufacturing industry and the importation of advanced technologies.

Additionally, the overseas RMB fund established in 2017 is likely to play a vital role. The fund positions itself as a medium- to long-term financing platform with businesses ranging from overseas RMB loans and equity investments to cross-border guarantees. Overseas loan services consist of overseas project financing, acquisition loans and short-term bridge loans. Equity investment and cross-border guarantee services are mainly provided for overseas projects and participating enterprises. It is estimated that a substantial proportion of RMB received by the fund's client countries will be used for importing goods and services from China, thereby creating a virtuous cycle that serves the real economy in which the RMB recycles through a 'capital outflow and trade inflow' mechanism.

References

Bank for International Settlements & World Bank. (2015). *Withdrawal from correspondent banking*. Retrieved from documents.worldbank.org/curated/en/113021467990964789/pdf/101098-revised-PUBLIC-CBR-Report-November-2015.pdf

Bao, S. & Li, G. (2015). *Case studies on Chinese firms going global*. Jinan, China: Shandong People's Publishing House.

Boston Consulting Group. (2015). *Gearing up for the new era of China's outbound M&A*. Retrieved from www.bcg.com.cn/cn/newsandpublications/publications/reports/report20150323001.html

China Economic Net. (2017). *CNPC's participation in China-Myanmar oil and gas pipeline project: Win-win cooperation among the six countries.* Retrieved from www.ce.cn/xwzx/gnsz/gdxw/201706/06/t20170606_23445750.shtml

China Mining Association. (2014). *Chinese companies' overseas investment accounted for 80% of losses in mining investment.* Retrieved from www.chinairn.com/news/20140624/134943294.shtml

Li, K. (2015). *Three challenges and coping strategies in relation to BRI projects.* Retrieved from finance.ifeng.com/a/20150627/13802234_0.shtml

Liu, K. (2012). A study on Japan's 'Capital Recycling Program'. *China Finance, 1*, 64–65.

Ministry of Commerce, National Bureau of Statistics & State Administration of Foreign Exchange. (2016). *2015 statistical bulletin of China's outward foreign direct investment.* Retrieved from finance.ce.cn/rolling/201609/22/t20160922_16181128.shtml

Ministry of Commerce, National Bureau of Statistics & State Administration of Foreign Exchange. (2017). *2016 statistical bulletin of China's outward foreign direct investment.* Retrieved from hzs.mofcom.gov.cn/article/date/201803/20180302722851.shtml

Organisation for Economic Co-operation and Development (OECD). (2011). *Arrangement on officially supported export credits.*

Organisation for Economic Co-operation and Development (OECD). (2015). *Eligibility for tied aid credits, trade policy note.*

Rong, B. (2017). Suggestions on how to increase the participation of Chinese banks in international syndicated loans. *Management Journal, 10*, 37.

United Nations Conference on Trade and Development (UNCTAD). (2016). *World investment report 2016.* Retrieved from worldinvestmentreport.unctad.org/wir2016/

United Nations Conference on Trade and Development (UNCTAD). (2017). *World investment report 2017. Investment and the digital economy.* Retrieved from unctad.org/en/pages/PublicationWebflyer.aspx?publicationid=1782

Wang, S. (2015). An analysis of overseas mining investment by 106 Chinese listed companies. *The Chinese Journal of Nonferrous Metals, 4*, 40–41.

Wang, Y. & Li, X. (2017). *Analysis of the characteristics of China's direct investment in countries along the Belt and Road.* Retrieved from www.iwep.org.cn/xscg/xscg_lwybg/201705/W020170531577889133101.pdf

Yin, Y. (2017). Financing associated with the Belt and Road Initiative should adhere to market principles. *Caixin Weekly, 21*. Retrieved from weekly.caixin.com/2017-05-27/101095492.html

Yuan, J. (2016). Research on demand for capital and investment and financing models of BRI infrastructure projects. *Intertrade, 5*. doi.org/10.14114/j.cnki.itrade.2016.05.011

Zhou, X. (2015). Central Bank Governor Zhou Xiaochuan: Redefining policy finance. *Ifeng*. Retrieved from finance.ifeng.com/a/20150820/13921126_0.shtml

Zhou, X. (2017). *Speech at the 2017 Lujiazui forum*. Retrieved from m.hexun.com/news/2015-08-21/178495641.html

www.ingramcontent.com/pod-product-compliance
Lightning Source LLC
Chambersburg PA
CBHW042319210326

41599CB00048B/7155